THE POLITICAL ECONOMY OF GROWTH

Ex dono Andrea Boltho
2007

The Political Economy of Growth

EDITED BY DENNIS C. MUELLER

YALE UNIVERSITY PRESS   NEW HAVEN AND LONDON

070323

Published with the assistance of the
Samuel W. Meek Publication Fund.

Designed by Sally Harris
and set in Times Roman type by
The Composing Room of Michigan, Inc.
Printed in the United States of America by
Edwards Brothers, Inc., Ann Arbor, Michigan.

Library of Congress Cataloging in Publication Data

Main entry under title:
The political economy of growth.

   Includes index.
   1. Economic development.   2. Economic policy.
3. Comparative economics.   I. Mueller, Dennis C.
HD87.P64   338.9   81 – 15955
ISBN 0 – 300 – 02658 – 7   AACR2
ISBN 0 – 300 – 03479 – 2 pbk.

10   9   8   7   6   5   4   3   2

Contents

Part III. Two Alternative Views of the Evidence

Part IV. Conclusion

Preface

This book arises out of a conference that took place in College Park, Maryland, in December 1978. The conference centered on a paper by Mancur Olson on the political economy of growth, and so does this volume. Several of the papers have been revised substantially since the conference took place. Mancur Olson has in the meantime expanded his paper into a recently published book entitled *The Rise and Decline of Nations: Economic Growth, Stagflation, and Social Rigidities*.

Olson's paper and the others in this volume contribute to a small but growing literature emphasizing the interaction between political and economic factors. The economic performance of a country cannot be fully understood without studying its political institutions. This literature gives equal weight to both parts of "political economy" as a branch of the social sciences. In the troubled economic waters of the 1980s, with each nation's government searching for political solutions to economic problems, this branch of social science should become increasingly more relevant.

Thanks are due first to the many participants of the original conference, both those whose papers were included in this volume and those whose papers and comments were not. The discussion that took place during the conference was most stimulating and led to the opinion that a part of it should be preserved in print. Many of the papers in this volume have benefited in revision from the comments of those not included here who were present at the conference.

Thanks are due secondly to both the Economics Division and the Innovation Processes Research Program of the National Science Foundation, which sponsored the conference and subsequent work on some of the papers.

Final thanks are due to Adele E. Krokes, who has carried the heavy burden of typing many parts of the manuscript, written at Maryland and elsewhere, and of keeping track of the various papers' and authors' whereabouts, so that a manuscript could be pulled together.

Introduction

DENNIS C. MUELLER

When World War II came to an end, few economists predicted the unprecedented era of growth that was to engulf Western economies for the next generation. Some even predicted a return to the era of stagnation that preceded the war, but this did not occur. All developed, capitalist economies grew at rates above their averages for this and the previous century. What caused this surprising surge?

While rapid growth was to be found across the Western, developed world, not all countries grew at anything like the same rate. Table I.1 indicates a great disparity in growth rates, with the Japanese growth rate more than three times that of the United Kingdom. What caused such a wide disparity? Why were the richest countries of the nineteenth and twentieth centuries the least able to benefit from this era of growth? And why, contrary again to what one would have predicted at the end of the sixties, did this process of growth suddenly go sour in the seventies?

To answer these questions economists have invested a great amount of time and energy developing and estimating various models of the growth process. During the sixties the growth rate of the ''growth literature'' far exceeded that of the phenomenon it tried to explain. Viewing the problem most simply, we can posit a neoclassical production function of the following sort:

$$Q = AL^\alpha K^\beta, \tag{1}$$

where Q is output, L is labor, K is capital, and A is a shift parameter reflecting technological change or similar factors that might improve the efficiency of the utilization of both factors simultaneously. Using lower-case letters to represent time derivatives we can rewrite equation 1 as

$$q = a + \alpha l + \beta k. \tag{2}$$

1

Table I.1.   Annual Average Rates of Growth of Aggregate Output, 1951–73 (percent)

Austria	5.0	Italy	5.1
Belgium	3.9	Japan[b]	9.5
Canada	4.6	Netherlands	5.0
Denmark[a]	4.2	Norway	4.2
France	5.0	United Kingdom	2.7
Germany	5.7	United States	3.7

a. 1954–73.
b. 1953–73.

SOURCE: John Cornwall, *Modern Capitalism* (London: Martin Robertson, 1977), table 4.4, p. 64, based on data from T. Cripps and R. Tarling, *Growth in Advanced Capitalist Economies, 1950–70* (Cambridge: Cambridge University Press, 1973); and *National Accounts of the OECD 1962–73*, vols. 1 and 2 (Paris: OECD, 1975).

Equation 2 represents an economy's growth rate as being composed of a weighted sum of the growth rates of the two (or more) factors of production and the growth of the technological and other factors captured by a. This equation must be viewed as an identity rather than a right–left causal relation. The work forces of several European countries have been expanded through the importation of ''guest'' workers from less developed countries *in response to* the growth in demand for their output. Thus, we cannot explain growth in output by simply pointing to the growth in labor force in these countries; a full account of what occurred would have to explain why some countries imported more labor or capital or technological change than others. Once one begins to view the question this way, it becomes obvious that institutional factors—for example, those that might explain why labor flows into one country and not another—may be an important part of the explanation of why growth occurs and why growth rates differ.

Efforts to break growth down into its component parts have typically attributed no more than 50 percent of growth in output to growth in labor and capital inputs, taking into account changes in the quality of these factors.[1] Thus, roughly half of the growth in output of most developed countries must be explained by the anomalous technological change and improvement in efficiency factor a in equation 2. Here again we see the potentially important role institutional factors may play in explaining growth. What makes one country more receptive to technological change

1. See John Cornwall, *Modern Capitalism* (London: Martin Robertson, 1977), ch. 3, and works cited there.

than another? What leads all countries to adopt new technologies more rapidly at one point in time than at another? What other factors determine productivity and the efficiency with which they combine to affect output across countries and over time?

The following essay represents an effort to shed some light on these questions by examining the influence of political factors on growth. In it Mancur Olson emphasizes the growth-retarding influence interest groups can have in our Western polyarchic democracies. Olson's essay focuses on the conflict between achieving allocative efficiency and growth and achieving the redistributive goals of interest groups. At first glance it might not be obvious that the sacrifice of allocative efficiency for redistributive goals need lead to reductions in growth as opposed to only a once-and-for-all loss in output (a fall in a as opposed to a fall in A). That the former can occur is shown in Sir John Hicks's note. Moses Abramovitz comments further on the logical and empirical support for the Olson thesis. Kwang Choi presents empirical evidence in support of the Olson hypothesis; Frederic Pryor presents evidence in conflict.

Olson's thesis is an ambitious effort to explain growth and differences in growth rates, taking into account institutional factors relating to a society's collective decision procedures. To appraise the Olson thesis one must therefore look not only at the broad array of cross-section results contained in part I; one must examine the institutional details of individual countries to see whether they too seem to fit the thesis. Part II contains essays that present a rich mosaic of institutional detail regarding the post–World War II growth histories of several developed, capitalist countries. As with Olson's thesis, the focus is upon the political and economic factors that affect growth, not on the economic factors alone. But not all authors of these essays agree with Olson as to the importance of interest-group conflict in explaining growth, and a variety of additional, sometimes contradictory, explanations emerge.

Part III returns to the analytic treatment of economic growth in the Olson thesis. The two essays by Bowles and Eatwell and Dean attack Olson's somewhat neoclassical approach, offering in its place a Marxist perspective. Once again, however, these essays emphasize and illustrate the importance of considering both economic and political factors simultaneously when trying to understand the growth and development process.

This theme is continued in the final essay, in which I reflect on some of the many threads that run through the intervening essays.

Part I: Theory and Empirical Evidence

1: The Political Economy of Comparative Growth Rates

MANCUR OLSON

The modern economist can draw upon at least two hundred years of cumulative theorizing and research and even on the ideas of a few men of undoubted genius. Whatever the limits of his own vision, he can say with Isaac Newton that, if he should sometimes see farther ahead, it is because he stands on the shoulders of giants. Nonetheless, when the economist is asked why some countries or regions are growing faster than others, he must concede that he does not see an answer even from his lofty perch. Economic theory tells us much more about resource allocation and income fluctuations in the short and medium terms than it does about long-run changes in technology, tastes, and economic organization. As others have said, it is much more like Newton's mechanics than Darwin's biology.

This limited nature of our understanding of why some countries and regions grow faster than others is perhaps not apparent until we remind ourselves of the distinction between the sources and causes of growth. The literature on the sources of growth is impressive; Denison's classic

So many people have made valuable comments on this essay that it is unfortunately not feasible to list their names here. I must, however, mention Kwang Choi, Gudmund Hernes, Robin Marris, Dennis Mueller, and Peter Murrell, whose work on complementary or collaborative projects is proving to be particularly helpful, and John Flemming, who provided most helpful comments at an early stage when that required special patience. I am also indebted to the Lehrman Institute, the National Science Foundation, and Resources for the Future for supporting my research. Parts of this essay are included in my book *The Decline and Fall of Nations: Economic Growth, Stagflation, and Social Rigidities* (New Haven: Yale University Press, 1982).

Though the argument in that book has been changed to take account of criticisms in this volume, the present essay has, with minor exceptions, been left as it was when the criticisms and extensions in this volume were proposed. The extent of my indebtedness to the contributors to the present volume will therefore be clear to the reader.

estimates of the relative contributions to growth of capital accumulation, of technical advance, and so on, were a major advance, and more recent estimates by Dale Jorgenson and others have taken advantage of the latest econometric techniques. Yet estimates of the sources of growth, however meticulous or sophisticated, do not tell us about the ultimate causes of growth. They do not tell us what incentives made the saving and investment occur, or what explained the innovations, or why there was more innovation or capital accumulation in one society or period than in another. They do not trace the sources of growth to their fundamental causes; they trace the water in the river to the streams and lakes from which it comes, but they do not explain the rain. This essay, by contrast, will emphasize the more fundamental determinants of growth rates and in particular will develop a model of some accumulating side effects of social and political stability that slow down the processes that generate growth. This model, if correct, explains the most notable variations in growth rates among those countries that are economically developed democracies, that is, those that are often loosely called the capitalist countries.

The limited nature of our understanding of the causes and retardants of growth is evident from a glance at those developed countries whose growth rates since World War II have surprised most economists. Consider first the rapid growth rates of the nations whose totalitarian governments were defeated in World War II. The rapid growth of Germany and Japan occurred not only shortly after the war, when these countries were recovering their prewar or "normal" levels of income, but also after their per-capita incomes surpassed prior levels and even those of some of the victorious countries.

Though it is not obviously anomalous, the performance of the French economy nonetheless also deserves some special attention. The estimates of the sources of growth confirm that the rate of capital accumulation has a significant effect on the rate of economic growth. Since new technologies are embodied in new capital equipment, some of the residual increase in productivity attributed to advances in knowledge would presumably also not have occurred without investment. Businessmen do, of course, have a political incentive to exaggerate their need for stable and predictable public policies, but there can be no doubt that their insecurities have some effect on both the level and type of investment in new capital. Virtually all economists accordingly agree that events, or even expectations, that discourage investment or that destroy productive capital will lower the level of income. Thus societies that are politically unstable or are often subjected to foreign invasion are likely to have less productive investment. There will be more flights of capital and fewer investments in plant or equipment that can pay off only in the long run. Savings are more likely to be hoarded in easily portable but socially unproductive assets such as gold. It follows that the level of per-capita income that France has achieved is probably also anomalous. In less than two centuries that country has experienced one of the most profound and protracted revolutions in human history, has gone through constitutions almost as though they were periodical literature, and has suffered partial or total occupation four times. Even in the late sixties and seventies near revolutions and fears of a popular-front government have brought about some capital flight. Given the extraordinary succession of political upheavals and foreign incursions, why did France have in 1970 a per-capita income decidedly above that of Great Britain, only a fourth lower than that of the United States, and about the same as that of West Germany,[1] another anomaly? Though the effects of World War II on the countries of Europe were in important ways different, France has, from a longer historical perspective, much in common with its former foes. Its experience is also different only in degree from that of Belgium and Holland.

Finally, there is of course the surprisingly slow growth of the United Kingdom, which has had the slowest growth of the major developed democracies in the years since World War II. Britain's relatively slow rate of growth goes back to the last two decades of the nineteenth century, and per-capita income in Britain is now decidedly lower than in most of the rest of Western Europe.

The Inadequacy of Ad Hoc Explanations

There are many ad hoc explanations for these puzzling differences in growth rates. Such explanations usually appeal only to laymen, but many economists studying relative growth rates have apparently found no alternative to them, unless it is to stress sociological and political factors without providing citations to any literature in which these factors are explained.

The remarkably rapid postwar growth of Germany and Japan, for ex-

---

1. Irving B. Kravis et al., *A system of International Comparison of Gross Product and Purchasing Power* (Baltimore: Johns Hopkins University Press, 1975), pp. 1–13.

ample, is often ascribed to the destruction of plants and equipment, which forced them to begin again with the latest technology. The rapid growth of Germany and Japan is similarly often ascribed to the unusual industriousness that is attributed to the populations of these countries, while in the same spirit the slow growth of Great Britain is ascribed to the allegedly exceptional British taste for leisure.

Perhaps because Britain has had an anomalous growth rate for a longer time, its economic performance has been the object of an unusual number of ad hoc explanations. The slow British growth is often laid to the strength or narrow-mindedness of British unions, to the resistance to change or uncooperative attitudes of British workers, or to socialistic governmental policies. Other explanations emphasize a lack of entrepreneurial drive and of willingness to innovate on the part of British managers; establishmentarian, anticommercial attitudes that keep the ablest and best-educated people away from business pursuits; and an addiction among the British ruling classes to Concorde-type purchases of national prestige. A common denominator of most of these ad hoc explanations of Britain's slow growth is that they emphasize the alleged rigidity of the British class system or some especially distinctive trait of one social class or another.

The foregoing folk wisdom is not set out as a straw man; on the contrary, the folk wisdom contains substantial elements of truth, and I will even endeavor to provide a more fundamental basis for some of the popular arguments. The point is to make it clear that even the most appealing ad hoc arguments cannot be sufficient.

One reason that these arguments are insufficient is that they are not directly testable against an array of data or experience broad enough to tell us whether they contain any truth. Each country is unique in many ways: the fact that a country with an unusually high or low growth rate has this or that distinctive trait provides no justification for the inference that there is probably a causal connection. Only the British have Big Ben and only the Germans eat a lot of sauerkraut, but no one suggests that the one is responsible for the slow British growth and the other for the fast German growth. An explanation of differences in growth rates cannot claim any more credence than can the Big Ben/sauerkraut argument unless it has stood up to testing against a broad range of data and, ideally, also has been derived from a theory which is based on assumptions that have proved robust or realistic enough to explain a range of phenomena.

Another reason why the ad hoc arguments are insufficient is that, because they are not related to any fundamental theory, they provide no guide to why the attribute that is alleged to explain the anomalous rate of growth came to characterize the country in question; and accordingly, they offer no clue to how a growth-inhibiting attribute might be eliminated or a growth-promoting attribute developed.

The limitations of ad hoc explanations and the importance of explaining the origin of any attribute that is alleged to explain growth rates can be beautifully illustrated in the economic history of Britain. In discussions of modern growth rates it is all too often forgotten that, just as Britain has had the slowest rate of growth of the developed democracies for quite some time, so apparently it had the fastest rate of growth in the world for almost a century. It was the British, of course, who invented modern economic growth with the Industrial Revolution. From approximately the middle of the eighteenth century until almost the middle of the nineteenth century, Britain had the fastest or, at the least, one of the fastest rates of growth in the world. *This means that no explanation of the current slow growth of the British economy in terms of some supposedly inherent or enduring characteristic of British society, or of any one of its social classes, could possibly be adequate.*

There is still further evidence of the need to go beyond ad hoc explanations and even a hint about what an adequate general theory would be like in the references to the British class structure in the economic history texts. The economic historians suggest that, in relation to much of the Continent, Britain had unusual social mobility, relatively little class consciousness, and a concern in all social classes with commerce, production, and financial gain that was sometimes notorious to its neighbors:

> More than any other in Europe, probably, British society was open. Not only was income more evenly distributed than across the Channel, but the barriers to mobility were lower, the definitions of status looser. . . .
>
> It seems clear that British commerce of the eighteenth century was, by comparison with that of the Continent, impressively energetic, pushful, and open to innovation. . . . No state was more responsive to the desires of its mercantile classes. . . . Nowhere did entrepreneurial decisions less reflect non-rational considerations of prestige and habit. . . . Talent was readier to go into business, projecting, and invention. . . .
>
> This was a people fascinated by wealth and commerce, collec-

tively and individually. . . . Business interests promoted a degree of intercourse between people of different stations and walks of life that had no parallel on the Continent.

The flow of entrepreneurship within business was freer, the allocation of resources more responsive than in other economies. Where the traditional sacrosanctity of occupational exclusiveness continued to prevail across the Channel . . . the British cobbler would not stick to his last nor the merchant to his trade. . . .

Far more than in Britain, continental business enterprise was a class activity, recruiting practitioners from a group limited by custom and law. In France, commercial enterprise had traditionally entailed derogation from noble status.[2]

It is not surprising that Napoleon once derided Britain as a "nation of shopkeepers" and that even Adam Smith found it expedient to use this phrase in his criticism of Britain's mercantilistic policies.[3]

Britain's gradual shift from first to last place in relative growth rates and the hints that the *relative* rigidity of its social structure also has changed make it seem likely that a correct explanation of British growth would focus upon gradual growth-reducing changes in British society. There is, however, one other logically possible explanation. This arises from the fact that *absolute* rates of growth have been increasing for the last century or two throughout the developed world. Indeed, the fastest rate of growth of per-capita income ever in Britain, as in other developed democracies, has occurred since World War II. A major reason for this is the increasingly rapid advance of pure science and technology, which all nations are generally able to share. (This advance in knowledge will have a major role in the argument developed here.) It is therefore logically possible that Britain's shift from the relatively fastest-growing to the relatively slowest-growing of the developed democracies could be explained by the emergence of some growth-promoting factor, or the weakening of some growth-repressing factor, that occurred elsewhere and did not occur at all or to the same degree in Britain. The fact that there are only two

---

2. David S. Landes, *The Unbound Prometheus* (Cambridge: Cambridge University Press, 1969), pp. 39–122. These quotations are taken from widely scattered sections of chapters 2 and 3.

3. I am grateful to Daniel Patrick Moynihan for reminding me of the purpose Smith had when using this expression: "To found a great empire for the sole purpose of raising up a people of customers, may at first sight appear a project only for a nation of shopkeepers; but extremely fit for a nation whose government is influenced by shopkeepers." *Wealth of Nations* (New York: Modern Library, 1937), p. 579.

forms that a correct explanation of British growth rates could possibly take is very important, for it immediately rules out most of the familiar explanations for Britain's slow growth and can keep us alert for any model that independently generates an explanation that has one of the two logically admissible profiles.

If what has been said in this section is correct, any adequate model not only must have one or the other of the possible profiles; it should also be framed in such a way that it applies to every country or region in at least one category, so that it will be refuted if it is contradicted by a majority of the cases in the relevant class. The basic model I set out here is directly applicable to the class of the developed democracies, and the model will be refuted if it is broadly inconsistent with experience in these countries. The model grows out of the "new political economy" or "public choice." Accordingly it focuses on some phenomena that economists have only recently begun to consider and which apparently never have been the focus of any analysis of comparative growth rates. The model nonetheless rests on familiar behavioral assumptions that have proven to be robust and useful in economic analyses generally.

The Logic of Collective Action

This analysis begins by considering those combinations or associations of firms or individuals that, as a result of their concerted action, obtain market power or political influence or both: labor unions, professional associations, farm organizations, trade associations, lobbies, cartels, and informally or even tacitly organized groups. These organizations will be called common-interest or special-interest groups, to call attention to the fact that all such combinations are supposed to serve the common interests of some collection of firms or individuals and to remind us that they represent only sections of the total society.

A defining feature of all these special-interest associations and collusions is that each provides some service to everyone in some category or group. If a union wins higher wages, every worker in the relevant category gets a higher rate of pay; if a cartel raises the price of some good, every firm that sells that good in the cartelized market gets the higher price; if a farm organization obtains legislation favorable to farmers, any farmer may take advantage of it. This means that every special-interest group provides what an economist must, to be consistent, define as a collective or public good: one that goes to everyone in some group if it goes to anyone in the group. The exclusion of nonpurchasers is not feasible. Though the expression "public good" is often applied only to goods provided by governments, this arbitrary usage obscures one fundamental respect in which governments and private associations are the same. Governments cannot sell their most basic services, such as defense or law and order, in a free market and rely instead on compulsory taxation. The individual has no incentive voluntarily to purchase basic government services; he would get a negligible share of the benefits of any public goods he chose to buy.

I have shown elsewhere[4] that associations in the private sector normally also cannot sell their basic services in a regular market, at least when the group they represent is sufficiently large. Each individual or firm will, when the group is large, again get only a minuscule share of the benefits of any action he takes in the group interest, and thus, if he should act in the group interest at all, such action will cease long before a group-optimal level of provision is achieved. When the group of firms or individuals that share a common interest is small, the external economy of individual action in the group interest will tend to be smaller, and Cournot-type behavior will come closer to achieving levels of provision that are Pareto-optimal for the group. In sufficiently small groups, moreover, the individuals can have an incentive to bargain with one another, and the strategic or oligopolistic interaction can sometimes lead to maximization of their joint interest. No more will be said about this logic here, since the argument has previously been set out more formally and fully.[5]

It follows inescapably that rational, self-interested individuals, at least in large groups, will not contribute significant amounts of time or money to an organization working in their common interest solely because they value the collective good such an organization could provide. Only a separate *selective* incentive, which discriminates between those who contribute to the provision of the collective good and those who do not, can induce large groups of individuals to act in their common interest. One selective incentive, as the analogy with taxation reminds us, is coercion: those who do not help finance the public good are subjected to some kind of sanction. Though there is a wide variety of coercive arrangements behind various special-interest groups, the best known are the picket lines

4. Mancur Olson, *The Logic of Collective Action* (Cambridge, Mass.: Harvard University Press, 1965, 1971).
5. Ibid., ch. 1.

and the closed shops of the labor unions. Individuals also may be induced to act in their common interest with positive selective incentives, that is, rewards to those who contribute to the provision of the collective good. A prototypical example is provided by American farm organizations, which often check off the dues in the lobbying organization out of the patronage dividends of tax-exempt farm cooperatives and mutual insurance companies. Other associations often exploit various tax advantages of non-profit organizations or various complementarities between special-interest groups and certain commercial activities to offer attractive publications, group insurance, charter flights, or club facilities to those who join the association.

If the group that shares a common interest is disposed to interact socially or can be subdivided into constituent groups that would interact, social selective incentives, both positive and negative, can be used. Those who act in the common interest can at little cost be accorded respect or even honor. Those who do not can be readily criticized or even ostracized. In societies in which solitary confinement is considered the harshest punishment short of death, the social incentive must surely sometimes be a powerful one.

As the late Reuben Kessel pointed out in his study of the relation between ethnic discrimination and price discrimination in the early history of organized medicine in the United States,[6] social pressure is more effective when the group at issue is more likely to interact socially because of similarities of background or other reasons. The significance of social homogeneity is also suggested by the theories of fiscal equivalence and optimal segregation, which emphasize the fact that all who receive a collective good tend to receive the same amount and type of good and that the nonrevelation of preferences for public goods prevents the attainment of Lindahl equilibria.[7] Thus, regrouping into jurisdictions or clubs with homogeneous tastes and incomes can sometimes increase welfare and reduce conflict. Both Kessel's argument and the fiscal equivalence type of reasoning suggest that special-interest groups are likely to emerge in homogeneous groups and that their leaders will have some tendency to maintain this homogeneity.

6. Reuben Kessel, "Price Discrimination in Medicine," *Journal of Law and Economics* (October 1968): 20–53.

7. Mancur Olson, "The Principle of Fiscal Equivalence," *American Economic Review, Proceedings*, vol. 59, no. 2 (May 1969): 479–89; Martin C. McGuire, "Group Segregation and Optimal Jurisdictions," *Journal of Political Economy*, vol. 82, no. 1 (January 1974): 112–32.

Though there has been no systematic international test of the implications of the argument that has just been described, the model was supported by a fairly detailed examination of all powerful interest groups in the United States in the early 1960s and has appeared roughly consistent with a wide variety of studies of special-interest groups done since that time.

Second-order Implications

The model outlined above has several general implications for the pattern of organization of interest groups in democratic societies. One is that the largest and most scattered interests presumably never will be able to organize in the mass. Consumers, taxpayers, the unemployed, and the poor have important common interests and would benefit substantially from effective mass organizations working on their behalf. But how can any organizer or political entrepreneur, without substantial assistance from the government, manage to coerce such groups? They do not assemble at any one spot the way workers at a mine or factory do, so that nothing resembling the picket line would be feasible. Nor is there apparently any way of getting enough resources in the private sector to induce the masses in such groups to act collectively. Thus it is not just an accident that there are not mass contributions to consumer, taxpayer, or poverty organizations in any of the economically developed democracies: their absence is due to the underlying logic of the situation.

Another implication of the model is that even those groups that can be organized usually will not be organized until some time after the common interests emerge. The organization of a labor union, for example, may wait until a jump in the demand for the relevant type of labor makes scabs hard to find and increases the potential loss to the employer from a strike. For example, in the United States, World Wars I and II saw exceptional union growth. Alternatively, a crisis may facilitate mass action and organization. In some cases, the creative political entrepreneur may be lacking. When interest groups must trade a private benefit of some kind for participation in efforts to obtain a public good, successful organization is likely to require exceptionally favorable conditions as well as good leadership. Simply setting up some kind of business whose profits can finance mass participation to obtain a public good will not suffice: profits are more easily sought than obtained, and if they are obtained the promoters may decide to keep them for themselves. The successful large-scale lobbying organizations that lack coercive power normally have had to find and exploit some tax advantage or special complementarity between the lobbying organization and the income-generating activity that finances participation in it.

Historical experience confirms that it takes quite a bit of time for groups with common interests to organize. Not until 1851, or virtually a century after the start of the Industrial Revolution, did the first true labor union (the Amalgamated Society of Engineers in Britain) emerge. Though in the United States many unions go back to the second half of the nineteenth century, the fastest growth of labor unions took place from 1937 to 1945, long after the country had achieved the industrialized condition favorable to unions. Some industrialized continental countries developed truly powerful unions only after World War II, and some have yet to develop them. The emergence of farm organizations also seems to take a long while. In the United States, for example, farmers constituted the largest part of the population and had significant common interests even at the founding of the Republic. Yet it was the late nineteenth century before any successful farm organization emerged, and not until World War I was the largest of farm organizations, the Farm Bureau, created by the Agricultural Extension Service of the federal government. The situation has not been greatly different in Britain or in some other societies. There is a need for systematic international research into the time it takes professional associations to emerge; it could be that they form less slowly. Small groups, such as trade associations and cartels, can of course emerge much more readily. But bargaining, given its time cost and the incentive to be a holdout, can take a long while and may initially be unsuccessful.

Once substantial common-interest organizations emerge, they are not likely to disappear. As Max Weber and others have pointed out, their leaders are likely to want to maintain them even if their initial function no longer needs to be performed. The selective incentives that support most common-interest groups will also normally ensure that they can maintain themselves indefinitely. It is difficult to think of powerful special-interest groups that have wasted away.

A second general implication of the model is therefore that developed democratic societies will accumulate more special-interest organizations as time goes on. Collective action is difficult and problematic, especially for large groups, and will occur if at all only under favorable conditions. The longer a society has stable freedom of organization, the greater the

likelihood that any given group with a common interest will find conditions in which it can work out selective incentives. Once such incentives
have been obtained, the organization is not likely to disappear, and the
number of such organizations increases over time. Nonetheless, our
model implies that some groups are never in a position to organize effectively, so that societies do not achieve complete or symmetrical organization of the groups within them: they never reach a stage in which all the
interests are similarly organized, so that their leaders could perhaps get
together and bargain with one another until an efficient or core allocation
of resources is achieved.

We must now ask what effects special-interest organizations and informal collusive arrangements have on the rate of growth. What incentive do
such organizations have to increase or to limit the rate of growth? The
answer is substantially dependent on whether the special-interest group is
small in relation to the economy as a whole or whether it encompasses a
significant fraction of the total work force or capital stock in the economy. Consider, for example, unions that (though they might have tens of
thousands of members) represent less than, say, one percent of the work
force, or trade associations that (though they may represent several major
corporations) account for a minute share of a nation's capital stock. Let us
abstract from exceptional cases in which such groups would not gain from
economic growth in their society, for example, that of sellers of inferior
goods. It then follows that, if it cost nothing to work for policies that
increased economic efficiency, the special-interest group would strive to
make the economy more efficient. Unfortunately, this work *does* cost
something. If a narrow special-interest group campaigns for the removal
of tax loopholes or socially inefficient tariffs, or lobbies for any nation-
wide public goods that will increase society's output, its members will
bear all the costs of their effort yet will get only a minuscule share of the
benefits, since they are by stipulation only a minute part of the economy.
The logic here is identical to that which showed that individuals in large
groups are less likely spontaneously to work for the common interest of
their group than are individuals in small groups, so the equations cited
previously still apply. If a common-interest group were unaccountably to
bring about the elimination of a public policy or market distortion of
which its own members were the principal beneficiaries, those members
would normally suffer a substantial loss, even if the total social gains
from the change were many times larger than the costs. Thus it would be
very surprising if narrowly based special-interest organizations or collu-

sive combinations gave high priority to measures that would benefit their members only to the extent that they get a minute share of the increase they bring about in the size of the national pie.

Almost the only case in which a narrow common-interest group could serve its clients' interests by enhancing economic efficiency and growth would be when its clients are the principal victims of some inefficient policy or institution. The construction lobby may oppose the usury law that keeps house buyers from getting credit, the farm organization may oppose a tariff on farm machinery, and the labor union may force a monopsonistic employer to treat the wage as the marginal cost of the labor he hires. Unfortunately, such cases are not very numerous. If all groups in the society were symmetrically organized, presumably there would be some organization to represent every group, including consumers, that would lose from each inefficient policy, and inefficient policies would then rarely pass. But if the prior argument is correct, there are no symmetrically organized societies.

The moment one asks how a special-interest organization can make its members better off by *reducing* economic efficiency, examples abound. Pressure groups often obtain tariffs that prevent the allocation of resources to lines in which they have a comparative advantage, price supports that raise the price of a commodity above its marginal social cost, or tax loopholes that encourage capital to crowd into activities in which its marginal social product will be unusually low. Each such inefficiency will, it is true, bring about only a one-time reduction in the absolute level of income rather than reduction in the rate of growth. But the accumulation of such inefficiencies that our model predicts lowers the rate of growth as well.

Special-interest groups also reduce the rate of growth along with the level of income when they use their power to block innovation. A labor union often has an incentive to repress labor-saving innovations that would reduce the demand for the group it represents or to demand featherbedding or other forms of overmanning. Similarly, whenever a firm develops an improved product or process that its competitors could copy only tardily, other firms will have an incentive to use their trade association or cartel, either directly or through its links with the government, to obstruct the innovation. Since a major technological advance will normally change both the optimal policy for a collusive group and the relative strengths of each of its members, the advance will also normally require new rounds of bargaining if the gains from combination are to be preserved. The chancy and sometimes protracted character of such bargaining may also induce the collusive group to discourage major innovations. Moreover, when an industry is nationalized, regulated as a public utility, or for other reasons subject to political dictation, and if the pertinent special-interest groups can veto changes or simply demand consultation about them, innovations will take longer to implement and the rate of growth will be slower. Indeed, in some cases even straightforward adaptations to new patterns of demand and the employment of commonplace modern machinery can be delayed, perhaps even for generations as the history of many of the older American railroads illustrates, so that a configuration of practices that might once have been optimal diverges ever further from the current ideal.

Above all, special-interest groups limit entry into markets they control either directly or by raising the price that must be paid in the controlled market. These entry barriers make an economy less efficient and lower the level of income. Do they also reduce the rate of growth? It would seem intuitively that they would do so in any circumstances in which an economy needs to adapt to changes in technology, tastes, or other conditions, and that was my initial opinion. A number of critics persuaded me at one point that a constant level of entry barriers would imply only a lower absolute level of income but not a lower rate of growth, since a constant degree of malallocation of resources should not offset the rate of increase in income due to technological advance or other factors. In fact, as Sir John Hicks has helpfully and rigorously proved in his essay in this volume,[8] barriers to resource reallocation will in general also reduce the growth rate. Notwithstanding the number of us who were wrong, the logic of the matter in this case (as in so many others) is very simple once it has been properly understood and explained. As Sir John Hicks's paper shows, any increases in productivity in different industries will normally change relative prices as well as income levels. There is the possibility that expenditures on each product, despite the income and price changes, might by chance be at just the level that induced all resources to remain in exactly the same employments. But unless all expenditures on each product happen to be at this improbable level, the increases in productivity will entail that resources must be reallocated if economic efficiency is to be maintained and the society is to take full advantage of the increases in productivity. The required resource reallocations will be prevented or delayed by the barriers to entry. A society with barriers to entry will there-

8. See chapter 2.

fore tend to get less growth out of a given advance in technological knowledge than will a society without such barriers. Hicks has further demonstrated that the magnitude of the reduction in the growth rate will vary with the extent to which the new pattern of expenditures deviates from the old and on the size of the industries in which resources are wasted because of the barriers to resource reallocation.[9] We can conclude that even if the strength of special-interest organizations and collusions should remain unchanged over time, an economy with a higher level of entry barriers will have a lower rate of growth as well as a lower absolute income.

The innovation-slowing and entry-limiting processes that have been described are important because of their profound impact on production functions, or what is sometimes called X-efficiency, and thus on the *evolution* of an economy. Innovation and experimentation in an economy are analogous to mutation in biological evolution. Profit seeking and the effort to avoid bankruptcy in any area of an economy are similar to the "survival of the fittest" in biology. This will be true even if competition is monopolistic—characterized by a high degree of product differentiation—so long as entrants are free to offer substitutes for the output of any existing firm. Both innovation and the Darwinian struggle are altered by any arrangements that control entry or subsidize failing firms. Accordingly, the hypothesis here proposes that common-interest groups substantially alter the evolution of an economy and slow its rate of growth. Though evolution continues, it centers increasingly on organizational or political struggles over distribution rather than on the search for new revenues or lower costs.

The extent to which this evolutionary emphasis transcends the usual microeconomic theory becomes clear as soon as we note that the textbook definition of monopoly—price above marginal cost—has not been listed here as one of the costs of common-interest groups and collusions. The reason is that, taken alone, this cost in conformity with Harberger's seminal estimates is presumed to be trivial, though monopolistic combinations will of course maximize joint profits by equating marginal revenue rather than price to marginal cost. But, as I have argued elsewhere,[10] the divergence between price and marginal cost is likely to be modest in the long

9. Strictly speaking, Hicks's proof applies only to a two-sector economy with labor as the only factor of production. The essence of the argument is nonetheless generalizable to economies with any number of industries or factors of production.

10. See my essay "On the Priority of Public Problems," in *The Corporate Society*, ed. Robin Marris (London: Macmillan, 1974), pp. 294–336.

run if there is unimpeded entry, since new entrants with substitute products will make firm demand curves more elastic and ultimately will improve the well-known tangency solution, in which monopoly profits are
zero and the difference between marginal cost and price is limited.[11]
When entry is blocked, by contrast, or when governments with coercive
power can create a difference between private and social cost of almost
any size, the losses that are amenable to comparative-static calculations
can be enormous and the evolutionary development of an economy can
also be altered.

When entry blockages and government intervention can create large
Harberger triangles, there is normally also a substantial redistributive effect. As Gordon Tullock, Anne Krueger, and others have shown, any
such substantial redistribution will engender extensive efforts and expenditures designed to win the rents that can accrue from entry barriers or
favorable legislation. Those who lose from the redistribution will also, if
organized, have an incentive to devote resources to defending their interests. As a result there will be a deadweight loss beyond that measured
in the Harberger triangle, consisting of the resources devoted to seeking
(or resisting the seekers of) the rents resulting from imposition of entry
barriers and government policies obtained by special interests.[12] The extent of this loss from rent-seeking will normally rise pari passu with the
degree of special-interest organization.[13]

The argument that special-interest organizations have substantial adverse effects on economic efficiency and growth does not necessarily
apply for those organizations that encompass a substantial fraction of the
population or resources of a society. The logic behind this conclusion is
the same as that which showed earlier that the members of very small

11. This hypothesis does not imply that laissez faire is Pareto efficient or necessarily even close to
optimality. A great many market imperfections may exist even in the absence of common-interest
organizations; the point is rather that common-interest organizations usually create new distortions
rather than end old ones. Air pollution, for example, is an important example of a market failure that
laissez faire does not solve. But the powerful common-interest organizations under discussion did not
start the campaigns against air pollution and on occasion have even opposed effluent fees and other
environment controls.

12. I am thankful to Dennis Mueller for calling the pertinence of rent-seeking to my attention.

13. The hypothesis that most common-interest organizations will have an adverse effect on rates of
growth of national product does not mean that such organizations are undesirable. They may perform
services that are not properly counted in the national income statistics. For example, they ensure a more
pluralistic political life and thereby protect democratic freedoms. Labor unions make employees feel
less subject to arbitrary actions of particular supervisors. The purpose here is not to argue for the
abolition of common-interest organizations but rather to put forth hypotheses that can be tested against
the existing statistics on economic growth.

groups are more likely than members of large groups to act voluntarily and spontaneously in their group interest. Just as the individual in a small group will tend to get a larger share of the gain from any action he takes in the group interest than the individual in a large group, so also the special-interest group that encompasses a large part of the society will tend to get a larger share of the benefits of an increase in national output than will a narrow common-interest group. The greater the size of the special interest that an organization represents, the smaller the external economy of action in the interest of society as a whole. More pertinently, the more inclusive the special-interest group, the greater will be the share of the social costs of any inefficient policies to be borne by its own membership. This internalization of external effects rises monotonically with the share of the population and other resources that a special-interest group includes. The parallel with strategic interaction in smaller groups also holds up. If there are only a handful of special-interest groups in a society, each with a noticeable percentage of the population and resources, their leaders may find it worthwhile to bargain with one another for the gains that socially efficient policies could bring.

If we define society in national terms, it follows that the national government encompasses everyone in a society. This means that though there are colossal and well-known difficulties in arriving at optimal collective decisions the national government would, if not influenced by lobbies, have an incentive to promote efficiency and growth. The argument here accordingly focuses not only on the absolute power of special-interest groups but also on the *relative* strength of the most encompassing group, the government, versus constituent groups that are much less encompassing. The efficiency of an economy may be increased either by making narrow special-interest groups weaker or by making the government stronger in relation to them. This logic must stand behind demands for political leaders with the popularity and resolve needed to "stand up to the vested interests" and must be especially important in understanding countries, such as Italy, with insecure governments.

Though the degree to which a common-interest group is encompassing necessarily affects the incentive to pursue efficient and growth-promoting policies, it does not necessarily affect the rate of growth itself. Any special-interest group may very well be mistaken about what will promote growth, just as a businessman might be mistaken about what investment is most likely to prove profitable. This is true both of organizations representing sectional interests and of governments. In societies with only a few highly inclusive organizations, there will tend to be fewer experiments and less intensive debates, so the chances that mistaken policies will be chosen could well be greater. When common-interest groups are unusually encompassing, and certainly when the central government is exceptionally strong in relation to all other organizations in the society, the chance that totalitarianism will ensue also tends to be greater. There can be no guarantee that sufficiently encompassing organizations will generate desirable outcomes. Nonetheless, there is always the possibility, if not the presumption, that the highly encompassing organization will in its own interest seek socially efficient policies, whereas very narrow common-interest groups never have an incentive to take the interests of the larger society into account. Indeed, in many cases, special-interest groups have such narrow bases that they do not even have an incentive to take much account of the interests of the industries or firms with which they deal. The argument here implies, for example, that industrial and enterprise unions will be less likely to pursue socially inefficient policies than will craft unions.[14] The presence of encompassing organizations will also eliminate costly disputes over demarcation or jurisdiction and will prevent the reduction in innovation that occurs when each of many groups has veto power over changes.

Third-order Implications

To summarize: Associations that provide collective goods are for the most fundamental reasons exceedingly difficult to establish, especially for larger groups; none will attract a significant percentage of scattered groups like consumers, taxpayers, the unemployed, or the poor; associa-

---

14. The merger or expansion of tiny organizations will not, however, necessarily increase social efficiency. Many special-interest organizations are so small in relation to the economy that even after great expansion they would control only a minute proportion of the society's resources. The degree to which such expansions internalize the national external diseconomies of growth-repressing policies is negligible, though there is the possibility that they would increase the sensitivity to social costs imposed on host firms or industries. The social value of this sensitivity may be more than offset by greater monopoly losses, if the expansion engrosses close substitutes for the factor or product in question. This is clearly a question that requires more research. Fortunately, when organizations encompass a substantial segment of the whole society, the situation is fairly straightforward. Such organizations normally represent clients in different industries; they are typically unions that represent most of the manual workers or business organizations that represent most of the substantial firms. Since usually it is not possible to exert much monopoly power across industry lines, such organizations won't employ more market power than separate industry-wide organizations would have done. Their members will bear a substantial cost of any growth-repressing policies, however, so they have an incentive to further their members' interests in ways that will not be very harmful to the whole society.

tions that can promote the common interests of some groups will be able to establish themselves, but only in favorable circumstances and thus often only long after the common interest arises; as associations with monopoly control or political power accumulate, they delay the innovations and reallocations of resources needed for rapid growth, though this need not occur if the associations encompass a substantial percentage of those who bear the costs of the delays.

It follows that countries whose special-interest groups have been emasculated or abolished by totalitarian government and foreign occupation should grow relatively quickly *after* a free and stable legal order is established. This helps to explain the marked underestimation of the growth that the war-torn economies would achieve after World War II, especially in the cases of Germany and Japan. In these countries, totalitarian governments were followed by Allied occupiers who were determined to promote institutional change and ensure that institutional life would start almost anew.[15] In Germany, Hitler had done away with independent unions as well as all other dissenting groups, whereas the Allies, through such measures as the decartelization decrees of 1947 and denazification programs, had emasculated cartels and organizations with right-wing backgrounds.[16] In Japan, the militaristic regime had kept down left-wing organizations, whereas the Supreme Commander of the Allied Powers imposed an antimonopoly law in 1947 and purged many hundreds of officers of Zaibatsu or other corporations for their wartime activities.[17]

Moreover, the special-interest organizations established after World War II in Germany and Japan were for the most part highly encompassing. This is true of the postwar labor union structure of West Germany and of the organization of businesses and employers that has played a dominant role in economic policy making in Japan. Whatever the reasons, the postwar growth rates of these two countries were likely enhanced not only by the absence of a dense accumulation of powerful

15. This is probably less true of Italy, though research on the Italian case has barely begun. Also, the very rapid rates of growth in postwar Italy have come to a temporary halt, perhaps under the pressure of common-interest groups. A severe and precocious sclerosis in Italy would raise the possibility that the model offered here is incomplete or incorrect: the precocity (if it exists) has to be predicted. An interesting question then is whether this Italian precocity is due to the application of the logic described in the previous section: to a weak, underdeveloped state that usually cannot resist common interest of even relatively modest strength.

16. Gustav Stolper et al., *The German Economy, 1870 to the Present* (New York: Harcourt Brace and World, 1967), pp. 258–61.

17. Richard E. Caves and Masu Uekusa, *Industrial Organization in Japan* (Washington: Brookings Institution, 1976).

special-interest groups but also by the encompassing character of many organizations that were created or reorganized after the war.[18]

The theory also offers a new perspective on French growth. Why has France had good postwar growth and achieved levels of income broadly comparable with those of other advanced countries, despite the fact that the investment climate has often been so inclement? Perhaps the foreign invasions and political instability that have hindered capital accumulation also have hindered the development of common-interest organizations and collusions, and on occasion have led to their reorganization on more encompassing bases as well. The deep divisions in French ideological life must owe something to the way one upheaval after another called into question the country's basic political and economic system; and the number and intensity of these ideological divisions must have further impaired the development of at least the larger special-interest organizations in that country. Such smaller groups as trade associations and the alumni of the most prestigious schools have, as the theory predicts, more often been able to organize, but their effects on growth rates in the last few decades have often been limited for reasons that will become clear when we extend the theory.

The logic of the argument implies that countries that have for the longest time had democratic freedom of organization without upheaval or invasion will suffer the most from growth-repressing organizations and combinations. This may explain why Britain, the major nation with the longest history of immunity from dictatorship, invasion, and revolution, has in this century had a lower rate of growth than other developed countries. Britain has precisely the powerful network of common-interest groups that the argument developed here would lead us to expect in a country with its record of military security and democratic stability. The number and power of its trade unions need no description. The venerability and power of its professional associations is also striking; consider the distinction between solicitors and barristers, which could not possibly have emerged in a free market innocent of professional associations or government regulations of the sort they often obtain. Britain also has a strong farmers' union and a great many trade associations. The word

---

18. I am grateful to Gudmund Hernes, with whom I am collaborating on an article on relatively encompassing organizations, for educating me on the apparently encompassing character of special-interest organizations in postwar Germany. I had initially given excessive emphasis to the more limited extent and power of common-interest organizations in countries that had been defeated in World War II.

"establishment" acquired its modern meaning there, and however often the word may be overused, it still suggests a substantial degree of informal organization that could emerge only gradually in a stable society. Many of the powerful special-interest groups in Britain are, moreover, narrow rather than encompassing. For example, often many essentially autonomous trade unions represent different workers in the same factory, and no one union encompasses a substantial fraction of the working population of the country.

As we recall, there are many ad hoc explanations. Some allege that the British, or perhaps only those in the working classes, do not work as hard as people in other countries. Some lay the unusually rapid growth of Germany and Japan to the special industriousness of their peoples. Taken literally, this type of explanation is unquestionably wrong, though related arguments may have value. The rate of economic growth is the rate of *increase* of national income, and though this could logically be due to an *increase* in the industriousness of a people, it could not, in the direct way implied in the familiar argument, be explained by their normal level of effort, which is relevant instead to their *absolute* level of income.[19] Even if the differences in willingness to work are part of the explanation, why are those in the fast-growing countries zealous and those in the slow-growing countries lazy? And since several countries, most notably Britain, have changed relative position in the race for higher growth rates, the timing of the waves of effort also needs explaining.

The most plausible explanation is that industriousness varies with the incentive to work to which individuals in different countries have become accustomed. These incentives, in turn, are strikingly influenced, whether for manual workers, professionals, or entrepreneurs, by the extent to which special-interest groups protect their members from the Darwinian processes described earlier. Thus the search for the causes of differences in the willingness to work, and in particular the question of why shirking should be thought to be present during Britain's period of slower-than-average growth but not when it had the fastest rate of growth, brings us back to the more fundamental explanation of differences in growth rates that is being offered here.

19. If we assume that the percentage of income saved rises with income, and that there are no inflows or outflows of capital, a country with a hard-working population will save and invest more than a country that is identical to it in everything except industriousness. It will accordingly grow faster. Another possibility is that more effort among those concerned with innovation could also increase the growth rate. I am thankful to Tatsuo Hatta and I. M. D. Little for help on these possibilities.

Another ad hoc explanation of the slow British growth focuses on a class consciousness that allegedly reduces social mobility and is often blamed for exclusive and traditionalist attitudes that discourage entrants and innovators and for maintaining medieval prejudices against commercial pursuits. We know from the fact that Britain had the fastest rate of growth in the world for nearly a century that its slow growth now could not be due to any inherent traits of the British character. We have also seen that eighteenth-century Britain appeared to be unique in Western Europe in the fluidity of its class structure, the weakness of its feudal ethos, the strength of its commercial spirit, and its hospitality to innovation. What explains the apparent shift in social structures and cultural attitudes?

We have already argued that instability, totalitarianism, and foreign occupation devastate established organizations and leadership groups and also make it harder for new special-interest organizations to emerge. In France, in much of what is now Germany, and in other parts of the Continent, feudal hierarchies and attitudes were apparently more rigid and highly developed than those in Britain. In France, for example, the nobility were exempt from taxation, whereas in Britain they were not. We saw earlier that in the eighteenth century Britain was distinguished from much of the Continent by its less rigid class structure and its greater receptivity to commerce. In some parts of Germany relatively detailed and hierarchical class structures were prescribed by law.

One reason that only remnants of medieval structures on the Continent remain today is that they are entirely out of congruity with the technology and ideas now common in the developed world. But there is another, more pertinent reason: revolution and occupation, Napoleonism and totalitarianism, have utterly demolished most feudal structures on the Continent and many of the cultural attitudes that they sustained. The new families and firms that rose to wealth and power often were not successful in holding on to their gains; new instabilities curtailed the development of new organizations and collusions that could have protected them and their descendants against still newer entrants. To be sure, fragments of the Middle Ages and chunks of the great fortunes of the nineteenth century still remain on the Continent; but, like the castles crumbling in the countryside, they do not hamper the work and opportunities of the average citizen.

The institutions of medieval Britain, and even the great family-oriented industrial and commercial enterprises of more recent centuries, are similarly out of accord with the twentieth century and have in large part crumbled. But would they not have been pulverized far more finely if Britain had gone through anything like the French Revolution, if a dictator had abolished its public schools, if it had suffered occupation by a foreign power, or if it had fallen prey to totalitarian regimes determined to destroy any organizations independent of the regime itself? The importance of the House of Lords, the Established Church, and the ancient colleges of Oxbridge has no doubt often been grossly exaggerated, but they are symbols of Britain's legacy from the preindustrial past or, more precisely, of the unique degree to which it has been preserved. There was extraordinary turmoil a century before the Industrial Revolution, and this probably played a role in opening British society to new talent and enterprise, but since then Britain has not suffered the institutional destruction, the forcible replacement of the elites, or the decimation of social classes that its Continental counterparts have experienced. The same stability and immunity from invasion have obviously also made it easier for the firms and families that advanced in the Industrial Revolution and the nineteenth century to organize or collude to protect their interests.

Here the argument is particularly likely to be misunderstood. It would be a logical error to suppose that a group as large as the British middle class could voluntarily collude to exclude others or to achieve any common interest.[20] Our framework of hypotheses does suggest that the unique stability of British life in the twentieth century must have affected social structure, social mobility, and cultural attitudes, but *not* through class conspiracies or coordinated action by any large class or group. The process is far subtler and must be studied at a less aggregative level.

We can see this process from a new perspective if we remember that concerted action usually requires selective incentives, that social pressure can often be an effective selective incentive, and that individuals of similar incomes and values are more likely to agree on the amount and type of collective good to purchase. Social incentives will not be very effective unless the group that values the collective good at issue interacts socially or is composed of subgroups that do. If the group does have its own social life, the desire for the companionship and esteem of colleagues and the fear of being slighted or even ostracized can at little cost provide a powerful incentive for concerted action. The organizational entrepreneurs who succeed in promoting special-interest organizations, and the managers

---

20. Olson, *The Logic of Collective Action*, pp. 98–110.

who maintain them, must therefore focus disproportionately on groups that already interact socially or that can be induced to do so. This means that special-interest groups will tend to have socially homogeneous memberships and that they will have an interest in using some resources to preserve this homogeneity. The fact that everyone in the pertinent group gets the same amount and type of a collective good also means, as we know from the theories of fiscal equivalence and optimal segregation, that there will be less conflict, and perhaps welfare gains as well, if those who are in the same jurisdiction or organization have similar incomes and preference orderings. This is important principally in organizations that are partly or entirely pressure groups, and that thereby need to agree on policies that may be controversial. The forces that have just been mentioned, operating simultaneously in thousands of professions, crafts, clubs, and communities, could by themselves explain some degree of class consciousness and even cultural caution about the fluctuating incomes and status of the businessman and the entrepreneur.

Unfortunately, the processes that have been described do not operate by themselves; they resonate with the fact that every special-interest organization or collusion that operates in the marketplace must, above all, control entry. There is no way a group can obtain more than the free market price unless it can keep outsiders from taking advantage of the higher price. Thus every special-interest group working in the marketplace is first and last an *exclusive* group:[21] a group that must exclude others if it is to serve any purpose for its members. Class barriers could not exist unless there were some groups capable of concerted action that had an interest in putting them up. We can see now that the special-interest organization or collusion that seeks advantage in the marketplace *must* exclude if it is to serve any function at all. Furthermore, if the organization is to have the inestimable benefit of socially selective incentives, it should be composed of people who have background and interests that are sufficiently similar to make them want to interact socially.

In addition to controlling entry, the successful cartelistic organization must also limit the output or labor of its own members; it must make all of the members conform to some plan for restricting the amount sold, however much this limitation and conformity might limit innovation.

As time goes on, custom and habit play a larger role. The special-interest groups use their resources to argue that what they do is what in

21. Ibid., pp. 36–43.

justice ought to be done. The more that pushy entrants and nonconforming innovators are repressed, the rarer they become, and what is not customary is "not done."

Nothing about this process should make it work differently at different levels of income or social status, though it may be particularly strong in professions in which public concern about unscrupulous or incompetent practitioners provides an ideal cover for policies that would in other contexts be described as "monopoly" or "greedy unionism."[22] The process takes place among the workers as well as the Lords; some of the first craft unions were in fact organized in pubs.

There is a temptation to conclude dramatically that this involutional process has turned a "nation of shopkeepers" into a land of clubs and pubs, but such a facile conclusion could be wrong and is certainly far too simple. Countervailing factors that may have greater quantitative significance are also at work. The rapid rate of scientific and technological advance encourages continuing reallocations of resources and brings about occupational, social, and geographical mobility. Perhaps the emergence of universal and largely free public education, in combination with what might be called impartial credentialism, also counters the involution. There is accordingly no presumption that the process described here has brought *increasing* class consciousness, traditionalism, or antagonism to entrepreneurship. The contrary forces may overwhelm the involution even when no upheavals or invasions destroy the institutions that sustain it. The only hypothesis on this point that can reasonably be derived from the model is that, of two societies that were in other respects equal, the one with the longer history of stability, security, and freedom of association would have more institutions that control entry and innovation, that these institutions would encourage more social interaction and homogeneity among their members, and that what is said and done by these institutions would have at least some influence on what people in that society find customary and fitting.

Unfortunately, it has not yet been possible to find suitable quantitative studies comparing social mobility in Britain and on the Continent. There is, however, one skillful quantitative comparison of the rates of social

---

22. One need not argue with George Bernard Shaw that "all professions are conspiracies against the laity" (*The Doctor's Dilemma*, 1906), yet one may believe that the honored place the professions have in modern society—and the fact that most intellectuals are in the professions—leads many to neglect their cartelistic aspects.

mobility in Britain and the United States.[23] This study finds, as have others, that neither society shows any signs of decreasing social mobility over time, but that, as the foregoing model would predict, the level of social mobility is somewhat lower in Britain.

At first sight, Sweden seems to contradict predictions based on the model since that country, though it industrialized late, has enjoyed freedom of organization and immunity from invasion for an unusually long time. The strength and coverage of special-interest organizations in Sweden, particularly of its labor movement, are what our model would predict. Why then does Sweden have one of the highest standards of living in the world? In particular, why, despite some recent reverses, has Sweden's economic performance been superior to Britain's, when its special-interest groups are also unusually strong? Does this divergence of performance argue not only against the familiar ad hoc argument that socialist economic policies are responsible for Britain's slow growth, but against our model as well?

It would, were it not for the fourth general hypothesis implied by the basic model, which states that sufficiently encompassing special-interest organizations will internalize much of the cost of inefficient policies and accordingly have an incentive to give greater weight to economic growth and to the interests of society as a whole. Sweden's main special-interest organizations are unusually encompassing, especially in comparison with those in Britain and the United States. For most of the postwar period, for example, practically all of the unionized manual workers in Sweden have belonged to one great labor organization. As our model predicts, Swedish labor leaders have often been distinguished from their counterparts in many other countries by their advocacy of such growth-increasing policies as subsidies to labor mobility and retraining rather than to inefficient plants. It is even conceivable that the partial integration of the Swedish labor organizations with the even more encompassing labor party, on a basis that contrasts with the corresponding situation in Britain, has at times accentuated the incentive to seek efficiency and growth,[24] though any definite statement here must await further research.

The reasons why Sweden (and Norway) have especially encompassing organizations also need to be explained. This task will be left for treat-

23. Donald S. Treiman and Kermit Terrill, "The Process of Status Attainment in the United States and Great Britain," *American Journal of Sociology* 81 (November 1975): 563–83.

24. I am thankful to Sten Nilson of the University of Oslo for this suggestion and for letting me see his draft on "Organizations in Norway after 1955."

ment at another time,[25] but one hypothesis follows immediately from our basic model: smaller groups are much more likely than large ones to organize spontaneously. This suggests that many relatively small common-interest groups—the British and American craft unions, for example—would be legacies of early industrialization, whereas special-interest groups that are established later, partly in emulation of the experience of countries that had previously industrialized, could be as large as their promoters could make them.

Implications for the United States

It is tempting to point to the relatively slow growth rate of the United States since World War II and to its good record of political stability and security against invasion, and then to conclude that the United States nicely fits the model offered here.[26] This conclusion is, however, premature, and probably also too simple. Different parts of the United States were settled at very different times and thus some have had a much longer time to accumulate special-interest groups. Some parts of the United States have enjoyed political stability and security from invasion for almost two centuries. By contrast, the South was not only defeated and devastated in the Civil War, and then subjected to federal occupation and carpetbagging, but for a century it reached no definitive outcome to the struggle over the racial policy that had been an ultimate cause of that war. There was no stable freedom of organization for black or racially integrated groups in the South until the passage of the acts extending voting rights and civil rights in 1964 and 1965.

Another complication arises in that since World War II the United States has had the highest per-capita income of all major nations. This was mainly because most of its industries had, at least in the early decades of the postwar period, a higher level of technology than those of other countries. This means that, at least for part of the postwar period, several other countries have had the opportunity to catch up by adopting superior technologies in use for some time in the United States as well as those developed in the current period, whereas in most industries in the

25. A paper on the Scandinavian experience is being prepared in collaboration with Gudmund Hernes of the University of Bergen.

26. I once did so, tentatively, in my "Comment" on Professor Thomas Wilson's paper in *The Market and the State*, ed. Thomas Wilson and Andrew Skinner (Oxford: Oxford University Press, 1976), p. 112.

United States any technical improvements could be only of the latter variety. Thus the growth rate of the United States should probably be adjusted upward for a fair test of the model offered here, but no one knows by how much.

Fortunately, since the United States is a large federation composed of separate states, often with very different histories and policies, a disaggregated test of the model is feasible. Moreover, the forty-eight contiguous states offer many more data points than can be obtained from aggregate data on the handful of developed democracies. The federal government also ensures that the income data for all the states are comparable. The analysis thus can not only rise above ad hoc explanations of growth rates of particular countries but can also weigh the hypothesis, as applied to national differences in growth rates, on a larger data base that will permit formal tests of statistical significance. These tests can be unusually straightforward because the hypothesized causal connection goes predominantly in only one direction: The length of time an area has had stable freedom of organization should affect its rate of growth, but there is at least for a first approximation no reason to suppose that the rate of growth of a region would on balance substantially change the rate at which the region accumulates common-interest groups. On the one hand, a booming economy may make barriers to entry and strikes more advantageous, but on the other, adversity can give a threatened group a reason to organize to protect customary levels of income. Thus simple, nonstructural regressions should be not only sufficient but perhaps better than any simultaneous-equation specification that is apparent now.

Since the model predicts that the longer an area has had stable freedom of organization, the more growth-retarding organizations it will accumulate, states that have been settled and politically organized the longest ought, other things equal, to have the lowest rates of growth. (We leave aside the states that were defeated in the Civil War.) The length of time a state has been settled and politically organized can be measured roughly by the number of years it has enjoyed statehood. Thus, excluding erstwhile members of the Confederacy, a simple regression between years since statehood and rates of growth should provide a preliminary test of our model.

If carried back into the nineteenth century, however, this test might be biased in favor of the model, since some states were then still being settled. The westward-moving frontier must have created disequilibria (the "gold rush" might be the most dramatic example) with unusual rates

of growth of total if not per-capita income. The frontier is generally supposed to have disappeared by the end of the nineteenth century, but where
agriculture and other industries oriented to natural resources are at issue,
some disequilibria may have persisted into the present century. Thus, the
more recent the period, the more likely that frontier effects are no longer
present. For this reason (and for another that will become apparent in
studying the South), the analysis deals with the years since 1965. Great
disequilibria are unlikely to remain three-quarters of a century after the
frontier closed, especially since many of the great agricultural areas in the
most recently settled states suffered substantial exogenous depopulations
during the agricultural depression of the twenties, the dust bowl of the
thirties, and the massive postwar migration from farms to cities. Tests
based on recent American experiences have the further advantage that
there has been stability in some states long enough for a significant degree
of institutional sclerosis to have developed in them; whereas there could
not have been much difference across states in this respect when even the
relatively older states were quite young.

The aforementioned regressions were run by Kwang Choi in complet-
ing his Ph.D. thesis, which contains a wide variety of statistical tests of
the theory offered here. Choi found that there is the hypothesized negative relationship between the number of years since statehood of all non-
Confederate states and their current rates of economic growth, and that
this relationship is statistically significant. This holds true whether or not
farm income and factor payments by governments are included in the
measure of growth.[27]

In a country with no barriers to migration of workers, migration should

27. $LPI = 9.576 - 0.0118\ STAHOD$
           (3.54) $R^2 = 0.26\quad n = 37$
    $NPI = 10.030 - 0.0149\ STAHOD$
           (4.49) $R^2 = 0.37\quad n = 37$

The first dependent variable, LPI, measures the income (but not transfer payments) received by labor or
by proprietors, irrespective of source. The other, NPI, measures only nonfarm income from private
sources. Unfortunately, there are no data on what proportion of the profits of corporations operating in
more than one state were generated in each state, so both measures exclude undistributed corporate
profits. There are data by state on dividends, interest, and rents received, but these factor payments will
often have been generated by activity in states other than that where the recipient lived. Indeed, if the
most profitable corporations are in the fastest growing areas and if their stockholders are dispersed
across states in proportion to absolute levels of income, attributing dividends or other corporate profits
to the state of the stockholder's residence will tend to understate the growth of production in the rapidly
growing states. Corporate profits should, however, vary roughly in accordance with wage and proprie-
tary income by state. Thus LPI should be a better measure for testing the hypothesis here than the
comprehensive measure of "national income" by state that could be estimated.

eventually make real per-capita incomes much the same everywhere, so the regressions use measures of total rather than per-capita income as dependent variables. When the corresponding measures of growth of states' per-capita income are used, however, the relationship remains negative and statistically significant.[28] Conceivably, the duration of statehood and political stability should not be measured on a ratio scale, and nonparametric tests focusing only on rank orders should be used instead, to guard against the possibility that the result might be an artifact of states at the far ends of the distribution or of other spurious intervals. Accordingly, Choi ran nonparametric tests on the same variables, and these equally supported the hypothesis derived from the model.[29]

Happily, there is a separate test that can provide not only additional evidence but also insight into whether it is the duration of stable freedom of organization and collusion, rather than any lingering "frontier" effect, that explains the results. Several of the defeated Confederate states were among the original thirteen colonies, so they are as far from frontier status as any of the United States. Yet the political stability of these Deep South states was profoundly interrupted by the Civil War and its aftermath, and full freedom of organization and political participation has come only in the last decade. If the model proposed here is correct, the former Confederate states should have growth rates more akin to those of the newer western states than to the older northeastern states, now that there has been a definitive and presumably stable answer to the question of whether the South can have significantly different racial policies from the rest of the nation and now that enough time has passed for the older stable states in the North to have accumulated extensive special-interest organizations. So, taking the years since the passage of the civil rights and voting rights acts of 1964–65, we must ask if the former Confederate states have a higher average growth rate than the other states.

They definitely do, according to both of our measures of growth. The exponential growth rate since 1965 for the ex-Confederate states is 9.37 percent for income from labor and proprietorships (LPI) and 9.55 percent

28. $PCLPI = 7.719 - 0.0051$ STAHOD
$\qquad\qquad\qquad (2.61) \qquad\qquad\quad R^2 = 0.16 \quad n = 37$
$\quad PCPN = 8.173 - 0.0082$ STAHOD
$\qquad\qquad\qquad (2.20) \qquad\qquad\quad R^2 = 0.22 \quad n = 37$

29. Spearman rank correlation coefficients between years since statehood and LPI, NPI, and per-capita LPI, NPI were respectively -0.52, -0.67, -0.52, and -0.52, and the correlation coefficients were in every case significant.

for private nonfarm income (PN), whereas the corresponding figures are 8.12 percent and 8.19 percent for the thirty-seven continental states that were not in the Confederacy. If variations in growth rates are normally distributed, the probabilities these two samples are from different populations can be calculated. Choi found that the difference in growth rates on this basis was statistically significant. A nonparametric test, the Mann-Whitney U-test, also indicated that the difference in average growth rates between the South and the rest of the continental United States was statistically significant. Again, this result holds true whether the growth of total or per-capita income is at issue. These findings obviously argue in favor of the model offered here and should also allay any fears that regression results involving years since statehood for the non-Confederate states were due to frontier settlement that might have taken place since 1865.

Since the ''southern'' and ''western'' results are essentially the same, and since parametric and nonparametric tests yield about the same results, it is reasonable to consider the data on the forty-eight states together and to use only standard ordinary least squares regression techniques. This has been done with the few score of Choi's regressions that are shown in the following tables. Though Choi's work is at an early stage and more elaborate tests may produce different conclusions, the results are nonetheless remarkably clear and consistent.

As the results with the separate treatment of the South and the other states suggest, any regressions that use the year of statehood to establish the earliest possible date for establishment of common-interest groups in non-Confederate states, and *any* year after the end of the Civil War to establish when the Confederate states came to have stable freedom of organization, will provide a statistically significant explanation of growth rates by state (table 1.1, equations 1–6). If the civil rights and voting rights acts mark the onset of universal freedom of organization and stability in the Deep South, this variable alone explains almost half of the variance in growth rates (equations 5 and 6). Since organizations that could most directly constrain modern urban and industrial life have had more time to develop in states that have been urbanized longer, the level of urbanization in 1880 was used as an independent variable. This variable again tends to have a significant *negative* influence on current growth rates. In combination with a dummy variable for defeat in the Civil War, it explains a fair amount of the variance (equations 9 and 10), but it is apparently not as significant as the duration of freedom of organi-

Table 1.1.   Determinants of Growth from 1965 to 1976

1. $LPI = 10.105 - 0.014$ STACIV1
$\qquad\qquad\qquad$ (4.38) $\qquad\qquad\qquad\qquad\qquad$ $R^2 = 0.29$

2. $NPI = 10.576 - 0.018$ STACIV1
$\qquad\qquad\qquad$ (5.31) $\qquad\qquad\qquad\qquad\qquad$ $R^2 = 0.38$

3. $LPI = \ \ 9.885 - 0.014$ STACIV2
$\qquad\qquad\qquad$ (5.83) $\qquad\qquad\qquad\qquad\qquad$ $R^2 = 0.43$

4. $NPI = 10.240 - 0.016$ STACIV2
$\qquad\qquad\qquad$ (6.89) $\qquad\qquad\qquad\qquad\qquad$ $R^2 = 0.51$

5. $LPI = \ \ 9.425 - 0.011$ STACIV3
$\qquad\qquad\qquad$ (5.98) $\qquad\qquad\qquad\qquad\qquad$ $R^2 = 0.44$

6. $NPI = \ \ 9.678 - 0.012$ STACIV3
$\qquad\qquad\qquad$ (6.81) $\qquad\qquad\qquad\qquad\qquad$ $R^2 = 0.50$

7. $LPI = \ \ 9.069 - 0.029$ UR1880
$\qquad\qquad\qquad$ (4.04) $\qquad\qquad\qquad\qquad\qquad$ $R^2 = 0.26$

8. $NPI = \ \ 9.406 - 0.040$ UR1880
$\qquad\qquad\qquad$ (5.79) $\qquad\qquad\qquad\qquad\qquad$ $R^2 = 0.42$

9. $LPI = \ \ 9.072 + 0.976$ CIVWAR $- 0.023$ UR1880
$\qquad\qquad\qquad$ (2.77) $\qquad\qquad\qquad$ (2.80) $\qquad$ $R^2 = 0.37$

10. $NPI = \ \ 9.653 + 0.707$ CIVWAR $- 0.038$ UR1880
$\qquad\qquad\qquad$ (2.01) $\qquad\qquad\qquad$ (2.80) $\qquad$ $R^2 = 0.47$

11. $LPI = \ \ 9.889 - 0.009$ STACIV1 $- 0.016$ UR1880
$\qquad\qquad\qquad$ (2.22) $\qquad\qquad\qquad$ (1.65) $\qquad$ $R^2 = 0.33$

12. $NPI = 10.208 - 0.009$ STACIV1 $- 0.027$ UR1880
$\qquad\qquad\qquad$ (2.29) $\qquad\qquad\qquad$ (2.97) $\qquad$ $R^2 = 0.48$

13. $LPI = \ \ 9.457 - 0.009$ STACIV3 $- 0.007$ UR1880
$\qquad\qquad\qquad$ (3.85) $\qquad\qquad\qquad$ (0.82) $\qquad$ $R^2 = 0.45$

14. $NPI = \ \ 9.764 - 0.009$ STACIV3 $- 0.019$ UR1880
$\qquad\qquad\qquad$ (3.70) $\qquad\qquad\qquad$ (2.34) $\qquad$ $R^2 = 0.55$

15. $LPI = \ \ 9.564 + 1.605$ CIVWAR $- 0.015$ STAHOD
$\qquad\qquad\qquad$ (5.57) $\qquad\qquad\qquad$ (4.01) $\qquad$ $R^2 = 0.45$

16. $NPI = 10.030 + 1.803$ CIVWAR $- 0.015$ STAHOD
$\qquad\qquad\qquad$ (6.34) $\qquad\qquad\qquad$ (5.15) $\qquad$ $R^2 = 0.53$

17. $PCLPI = \ \ 8.236 - 0.008$ STACIV1
$\qquad\qquad\qquad\qquad$ (3.3) $\qquad\qquad\qquad\qquad\qquad$ $R^2 = 0.19$

18. $PCPN = \ \ 8.707 - 0.011$ STACIV1
$\qquad\qquad\qquad\qquad$ (3.0) $\qquad\qquad\qquad\qquad\qquad$ $R^2 = 0.16$

19. $PCLPI = \ \ 8.039 - 0.007$ STACIV3
$\qquad\qquad\qquad\qquad$ (6.6) $\qquad\qquad\qquad\qquad\qquad$ $R^2 = 0.48$

20. $PCPN = \ \ 8.292 - 0.009$ STACIV3
$\qquad\qquad\qquad\qquad$ (4.52) $\qquad\qquad\qquad\qquad\qquad$ $R^2 = 0.31$

21. $PCLPI = \ \ 7.815 - 0.022$ UR1880
$\qquad\qquad\qquad\qquad$ (4.67) $\qquad\qquad\qquad\qquad\qquad$ $R^2 = 0.32$

22. $PCPN = \ \ 8.153 - 0.032$ UR1880
$\qquad\qquad\qquad\qquad$ (4.52) $\qquad\qquad\qquad\qquad\qquad$ $R^2 = 0.31$

23. $PCLPI = \ \ 7.789 + 0.956$ CIVWAR $- 0.016$ UR1880
$\qquad\qquad\qquad\qquad$ (5.04) $\qquad\qquad\qquad$ (3.64) $\qquad$ $R^2 = 0.59$

24. $PCPN = \ \ 8.368 + 0.688$ CIVWAR $- 0.031$ UR1880
$\qquad\qquad\qquad\qquad$ (2.36) $\qquad\qquad\qquad$ (4.58) $\qquad$ $R^2 = 0.48$

Table 1.1. (*continued*)

25.   PCLPI =   7.646 + 1.210 CIVWAR − 0.005 STAHOD
                      (6.65)   (2.46) $R^2 = 0.50$
26.   PCPN =   8.112 + 1.409 CIVWAR − 0.008 STAHOD
                      (4.32)   (2.33) $R^2 = 0.30$

NOTE: n = 48, all equations.

SYMBOLS:
CIVWAR: Dummy variable 1 for Confederate (defeated) states and 9 for non-Confederate states.
YEAR: For Confederate . . . 100.
           For non-Confederate . . . length of time since statehood.
YEAR2:   For Confederate . . . 50.
           For non-Confederate . . . length of time since statehood.
YEAR3:   For Confederate . . . 0.
           For non-Confederate . . . length of time since statehood.
STACIV1 = YEAR/178   STACIV2 = YEAR2/178   STACIV3 = YEAR3/178
   [178 = 1965 − 1787 (earliest year of statehood)]
STAHOD: Years since statehood.
SOURCES: Date of Statehood: Council of State Governors, *The Book of the States* (Lexington, Ky., 1976); Civil War Information: Peter J. Parish, *The American Civil War* (New York: Holmes and Meier, 1975).

LPI: Exponential rate of growth of income of labor and proprietors, 1965–76.
NPI: Exponential rate of growth of private nonfarm income, 1965–76.
PCLPI: Exponential rate of growth of per-capita labor and proprietors' income, 1965–76.
PCPN: Exponential rate of growth of per-capita private nonfarm income, 1965–76.
SOURCES: Printouts from the Office of Regional Analysis, Bureau of Economic Analysis, U.S. Department of Commerce. These data show income by state of employment rather than of residence, which is better for present purposes. Essentially the same results were obtained using published data from the *Survey of Current Business* and the *Statistical Abstract*.

UR1880 and UR1970. Percentages of people who resided in cities in the corresponding year.
SOURCE: U.S., Department of Commerce, Bureau of the Census, *Historical Statistics of the U.S.—Colonial Times to 1970* (Washington: Government Printing Office, 1976).

NOTE: Figures in parentheses are the standard errors.

zation. The same patterns hold regardless of which measure of growth of income we use and of whether the growth of total or per-capita income is at issue.

Since the model predicts that special-interest organizations should be more powerful in places that have had stable freedom of organization, we can get an additional test of its validity by looking at the spatial distribution of the membership of such organizations. Unfortunately, the only special-interest organizations on which we have so far found state-by-state membership statistics are labor unions. In view of the widespread neglect of the parallels between labor unions and other special-interest groups, it is important not to attribute all of the losses caused by special-interest organizations and collusions to labor unions. It is probably appropriate, however, to treat labor union membership as a proxy measure for membership and strength of all common-interest groups in urban areas[30] and this is what we shall do.

Table 1.2 suggests immediately that special-interest group membership is greatest in the states that have had stable freedom of organization longest. Urbanization in 1880 is also a statistically significant predictor of union membership from 1964 on. Indeed, the crucial importance of the *duration* of freedom of organization is shown by the fact that urbanization in the 1880s is a better predictor of union membership in the 1960s and 1970s than is urbanization in 1970 (equations A1–A9). The number of years of freedom of organization is often a better predictor still (equations A10–A13).

As the previous results and the model suggest, there is also a statistically significant *negative* relationship between common-interest organization membership in 1964 and 1970 and rates of economic growth since 1965. This result holds for both measures of income and for both total and per-capita changes in those measures (table 1.2, part B). Thus there is not only statistically significant evidence of the connection between the duration of stable freedom of organization and growth rates predicted by our model, but also, as far as labor unions are concerned, distinct and statistically significant evidence that the process the model predicts is going on, that is, that the accumulation of common-interest organizations is occurring and that common-interest groups do on balance have the hypothesized negative effect on economic growth. Every properly specified test that has so far been run produces results that are clearly consistent with the model. This evidence, when combined with the earlier international comparisons, makes it clear that the present model is consistent with a vastly greater quantity and variety of information about growth rates than any known alternative.

---

30. This is not true for farm organizations. They focus, however, almost exclusively on the farm policies of the federal government, and any losses in output due to them must fall mainly on consumers throughout the United States rather than in the state in which the farmers are organized; so farm organization membership probably should not be included in tests on the forty-eight contiguous states. Some of the losses in output due to other common-interest organizations also fall outside the state in which the combination occurs, but the victims of any barriers to entry or restrictive practices are likely to be disproportionately from the area in which the common-interest organization operates.

Table 1.2. Common-Interest Groups

A. Membership as Dependent Variable

1. $\text{UNON64} = 18.536 + 0.262 \text{ UR1880}$
   (3.64) $R^2 = 0.22$

2. $\text{UNON70} = 18.842 + 0.212 \text{ UR1880}$
   (3.21) $R^2 = 0.19$

3. $\text{UNON74} = 16.586 + 0.234 \text{ UR1880}$
   (3.79) $R^2 = 0.24$

4. $\text{UNON64} = 9.820 + 0.223 \text{ UR1970}$
   (2.25) $R^2 = 0.10$

5. $\text{UNON74} = 9.663 + 0.185 \text{ UR1970}$
   (2.16) $R^2 = 0.09$

6. $\text{UNON64} = 22.924 - 9.974 \text{ CIVWAR} + 0.167 \text{ UR1880}$
   (3.28)   (2.34) $R^2 = 0.38$

7. $\text{UNON74} = 19.922 - 7.584 \text{ CIVWAR} + 0.162 \text{ UR1880}$
   (2.82)   (2.57) $R^2 = 0.35$

8. $\text{UNON64} = 17.687 - 11.780 \text{ CIVWAR} + 0.143 \text{ UR1970}$
   (4.01)   (1.63) $R^2 = 0.30$

9. $\text{UNON74} = 15.984 - 9.465 \text{ CIVWAR} + 0.122 \text{ UR1970}$
   (1.55) $R^2 = 0.29$

10. $\text{UNON64} = 12.107 + 0.104 \text{ STACIV1}$
    (3.06) $R^2 = 0.17$

11. $\text{UNON64} = 12.178 + 0.114 \text{ STACIV2}$
    (4.63) $R^2 = 0.32$

12. $\text{UNON64} = 15.441 + 0.094 \text{ STACIV3}$
    (5.19) $R^2 = 0.37$

13. $\text{UNON74} = 14.044 + 0.081 \text{ STACIV3}$
    (5.19) $R^2 = 0.37$

B. Membership in Common-Interest Groups and Growth

1. $\text{NPI} = 10.261 - 0.072 \text{ UNON64}$
   (5.64) $R^2 = 0.41$

2. $\text{LPI} = 9.667 - 0.052 \text{ UNON64}$
   (3.84) $R^2 = 0.24$

3. $\text{NPI} = 10.338 - 0.078 \text{ UNON70}$
   (5.27) $R^2 = 0.38$

4. $\text{LPI} = 9.737 - 0.056 \text{ UNON70}$
   (3.70) $R^2 = 0.23$

5. $\text{PCPN} = 8.730 - 0.053 \text{ UNON64}$
   (3.96) $R^2 = 0.25$

6. $\text{PCLPI} = 8.135 - 0.033 \text{ UNON64}$
   (3.67) $R^2 = 0.23$

NOTE: n = 48.

SYMBOLS:
UNON64, UNON70, and UNON74: Union memberships as a percentage of employees in nonagricultural establishments in 1964, 1970, and 1974.
SOURCE: U.S., Department of Labor, Bureau of Labor Statistics, *Directory of National Unions and Employee Associations*, 1967 and 1971; U.S., Department of Commerce, Bureau of the Census, *Statistical Abstract of the United States*, 1976.

Nonetheless, the evidence in favor of the model is very far from sufficient to establish its validity. This article is only the beginning of what is
hoped will be a wide series of investigations to determine how the model
relates to the growth process in many different industries, states, and
countries. Even if the model is completely correct, it cannot be the whole
story. The model is not intended as a monocausal explanation; the most
that could possibly be hoped is that, like the dog that didn't bark, it might
provide the clue to a better understanding of the whole story.

Most important, the model considers only growth-retarding forces.
There is obviously also a need for a conception of growth-inducing factors and, most notably, of the opportunities for growth. Different regions
and countries face different growth opportunities. The most important
and systematic of these arise from the fact that some regions and countries
have not come close to exploiting the full potential of modern technology
or of their own natural and human resources. The areas that have many
unexploited opportunities can, other things being equal, grow faster than
those that have very few; thus we arrive at the well-known hypothesis that
poorer and technologically less advanced areas can, as they catch up,
grow faster than richer and technologically advanced areas.[31] I have argued elsewhere that the catch-up hypothesis is a particularly congenial
partner for the present model, that there are probably severe specification
problems if the two are not tested together, and that there are reasons to
hope that between them they might explain most variations among growth
rates in the developed democracies.[32] Obviously, the catch-up hypothesis
cannot explain, for example, the differences between German and Japanese postwar rates of growth, on the one hand, and British rates of
growth, on the other. But that does not mean that the catch-up process
wasn't operating.[33]

The forty-eight states also provide a uniquely rich and comparable data
base for testing the common-interest and the catch-up models together.
Choi has calculated how much the per-capita income deviated, in terms of
each of our measures of income, from the average for the forty-eight
states in a given year. If the catch-up hypothesis is true, this deviation
should then be negatively associated with the state's growth rate. In all of

31. I am grateful to Moses Abramovitz, Geoffrey Brennan, and Simon Kuznets for giving me a
fuller appreciation of the salience of this distinction.

32. Mancur Olson, "Thoughts on Catch-Up," unpublished manuscript.

33. See Moses Abramovitz, "Notes on International Differences in Productivity Rates," chapter 4
in this volume; and Robin Marris, "Some New Results on 'Catch-Up,'" mimeo. University of
Maryland, College Park, 1978.

Table 1.3.   Growth with Catch-up Variables Added

1. $\quad$ NPI $= 5.63 + 4361.81$ INVNPI
$\qquad\qquad$ (5.73) $\qquad\qquad\qquad\qquad\qquad$ $R^2 = 0.42$

2. $\quad$ LPI $= 5.56 + 5682.74$ INVLPI
$\qquad\qquad$ (3.64) $\qquad\qquad\qquad\qquad\qquad$ $R^2 = 0.22$

3. $\quad$ NPI $= 8.47 - 0.0020$ DEVNPI
$\qquad\qquad$ (6.92) $\qquad\qquad\qquad\qquad\qquad$ $R^2 = 0.51$

4. $\quad$ LPI $= 8.47 - 0.0014$ DEVLPI
$\qquad\qquad$ (3.78) $\qquad\qquad\qquad\qquad\qquad$ $R^2 = 0.24$

5. $\quad$ NPI $= 7.83 - 0.0087$ STACIV3 $+ 2278.86$ INVNPI
$\qquad\qquad$ (4.06) $\qquad\qquad\qquad$ (2.73) $\qquad\quad$ $R^2 = 0.57$

6. $\quad$ LPI $= 9.05 - 0.0101$ STACIV3 $+ 634.392$ INVLPI
$\qquad\qquad$ (4.15) $\qquad\qquad\qquad$ (0.35) $\qquad\quad$ $R^2 = 0.44$

7. $\quad$ NPI $= 7.32 - 0.025$ UR1880 $+ 2647.22$ INVNPI
$\qquad\qquad$ (3.01) $\qquad\qquad\qquad$ (2.93) $\qquad\quad$ $R^2 = 0.51$

8. $\quad$ LPI $= 7.34 - 0.021$ UR1880 $+ 3032.45$ INVLPI
$\qquad\qquad$ (2.23) $\qquad\qquad\qquad$ (1.58) $\qquad\quad$ $R^2 = 0.30$

9. $\quad$ NPI $= 9.19 - 0.0074$ STACIV3 $- 0.0013$ DEVNPI
$\qquad\qquad$ (3.57) $\qquad\qquad\qquad$ (3.69) $\qquad\quad$ $R^2 = 0.62$

10. $\quad$ LPI $= 9.34 - 0.0098$ STACIV3 $- 0.0003$ DEVLPI
$\qquad\qquad$ (4.05) $\qquad\qquad\qquad$ (0.59) $\qquad\quad$ $R^2 = 0.44$

11. $\quad$ NPI $= 8.82 - 0.0198$ UR1880 $- 0.0014$ DEVNPI
$\qquad\qquad$ (2.46) $\qquad\qquad\qquad$ (3.90) $\qquad\quad$ $R^2 = 0.57$

12. $\quad$ LPI $= 8.88 - 0.0197$ UR1880 $- 0.0008$ DEVLPI
$\qquad\qquad$ (2.11) $\qquad\qquad\qquad$ (1.69) $\qquad\quad$ $R^2 = 0.31$

13. $\quad$ NPI $= 7.79 + 2647.31$ INVNPI $- 0.0422$ UNON64
$\qquad\qquad$ (2.71) $\qquad\qquad\qquad$ (2.59) $\qquad\quad$ $R^2 = 0.49$

14. $\quad$ LPI $= 7.62 + 3321.43$ INVLPI $- 0.0338$ UNON64
$\qquad\qquad$ (1.64) $\qquad\qquad\qquad$ (1.97) $\qquad\quad$ $R^2 = 0.29$

NOTE: n $= 48$.

SYMBOLS:
INVNPI, INVLPI: Inverse of per-capita NPI and LPI in 1965
DEVNPI, DEVLPI: Deviation of per-capita NPI and LPI from U.S. average in 1965

the equations reported in table 1.3, the catch-up coefficient has the hypothesized negative sign and in several regressions it has statistical significance as well. The catch-up factor appears to have less significance than the amount of time a state has had to develop organizations pertinent to modern urban conditions,[34] but since the two hypotheses are compati-

---

34. As was argued earlier, differences in per-capita income induce migration that tends to eliminate the differentials. Thus within any country with freedom of movement the model here should be tested on changes in total rather than per-capita income. The significance of migration is shown by the fact that the catch-up hypothesis performs much better with per-capita than total income as the dependent variable; indeed, it then decisively outperforms the independent variables suggested by our model.

ble it would be absurd to reject one of them simply because it may have a weaker effect than the other.

Further research should look at cities as well as states. For example, putting aside the shortcomings of leaders and other idiosyncratic factors, could the problems of New York City, one of the oldest of the large American cities, be explained in part by the logic developed here? Would the fascinating parallels between Britain and New York City drawn by Norman Macrae in "Little Britain in New York"[35] stand up to a systematic examination?

Internal Contradictions

If the argument here is correct, what is sometimes called the "English disease" is not an ailment unique to one country but is rather the most advanced manifestation of an evolutionary process going on in all developed democracies, which has naturally reached its furthest point in the country with the greatest maturity in both industrialization and democracy. There is, in other words, an internal contradiction in the evolution of the developed democracies. This is not the contradiction that Marx claimed to have found, helpful as his terminology may be in evoking it. The contradiction[36] is between the desire for stability and peace and the desire to realize our full economic potential. For those, like this writer, who are so devoted to democratic freedoms and peace that they would retain them even at the cost of all further growth, this is a disturbing finding. To some degree, the contradiction is inescapable in that there is no way to avoid it entirely.

If the evolutionary or, more precisely, involutional process is understood, however, its outcome can be changed substantially. Some may suppose that the policy implication of the present argument is that a nation ought to invite a violent revolution, a somehow temporary totalitarianism, or a war that will end with its defeat and occupation. This makes as much sense as the suggestion that war and pestilence ought to be encouraged because they lessen overpopulation. In fact, the model here suggests a variety of less costly policies that can limit the losses arising from common-interest organizations and collusions. Moreover, as I shall

35. *America's Third Century* (New York: Harcourt Brace, 1976), pp. 72–74.

36. For a related argument about "contradictions," see Samuel Brittan, "The Economic Contradictions of Democracy," *British Journal of Political Science* 5: 129–59, reprinted as chapter 23 of Brittan, *The Economic Consequences of Democracy* (London: Temple Smith, 1977).

show elsewhere, when the model is appropriately extended, it implies that nondemocratic societies are subject to a subtler but no less debilitating aging process and thus contributes nothing at all to the case for dictatorial government.

An obvious policy implication is that the restrictive, entry-limiting practices of special-interest groups should be outlawed or made subject to Pigouvian taxes or other countervailing measures and that special-interest legislation that distorts resource allocation be repealed. Of course, each organized interest, though outnumbered by those who would gain from such changes, may be able with its disproportionate political power to block reform: that is why there is no complete cure. The situation is not, however, as bleak as it seems.

Most important, the further a society falls short of its potential output, the greater the gains from removing the inefficiencies. Thus the more special-interest organizations and collusions a society has accumulated, and the longer they have resisted socially efficient readjustments that reflect technological advances and other changes, the greater the shadow prices of maintaining these inefficient arrangements.[37] This suggests that the degree of resentment of these arrangements in the society and the gains to political entrepreneurs and others who can replace or bypass the inefficiencies will increase over time in a stable democracy. Thus the gap between actual and potential output need not expand forever. Unfortunately, a violent cataclysm is possible when the gap becomes too large. It is also possible that, as both the special-interest groups and the society's incentives to defend itself against them increase, there will be a standoff, with some abuses being ameliorated or corrected and others being added. Finally, there is the appealing possibility that, as the social cost of the distortions rises, a society will be able democratically to overcome the resistance to sweeping reforms. There are some reasons to believe that this last outcome is a practical possibility.

As Keynes eloquently said, ideas influence policy. Perhaps he exaggerated their importance in comparison with vested interests, at least when particular microeconomic choices rather than overall monetary and fiscal issues are at stake; but the impact of his own writings demonstrates that ideas can have a significant independent influence. Accordingly, one

---

37. I am thankful to J. S. Flemming for bringing the relationship between the magnitude of the losses and the pressures for reform or revolution, and the variety of possible manifestations of this relationship, to my attention.

may reasonably hope that, if further research on the issues we are discussing should have resonance, this would influence education and the higher journalism, and thus ultimately public opinion and political action.

The compensation principle also may be exploited in the spirit of the "new political economy" or "public choice." If any reform is truly Pareto-superior, there will by definition always be enough gain from the reform fully to compensate the losers plus something left over. Thus, if the losing group and the size of the losses are well defined, creative organizational or political leaders may be able to get a consensus for a package that removes the inefficiency and at the same time compensates those who gained from it. This method is more difficult, even impossible, to apply when the losers or the sizes of their losses aren't readily calculable, and it is accordingly impossible in practice to compensate every one of the losers fully, so unanimity cannot be obtained. Yet as a practical matter, existing democratic governments require little more than majority approval rather than unanimity to make changes, so imaginative if rough-and-ready proposals that buy off the main groups that would lose from reform can often pass despite scattered opposition.

There is also a good chance that economic efficiency could be improved by making special-interest groups more encompassing. Since the groups involved should often be able to gain from this, it is by no means always an unrealistic possibility. Casual observation suggests that some special-interest organizations may already be becoming more encompassing over time. This should occur more often if the relevant principle were widely understood, and politically feasible legislation could promote the evolution of structures of special-interest organizations with a greater incentive to take account of the effects of their actions on the welfare of society.

Another way to deal with institutional sclerosis is through immigration and guest-worker policies. The existing restrictions on immigration and guest workers in some countries are promoted in substantial degree by special-interest groups that represent the domestic factors of production that would face competition from in-migrants; labor unions obtain limitations on the inflow of manual workers, medical societies impose stricter qualifying examinations for foreign-trained physicians, and so on. The separate states of the United States, for example, normally control admission not only into most professions, but sometimes also into such diverse occupations as cosmetology, acupuncture, barbering, and lightning rod sales, and these controls are frequently used to keep out practitioners from other states. The nations of Western Europe also vary greatly in the proportion of migrants and guest workers they have admitted. Though many other factors are involved, the preliminary impression is that countries with weaker labor unions have accepted relatively larger inflows of labor.

The law of diminishing returns suggests that the rate of growth of income per capita or per worker would be reduced when an already densely populated country imports more labor. However, as Charles Kindleberger has intriguingly argued,[38] the developed industrial economies in which per-capita income has grown most rapidly are often those which have absorbed the most new labor. Kindleberger explains this in terms of Sir Arthur Lewis's famous model of growth with "unlimited supplies of labor," and this seems to be a useful hypothesis. The Lewis-Kindleberger approach does not, however, attempt to explain *why* some countries take in more migrants than others. A good question for further research, then, is whether our model of special-interest organization can help to explain the systematic differences in hospitality to foreign labor among countries and other jurisdictions. If it can, and the Lewis-Kindleberger explanation should also prove to be correct, the two models should be integrated, and the explanation of openness to foreign labor would be an important special application of the model developed here.

Just as the policies about admission of labor must affect the size of the inflow, so the magnitude of the inflow in turn affects the strength of the common-interest groups. The labor union and the professional association will not be able to exercise so much monopoly power if a large pool of outside labor is readily available. The cooptation of the labor from afar will usually be obstructed by linguistic or cultural differences or by the temporary character of the interest of guest workers. This is presumably one of the reasons why, despite the law of diminishing returns, the countries with disproportionate inflows of labor often have unusually rapid rates of growth of per-capita income.

Similarly, organized business interests often get governments to exclude or restrict foreign firms, and these foreign firms in turn may undercut existing oligopolistic arrangements. The unpopularity of multinationals is not an accident, nor is the fact that they often introduce new ways of doing things.

38. Charles P. Kindleberger, *Europe's Postwar Growth* (Cambridge, Mass.: Harvard University Press, 1967).

The fact that an influx of labor or firms constrains or weakens some common-interest organizations provides another policy option for dealing with institutional sclerosis. If this sclerosis can be serious, the case for liberal policies toward immigrant workers and firms is greatly strengthened. Perhaps there are social or political costs and dangers of violence that arise from alien workers or foreign managements. But institutional sclerosis and slow growth bring costs and dangers too, so that whatever the optimum may be, sclerosis must push it at least marginally in a liberal direction. To be sure, the special-interest groups that will be constrained by the inflow of new factors are likely to oppose it. But the special-interest groups that represent complementary factors of production, which gain disproportionally from the inflow, may readily be persuaded to favor more liberal policies, and possible public support for various suprajurisdictional entities (the Common Market, the British Commonwealth, a reunified Germany, and the like) may at times work to lessen sclerosis.

We are now in a better position to assess the ad hoc argument that Britain's economic plight is due to its trade unions. At the first level of reasoning, this argument is absurd, since combinations of firms (being fewer in number) are more likely to be able to collude in their common interests than large groups of employees are. The ad hoc antiunion argument also overlooks professional associations, class structure, and anti-entrepreneurial attitudes, which are grounded in the same logic and history that underlie the British pattern of trade unions. Despite all its shortcomings, the blame-it-on-the-unions argument does have one virtue (if the professional associations are counted as unions). That is the fact that the net migration of labor into the United Kingdom has been fairly limited, whereas falling transport costs and multilateral tariff-cutting agreements have brought about a substantial increase in international trade. Accordingly, though big businesses are in general more likely than workers to combine, many have been prevented from colluding successfully because they compete in a world market that is too large and diverse to organize. This suggests that the sclerosis should be most serious for goods and the factors of production that do not face foreign competition. Thus retail trade, domestic services, construction, agriculture, the professions, and, as the ad hoc argument states, labor unions probably account for a disproportionate share of the sclerosis in the British economy.

The foregoing account suggests a perspective from which we can see an ancient policy prescription in a better light. If the literature is a fair guide, most economists not only believe that free trade is the best policy in most situations, but also that the degree of protection or openness is a matter of great importance. These views have persisted despite empirical findings that the social costs of tariffs, as a percentage of national income, are usually negligible. As with Harberger-type estimates of the losses from monopoly, the fact that the resources that have been diverted from their socially most productive uses through a tariff or monopoly are also useful, if less so, in other lines of activity means that the loss from the tariff is usually relatively small on any comparative statics calculation.

If the argument offered here is correct, tariffs that are of only small significance in a comparative statics framework could still have profound quantitative importance, because they encourage, and free trade prevents, institutional sclerosis. It isn't easy to organize special-interest groups across national borders, and most trade associations and cartels are confined to one country. The number that must achieve a consensus about policy rises greatly when a common-interest organization or collusion has to take on an international, let alone a world-wide, scale; as was demonstrated earlier, the difficulties of collective action rise exponentially with rising numbers. In the absence of world government, moreover, a symbiotic relation between an international cartel or trade association and a government that can enforce coordination is normally out of the question. Thus if there is free and substantial international trade in a manufactured product that is produced in several countries, no effective cartel is likely to emerge. With essentially undifferentiated, easily defined primary products, the relevant governments, being limited in number, may occasionally form an effective cartel, but effective and enduring world-wide cartelization of manufacturing is not now usually feasible. If international cartelization or collusion is not likely, but national cartelization or collusion is, then tariffs can encourage, and free trade prevent, institutional sclerosis among any enterprises producing goods that are traded internationally.

International competition among these enterprises also indirectly constrains combinations of factor suppliers, such as labor unions, because it limits the monopoly rents which the combination of factor suppliers must normally tap if it is to offer large gains to its members. The union or other combination that sells a major factor of production to a firm that faces international competition will find the demand for its services constrained by the competition the firm faces from foreign producers, at least when the foreign competitors do not face similarly restrictive combinations.

Our model and the perspective on international trade and factor mobility that it offers accordingly provide another reason why many of the countries of continental Europe grew so rapidly after World War II, and especially in the 1960s. The combination of reduced transport costs and the more liberal policies for trade and factor mobility resulting from the Common Market and the Kennedy round of tariff cuts must have notably limited the power of organized groups, particularly of manufacturing firms. This effect was probably most notable in some of the original six Common Market countries, such as France and Italy.[39]

One well-known policy proposal directed particularly at the British economy can now be assessed more judiciously. Some economists suggest that Britain needs substantial tariffs and import controls, at least for a time, to solve its growth problems. These measures are sometimes likened to hospitalization for a sick man on the ground that they would provide a protected environment suitable for recovery.[40] Our model suggests that this recommendation is akin to prescribing bed rest as a cure for obesity: it would eliminate one of the few constraints on the process that has changed Britain from the fastest-growing to the slowest-growing of the major developed nations. This policy would also have one other consequence that may surprise its opponents as well as its proponents. Though by indirect means the protectionist policy would to a degree strengthen unions, the most significant gains would accrue to the owners and management of the firms in the industries whose collusion or organization has been hindered by foreign competition. Protection would increase the degree of special-interest organization by industry among business firms, especially manufacturing firms in relatively concentrated industries.

Though the model offered here appears to fit the gross variations in relative growth rates among the major developed democracies and the forty-eight contiguous states better than any known alternative theory, the emphasis must still be on the most tentative nature of the results and on the need for detailed testing of the model. There are many reasons why caution and further research are in order. The first but by no means the most serious problem is that the real national income statistics used to measure economic growth are most imperfect measures of the change in

39. See Jean-François Hennart, ''The Political Economy of Comparative Growth Rates: The Case of France,'' chapter 9 in this volume.
40. I am thankful to John Eatwell for calling my attention to this analogy and to some of its shortcomings.

true income or welfare we are really interested in. Though the allegation that economic growth, as it is conventionally measured in the income statistics, is not worth having, is absurd,[41] there is reason to fear that the statistics sometimes overstate the improvement in rapidly growing as compared with slowly growing countries.[42]

The problems with the dependent variable in this analysis are as nothing compared to the difficulty of measuring the independent variables. This latter difficulty is a classic illustration of one reason why economics and other social sciences are usually more difficult than the natural sciences—the heterogeneity of the entities considered. Iron molecules resemble one another much more than, say, firms or special-interest organizations do. International data on the proportion of the work force that is unionized, for example, tell us very little, since the power and character of unions varies dramatically from country to country. The difficulties with other types of special-interest groups are even greater. Thus initial assessments of the model must rely on ingenious indirect statistical tests, such as those conducted by Peter Murrell,[43] and on the judgments of experts on each of the relevant countries. Firm conclusions must await detailed and comparable studies of many different countries.

A final difficulty arises from the fact that the model is by no means monocausal. This means that individual countries that appear to fit the model's predictions may occasionally in fact not do so, but may in truth reflect the operations of some other causal variable, and that, conversely, occasional contrary observations may occur because the effect of omitted variables has more than offset the force that the model here describes. This means that hypotheses about the growth-retarding forces offered here should be tested in combination with other hypotheses, particularly those that, like the catch-up hypothesis, focus on the opportunities for growth.

The task of testing the model is, however, somewhat eased by the fact that the model can be extended or integrated with other models in such a

41. This strong statement grows out of many years of work on this problem; see my essays "The Treatment of Externalities in the National Income Statistics," in *Public Economics and the Quality of Life*, ed. Lowdon Wingo and Alan Evans (Baltimore: Johns Hopkins University Press, for the Center for Environmental Studies and Resources for the Future), pp. 219–49; and "The Plan and Purpose of a Social Report," *The Public Interest*, no. 15 (Spring 1969): 85–97; also Mancur Olson and Hans Landsberg, eds., *The No-Growth Society* (New York: Norton, 1974; London: Woburn, 1975).

42. The reasons will be set out in a forthcoming book that I have tentatively titled *Beyond the Measuring Rod of Money*.

43. See Peter Murrell, "The Comparative Structure of the Growth of the West German and British Manufacturing Industry," chapter 6 in this volume.

way that it offers testable predictions about several other matters besides the growth rates of the developed democracies. Extended versions of the model generate testable predictions about the severity of what is loosely called "stagflation" in different countries and on how the macroeconomic problem should change over time in stable societies; about the development profile of guilds in medieval and early modern Europe and the geographical pattern of early modern European economic growth; about what some political scientists call the "ungovernability" of many modern societies; and even about the characteristics of the Indian caste system. If the model, or an extended model including the same assumptions, is not consistent with the facts, it calls what has been said in this paper into question, whereas a wider range of supporting observations should generate more confidence in what has been said here.

If further investigations should support the argument offered here, the model would then be an appropriate beginning for the effort to enlarge economic theory so that it can systematically encompass evolutionary and historical change. Any such support would also suggest that the inadequacy of the economist's understanding of the causes and retardants of growth was due not to any want of stature of our predecessors in the field but rather to the narrow, static, and unhistorical character of our own preoccupations. Perhaps there is a lesson in this for those who are inclined to rebel against modern economics; the need is not to spurn what the giant economists of the last two centuries have learned about the workings of the markets in the short and medium run, when the technology, tastes, and institutional environment may be unchanged. The need, rather, is to develop the vision to see these markets in the context of the organizational, social, and Darwinian processes that surround and pervade them and largely to explain the evolution of the societies in which they are found.

2: Structural Unemployment and Economic Growth: A "Labor Theory of Value" Model

JOHN HICKS

The model developed here is designed to investigate the consequences for economic growth of imperfect transferability of labor between industries. In order to isolate the working of this, I shall simplify the model in every possible way. Thus I shall assume that labor is the only element in costs and that there are just two industries which comprise the whole economy, no distinction being made between consumption and investment industries. The wages earned in the two industries constitute the whole of income, and the whole of that income must be spent on the products of one industry or the other. I compare the behavior of the economy in a base year and in one year following it.

In the base year the labor employed in the two industries is respectively L_1 and L_2. I choose units in such a way that in each industry one unit of product is produced by one unit of labor. The wage of labor is thus one unit, in whichever product it is measured. Thus outputs are L_1, L_2, and

$$\text{Total income} = \text{total output} = L_1 + L_2,$$

all this in the base year.

In the second year productivity has increased, so that G_1 of product one and G_2 of product two are produced per unit of labor. If the wage remained unchanged at unity, prices would fall to $1/G_1$ and $1/G_2$. If the labor employed was unchanged at L_1 and L_2 outputs would be G_1L_1 and G_2L_2, and total output valued at the new prices would be $L_1 + L_2$ (unchanged). So an income of $L_1 + L_2$ would be spent at the new prices $1/G_1$ and $1/G_2$.

Two prices have changed, so that there is an income effect, due to the general fall in prices, and a substitution effect, due to the change in relative prices. The latter should be favorable to increased demand for the product whose relative price has fallen, but the former may go either way. It will be useful to take as a point of reference the case in which demand expands in such a way as to leave expenditure on each product unchanged (this is not the case of unit elasticity, since the prices of both products have changed). In this *neutral* case there can be equilibrium with unchanged employment in each industry.

Now suppose that the distribution of expenditure in the second year is not such as to make this possible. Instead of being divided in proportions $L_1 : L_2$ as in the neutral case, it is divided in proportions $E_1L_1 : E_2L_2$, where E_1/E_2 is not equal to unity. For equilibrium, there must be changes d_1 and d_2 in employment, from L_1 and L_2 to $L_1 + d_1$ and $L_2 + d_2$. Outputs will then be $G(L + d)$ in each industry; at prices $1/G$, the values of outputs will be $(L + d)$, or $L_1 + d_1, L_2 + d_2$. For equilibrium, these must be in the ratio $E_1L_1 + E_2L_2$. Thus we have as equilibrium conditions

$$L_1 + d_1 = \beta \, E_1E_1$$

$$L_2 + d_2 = \beta \, E_2E_2 \tag{1}$$

for some value of β.

It is evident that if $E_1 = E_2$, these conditions are satisfied by $d_1 = d_2 = 0$, as they should be. But if $E_1 > E_2$, $d_1/L_1 > d_2/L_2$ so that there must be a *relative* expansion in employment in industry one. We shall assume that $E_1 > E_2$, so that industry one is the expanding industry.

If the equilibrium conditions are to be satisfied with both d_1 and d_2 positive, there must be a general expansion in employment, so that the total supply of labor must be expanding. If the total is not expanding, the relative change can only be brought about by a contraction in industry two so that d_2 must be negative.

I shall take it, in continuing, that total supply of labor is not expanding, so that labor can only be drawn into industry one from industry two. I shall assume further that labor is not perfectly transferable, so that no more than a fraction of the labor that is displaced is reabsorbed. So $d_1 = -kd_2$, where k lies between 0 and 1.

We can then eliminate d_1 and d_2 from the equilibrium equations, multiplying the second by k and adding to the first.

$$L_1 + kL_2 = \beta \, (E_1L_1 + k \, E_2L_2) \tag{2}$$

Actual employments, and actual outputs, in the two industries can then be read off from equations 1.

The total output of the economy in the second year, when valued, as is customary in the calculation of growth rates, at base-year prices, is

$$G_1(L_1 + d_1) + G_2(L_2 + d_2);$$

for the base-year prices, it will be remembered, are unity. By equations 1 this equals

$$\beta \left(\frac{G_1E_1L_1 + G_2E_2L_2}{L_1 + L_2} \right) = \beta \gamma = G^*.$$

It will be noticed that E_1 and E_2 occur linearly in the numerator of γ and in the denominator of β. Thus G^*, the growth rate of the whole economy, depends on the *ratio* of E_1 to E_2, as it should.

The variable k does not occur in γ; it occurs only in β. From equation 2,

$$E_2 \beta = 1 - \frac{L_1(E_1 - E_2)}{E_1L_1 + kE_2L_2} .$$

Thus $E_2\beta$, and consequently G^*, is steadily larger the larger is k.

We can find the maximum effect of a change in k by comparing the values of G^* for $k = 0$ and $k = 1$. If $k = 1$,

$$\beta = (L_1 + L_2)/(E_1L_1 + E_2L_2),$$

so that

$$G^*(k = 1) = (G_1E_1L_1 + G_2E_2L_2)/(E_1L_1 + E_2L_2).$$

The growth rate of the whole economy is just a weighted average of the separate growth rates, the weights being the shares of the industries in total expenditure in the second year.

If $k = 0$, $\beta = (1/E_1)$, so that

$$G^*(k = 0) = (G_1E_1L_1 + G_2E_2L_2)/E_1(L_1 + L_2).$$

Thus the ratio of $G^*(k = 0)$ to $G^*(k = 1)$ is, say,

$$\frac{E_1L_1 + E_2L_2}{E_1(L_1 + L_2)} = 1 - \frac{(E_1 - E_2)L_2}{E_1(L_2 + L_2)} = 1 - D.$$

If we write g_0 and g_1 for growth rates at $k = 0$ and $k = 1$,

$$1 + g_0 = (1 + g_1)(1 - D),$$

so that $g_0 = g_1 - D(1 + g_1)$. D (which, it will be noticed, is independent of the separate industrial growth rates) is larger the larger is the switch $(1 - (E_2/E_1))$ and the more important is the declining industry in initial total expenditure.

It is easy to take a numerical example. Suppose that the switch is 10 percent and the share of the declining industry (as just defined) is 30 percent. Then D is 3 percent. The maximum effect of lack of transferability is thus that the growth rate may drop by 3 percent, from, say, 7 percent to 4 percent. Even if there is some transferability, the effect could still be considerable.

3: A Statistical Test of Olson's Model

KWANG CHOI

My main purpose here is to test Mancur Olson's theory of political economy of comparative growth rates to ascertain whether the new theory provides useful insights into the causes of different rates of economic growth. Though growth models abound, no convincing theory has been put forward to explain the causes of different growth performances among nations. Many of the deficiencies in the conventional theories will be removed if Olson's new theory can explain the empirical evidence.

The organization of the essay is as follows: First, I summarize the Olson theory briefly in the form of operation hypotheses. Then, I examine whether these hypotheses are consistent with the cross-national evidence of eighteen advanced democratic countries. An effort is made to develop and construct an index of institutional sclerosis close to that implied by the theory, and the index is then used in testing the theory.

Olson's Theory

The Olsonian model takes account of a factor that other growth models ignore: the associations of firms or individuals which together have monopoly power or political influence or both. Among the obvious common-interest groups are labor unions, professional associations, farm organizations, trade associations, lobbies, and cartels. The informally, or even tacitly, collusive groups that are not formally organized are less obvious but should be included.

I thank Professor Mancur Olson for his helpful suggestions and invariably constructive criticisms. Professor Peter Murrell discussed the first draft of the essay with me and suggested certain clarifications. Any errors that remain are my responsibility.

Regarding the characteristics of organizations and formation of common-interest groups, Olson put forward the following two hypotheses.[1]

HYPOTHESIS 1.   *Some groups in democratic societies will not be effectively organized to promote their common interests, even when gains to the group as a whole from such organization would far exceed the costs, no matter how long a period is available to promote common-interest groups.*

HYPOTHESIS 2.   *Common-interest groups accumulate gradually in societies with continued freedom of organization.*

The expected functional relationship between the common-interest groups and economic growth is stated in Hypotheses 3 and 4.

HYPOTHESIS 3.   *Common-interest groups and informally coordinated collusive groups that do not control a sizable share of a society's resources will have an adverse net effect on the rate of economic growth.*

HYPOTHESIS 4.   *Highly inclusive groups will have policies that are less restrictive of growth than common-interest groups or collusions that control only a negligible proportion of resources in a society.*

Hypotheses 2 and 3 are of most concern in the study of comparative rates of growth. If these are correct, however, we would also expect the following hypothesis to be supported:

HYPOTHESIS 5.   *The longer the period in which a country or a region has had a modern industrial pattern of common interests concurrent with democratic freedom of organization without upheaval or invasion, the greater the extent to which the growth rate will be slowed by organized interests.*

Specifically:

HYPOTHESIS 5A.   *There exists a positive association between the power of common-interest groups and the length of time interest groups have been in existence.*

HYPOTHESIS 5B.   *Both the length of time interest groups have been in*

---

1. For his analysis of the formation of common-interest groups, see his earlier book, *The Logic of Collective Action* (Cambridge, Mass.: Harvard University Press, 1965).

> *existence and their power have a negative relationship with economic*
> *growth of the community.*

Ideally the problems associated with economic growth ought to be analyzed by building a highly complicated structural model, which includes direct and indirect factors, economic as well as noneconomic determinants. I do not construct such a model here. Instead, I defend an unusually straightforward, simple formulation and testing of the Olsonian model by noting that the hypothesized causal connection goes in only one direction: the strength of institutional sclerosis due to the accumulation of group interests should affect the rate of growth, but there is no theoretical reason why the rate of growth of a region would on balance change the rate at which it accumulates common-interest groups, at least in the short run.

Testing with Cross-national Data

I tested the negative relationship between economic growth and institutional sclerosis implied by Olson's theory using various measures of the dependent and explanatory variables. The dependent variable for cross-country analysis is easy to identify and measure. One natural choice for the growth measure would be the rates of growth, either in gross domestic product (GDP) or gross national product (GNP). In this study I chose to employ the growth rates of GDP, total and per capita, from eighteen advanced democratic countries for the period 1950–73.[2] Six countries— Iceland, Luxembourg, Greece, Portugal, Spain, and Turkey—from twenty-four OECD member countries were excluded from our sample. The last four countries have not enjoyed political stability and freedom of organization as the included countries have, and the first two countries are excluded because they are relatively small.

Unlike the dependent variables, the independent variables in Olson's theory are hard to measure and the data are not readily available. I begin with rough proxies, and then progress to more refined measures.

One important variable in Olson's theory is the power of common-interest groups in a country or the strength of institutional sclerosis due to the accumulation of group interests. This power or strength is difficult to measure. Since, other things being equal, the longer the period a country

---

2. While the differences between GNP and GDP are important in understanding some international differences, either of these two measures of aggregate output will suffice. In most poor countries GDP is larger than GNP; the reverse is true in most developed countries.

has enjoyed political stability and freedom of organization, the greater the extent to which common-interest groups build up power or cause institutional sclerosis, the institutional age of a nation is, as a first proxy, employed to measure the power of common-interest groups or institutional sclerosis.

Given the importance of studying institutional development, especially in political science, it is curious, if not dismaying, that so little work has been done in measuring the age of modern political entities. One effort to provide an indicator of institutional age was made by C. E. Black.[3] He classified countries according to the dates of consolidation of modernizing leaderships. The consolidation is marked by three characteristics: the assertion of the determination to modernize; an effective and decisive break with the institutions of an agrarian way of life; and the creation of a national state with an effective government and a reasonably stable consensus on political means and ends by inhabitants.

In the absence of better data, it is postulated that the earliest development of common-interest groups concurs with such consolidation. Since the longer the period a country has enjoyed freedom of organization without disruption the stronger is the power of common-interest groups in the country, the length of time since the beginning of the consolidation is taken as a first proxy to measure the power of common-interest groups. Refinements of this proxy, as will be seen, afford a more germane index.

In the first test, I computed a simple linear regression by the method of least squares, with the growth rates of GDP of eighteen countries from 1950 to 1973 as the dependent variables and the length of time since the consolidation of modernizing leadership (CML) as the independent variables, and obtained the following equation:

$$Y_t = 6.7366 - 0.0139 \text{ CML}$$
$$(6.27) \quad (1.97) \quad\quad R^2 = 0.19$$
$$Y_p = 5.8181 - 0.0146 \text{ CML}$$
$$(5.26) \quad (2.00) \quad\quad R^2 = 0.20,$$

where Y_t and Y_p are growth rates of total GDP and per-capita GDP, respectively, and the numbers in the parentheses are the value of the t-statistic for the coefficients estimated.

The regression results show that the coefficients of determination, R^2,

---

3. C. E. Black, *The Dynamics of Modernization: A Study in Comparative History* (New York: Harper and Row, 1966).

and the statistical significance of the estimated coefficient are not impressive, but the signs of the coefficients are in the expected direction. Because Japan is recognized by several economists as an exceptional case which fits various hypotheses, I follow them in excluding Japan. When Japan is excluded from the sample, the two equations above become:

$$Y_t = 5.3913 - 0.0065 \text{ CML}$$
$$ (7.73) \quad (1.44) \qquad R^2 = 0.12$$
$$Y_p = 4.5467 - 0.0075 \text{ CML}$$
$$ (5.55) \quad (1.42) \qquad R^2 = 0.12.$$

While the negative relationship between economic growth and the length of time a country has had institutional stability remains in force, it is not significant in terms of R^2 and t-ratios. These poor results are mainly due to the poor proxy measure of the independent variable.

One important aspect of institutional development which the proxy does not account for is disruption and consequent reduction in strength and power of the common-interest groups since they began to accumulate. One simple way of dealing with these disruptions is to use a dummy variable. When a dummy is assigned to all countries which have undergone such social disruptions as upheaval, invasion, or occupation, the following equations result:

With Japan included,
$$Y_t = 5.9014 - 0.0128 \text{ CML} + 1.2083 \text{ Dummy}$$
$$ (5.48) \quad (1.95) \qquad\qquad (1.96) \qquad R^2 = 0.36$$
$$Y_p = 4.7967 - 0.0132 \text{ CML} + 1.4778 \text{ Dummy}$$
$$ (4.57) \quad (2.07) \qquad\qquad (2.46) \qquad R^2 = 0.43.$$

With Japan excluded,
$$Y_t = 4.9335 - 0.0063 \text{ CML} + 0.8075 \text{ Dummy}$$
$$ (7.51) \quad (1.56) \qquad\qquad (2.19) \qquad R^2 = 0.34$$
$$Y_p = 3.9142 - 0.0073 \text{ CML} + 1.1124 \text{ Dummy}$$
$$ (5.43) \quad (1.64) \qquad\qquad (2.75) \qquad R^2 = 0.43.$$

This gives a much improved fit and a significant coefficient for the dummy variable at the 95 percent confidence level.

One of the main conclusions of Olson's theory is that common-interest groups have adverse effects on economic growth unless they are sufficiently small or highly "encompassing." To test this conclusion it was necessary to measure the power of common-interest groups or the degree of institutional sclerosis due to the accumulation of powerful interest groups. It is difficult to measure this power or this degree of sclerosis, and data which might be used to measure them are not available for all types of common-interest groups.

Since common-interest groups accumulate gradually in societies with continued freedom of organization, there exists a positive association between the power of common-interest groups, or the degree of institutional sclerosis, and the length of time interest groups have been in existence. However, the measurement of institutional sclerosis by mere length of time that interest groups have been in existence does not allow for a decrease in the power of interest groups or reduction in institutional sclerosis due to the control of a society by a totalitarian government, an occupation by foreign forces, or social upheavals, all of which deter the accumulation of common-interest groups or abolish the vested interests enjoyed by these groups.

Previously, I put a dummy variable in the regression to account for disruptions of various kinds and obtained good and improved results. One major problem with this dummy variable technique is that the degree and duration of major disruptions have not been taken into account. Therefore I constructed an index which makes due allowance not only for disruptions per se, but also for the degree and duration of major disruptions. The construction of the index is based on the idea that institutional sclerosis increases as a logistic curve unless disruptions develop, in which case increase is slowed or sclerosis is in part destroyed.

The choice of the logistic curve for the accumulation function is arbitrary, but there are some good reasons why institutional sclerosis follows a path that is akin to the logistic. A common-interest group can be seen as an organism. Any change in the common-interest group can be viewed as an inevitable growth and decay process intrinsic to the organism. The development of the organism usually follows an *S*-shaped growth path. Within a given cycle, or over a lifetime, the growth rate of an organism is not constant; at first the organism grows slowly, but its rate of growth constantly increases to a maximum, then becomes progressively slower, finally tapering off. There are several *S*-shaped functions. The cumulative normal distribution density curve and the logistic curve are used most widely. As there is almost no difference between the two, the logistic was chosen because it is simpler to fit and easier to interpret.[4]

4. The logistic curve is not employed so often in economics as in such other social science applications as theory of social change and population growth analysis. In economics the logistic curve was used by S. Kuznets in his study of long-term growth of industry, and by Zvi Griliches in his

The basic idea is portrayed in figures 3.1, 3.2, and 3.3. They represent the typical cases. In each figure the vertical axis measures the degree of institutional sclerosis while the horizontal axis denotes chronological (historical) time. Our objective is to measure the degree of institutional sclerosis at a point X of time, say, as of 1950. The country represented by figure 3.1 has enjoyed political stability, and common-interest groups in the country have accumulated power since they were given the freedom to organize. At time X, the country has accumulated institutional sclerosis to the degree of AX.

Common-interest groups in the country represented by figure 3.2 began to accumulate at the same time as those in figure 3.1. However, two major disruptions, at times t_1 and t_2, destroyed parts of the accumulated power of growth-retarding forces, the degree of destruction at each time being indicated by BC and DE, respectively. Without these two upheavals, invasions, or occupations, the country in figure 3.2 should have had institutional sclerosis as measured by the distance FX. If the country had undergone only one disruption, at time t_1, it would have accumulated growth-retarding power up to XG. The disruption at time t_2 leads the country to reach institutional sclerosis to the degree of XH instead of XG, given the first disruption at time t_1.

The country represented in figure 3.3 is a late starter as a newly settled country: accumulation of common-interest groups began at time t_3. One major disruption occurred in this country at time t_4. Unlike the disruptions in figure 3.2, which were instantaneous in nature and produced a once-and-for-all reduction in the power of common-interest groups, the disruption in figure 3.3 lasted over the period from t_4 to t_5. By time X the country reached institutional sclerosis up to the level XN. Were it not for the continued suppression of growth-retarding activities of the common-interest groups during the period from t_4 to t_5, the country would maintain an XM level of institutional sclerosis.

In summary, figures 3.1, 3.2, and 3.3 represent the evolution of institutional sclerosis due to the accumulation of common-interest groups in societies which experienced different historical developments. It is not claimed that the figures cover all notable cases, but it is believed that they describe the cases most relevant to my purpose. It should be noted that the

investigation of how technological change is generated and propagated. See S. Kuznets, *Secular Movements in Production and Prices* (Boston: Houghton Mifflin, 1930); and Zvi Griliches, "Hybrid Corn: An Exploration in the Economics of Technological Change," *Econometrica* 25 (October 1957): 501–22.

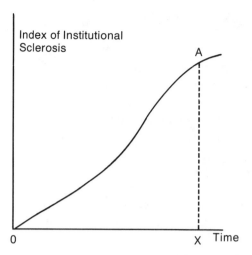

Figure 3.1. Pattern of Institutional Sclerosis (I)

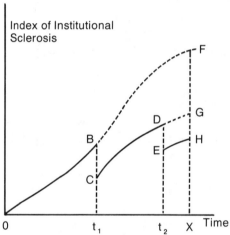

Figure 3.2. Pattern of Institutional Sclerosis (II)

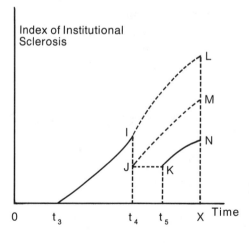

Figure 3.3. Pattern of Institutional Sclerosis (III)

derivation of a numerical index of institutional sclerosis requires the following data:

1. when common-interest groups in each country began to accumulate
2. what the major disruptions were, when they occurred, and how long they lasted
3. how strong each disruption was
4. a formula for the logistic curve along which the accumulation follows.

As a first step toward the construction of an index of institutional sclerosis it was necessary to choose a beginning year for institutional sclerosis. Nations differ in their degrees of institutionalization, civil order, and polit-

Table 3.1. Alternative Years for Onset of Institutional Sclerosis

Country	Beginning Year of Consolidation of Modernizing Leadership	Beginning Year of Economic and Social Transformation	Year of First Constitution	Beginning Year of Take-off (Rostow)
Australia	1801	1901	1900	1901
Austria	1848	1918	1920	n.a.
Belgium	1795	1848	1831	1833
Canada	1791	1867	1867	1896
Denmark	1807	1866	1849	n.a.
Finland	1863	1919	1919	n.a.
France	1789	1848	1791	1830
Germany	1803	1871	1848	1848
Ireland	1870	1922	1922	n.a.
Italy	1805	1871	1848	1895
Japan	1868	1945	1889	1885
Netherlands	1795	1848	1795	n.a.
New Zealand	1826	1907	1852	n.a.
Norway	1809	1905	1814	n.a.
Sweden	1809	1905	1720	1868
Switzerland	1798	1848	1898	n.a.
United Kingdom	1649	1832	1688	1783
United States	1776	1865	1787	1843

SOURCES: Columns 1 and 2—C. E. Black, *The Dynamics of Modernization: A Study of Comparative History* (New York: Harper and Row, 1966), pp. 90–91.
Column 3—Dankwart A. Rustow, *A World of Nations: Problems of Political Modernization* (Washington, D.C.: The Brookings Institution, 1967), p. 230.
Column 4—W. W. Rostow, *The World Economy: History & Prospect* (Austin: University of Texas Press, 1978), pp. 373–465; and idem, *The Stages of Economic Growth: A Non-Communist Manifesto* (London: Cambridge University Press, 1960), p. 38.

ical stability, in the extent of freedom allowed, and in their levels of organization. So, finding such a year for every country in our sample demanded a detailed examination of the history of each country; complete agreement on any year if chosen by various experts in the field may not be possible. A group of political scientists who were engaged in the study of modernization and political development among nations have produced some interesting series, as shown in table 3.1. Four indicators of institutional age are presented there: beginning year of consideration of modernizing leadership, beginning year of economic and social transformation, year of the first constitution, and beginning year of take-off as compiled by W. W. Rostow. Dates of take-off (the last column) are not available for all countries in the sample. Given that only a limited number of series is available and that an ideal series is not within my grasp, I judged it best to take the consolidation of modernizing leadership as a proxy for the onset of

Table 3.2.   Major Disruptions

Australia	None
Austria	Occupation (1938–55)
Belgium	Occupation during WW I and WW II
Canada	None
Denmark	Occupation during WW II
Finland	None
France	Revolutions (1789–1814, 1830, 1848–52); authoritarian government (1852–60); occupation during WW II
Germany	Defeat during WW I; totalitarian government (1933–45); defeat and occupation (1943–49)
Ireland	None
Italy	Totalitarian government (1922–45); defeat during WW II
Japan	Totalitarian government and defeat during WW II; occupation (1945–52)
Netherlands	Occupation during WW II
New Zealand	None
Norway	Occupation during WW II
Sweden	None
Switzerland	None
United Kingdom	None
United States	Civil War (1861–65); large portions settled after 1865

SOURCES: William Langer, ed., *An Encyclopedia of World History* (Boston: Houghton Mifflin, 1972); Bruce M. Russell, J. David Singer, and Melvin Small, "National Political Units in the Twentieth Century: A 'Standardized List'," *American Political Science Review* 62 (September 1968): 932–51.

common-interest group accumulation. This consolidation is a dividing line between preindustrial feudal and industrial modern environments.

Index construction demands a detailed examination of major disruptions in each country which might have deterred or destroyed the accumulation of common-interest groups. I emphasize only those events that have had strong influence on the augmentation or reduction of the power accumulated by common-interest groups since the consolidation of modernizing leadership. The events chosen to represent this disruption are occupation by foreign forces, indigenous totalitarian government control, defeat during major wars, and revolutions. The major relevant disruptions are listed in table 3.2.

Under the assumption that institutional sclerosis develops along a logistic curve, it was necessary to formulate an equation for the logistic curve. In a most general form this logistic curve can be specified as

$$Y = \frac{K}{1+Ae^{-bt}}, \tag{1}$$

where K, A, and b are parameters which will determine the shape of the curve and t is the variable. Under this general form Y will take an asymptot-

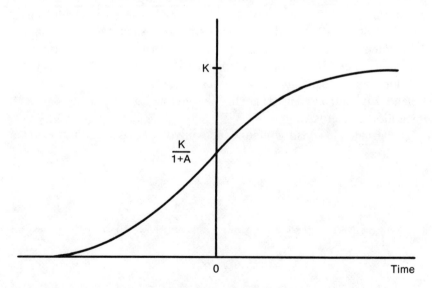

Figure 3.4.   A Logistic Curve

ic maximum value of K and Y is equal to $K/(1+A)$ when $t = 0$, as shown in figure 3.4.

A particular form of the logistic curve is chosen for our purpose.[5] That is

$$I = \frac{200}{1+e^{-bt}} - 100, \tag{2}$$

and the shape of the logistic curve under this formulation is shown in figure 3.5. The index of institutional sclerosis, I, will have an asymptotic value of 100 and start at the origin. The slope of the curve depends on the parameter b and still has to be determined. I chose a value of b such that the country which has the longest history of the accumulation of common-interest groups, the United Kingdom, reaches the institutional sclerosis level of about 90 in 1950. This assumption gives us a value of b equal to 0.01;[6] so institutional sclerosis develops along the curve

$$I = \frac{200}{1+e^{-0.01t}} - 100. \tag{3}$$

Using for t in equation 3 the period from the consolidation of modernizing leadership, shown in the first column of table 3.1, to 1950, which is the beginning year of our growth rate sample period, gives the value of the index, as shown in the first column of table 3.3. The value in the first column indicates the degree of institutional sclerosis each country might have reached if there had been no disruptions since the consolidation. Adjustments for the disruptions experienced by a number of countries have not been made. Based on this unadjusted index the U.K., the U.S., Belgium, and Canada are the top four countries in our index, and Japan, Ireland, Finland, and Austria are the bottom four countries in the degree of institutional sclerosis.

The last step in constructing the index involves making adjustments for

5. The derivation is as follows:

By adding a new term the curve is shifted to start at the origin:

$$Y = \frac{K}{1+Ae^{-bt}} - \frac{K}{1+A}.$$

Setting A equal to 1 for simplicity and K equal to 200 so that the maximum value of Y becomes 100, we have

$$I = \frac{200}{1+e^{-bt}} - 100.$$

6. For the U.K. the beginning year of the consolidation of modernizing leadership is 1649; so the period during which common-interest groups built themselves is $t = 1950 - 1649 = 301$; solving the equation $90 = [200/(1+e^{-301 \times b})] - 100$ we obtain a value of b equal to 0.01.

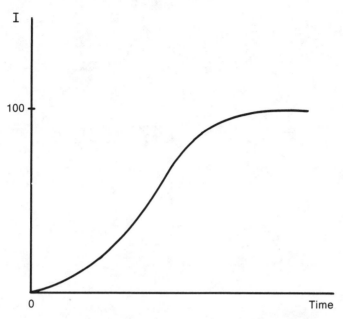

Figure 3.5.   Logistic Curve for Institutional Sclerosis

the major disruptions listed in table 3.2. Since different people will put different weights on different events and arbitrary elements cannot be entirely eliminated, I try to apply a simple rule. This is that the degree of each disruption is proportional to the duration of that disruption. Once I obtain an average degree of disruption per year, multiplication of the average by the length of any particular disruption provides the total degree of adjustment for the disruption in question. An average degree of accumulation has been calculated in two alternative ways. The first is to apply the average degree of accumulation per unit of time for the U.K., which is the reference country, to the other sample countries. The second is to calculate an average degree of accumulation per year for each country. The average degree of accumulation by the second method is obtained by dividing the unadjusted index, shown in the first column of table 3.3, by the total number of years without disruption since consolidation, shown in the second column of the same table.[7]

7. Using symbols and simple mathematics the procedure applied to obtain the total degree of adjustment for disruptions can be put as follows. Suppose there are two countries: A, which has not been subjected to any disruption from time t_0 to time t_n; and B, which has undergone one disruption

Table 3.3. Index of Institutional Sclerosis

Country	Unadjusted Index of Institutional Sclerosis	Sum of Years without Disruption since Consolidation	Sum of Years with Disruption since Consolidation	Adjustment for Disruption Using U.K. Weights	Adjustment for Disruption Using Country's Own Weight	Adjusted Index of Institutional Sclerosis A	Adjusted Index of Institutional Sclerosis B
Australia	62.36	149	0	0.00	0.00	62.36	62.36
Austria	41.48	90	12	3.59	5.53	37.89	35.95
Belgium	65.72	145	10	2.99	4.53	62.73	61.19
Canada	65.26	159	0	0.00	0.00	65.26	65.26
Denmark	59.77	138	5	1.49	2.17	58.27	57.60
Finland	40.26	87	0	0.00	0.00	40.26	40.26
France	54.10	118	23	6.88	10.54	47.22	43.56
Germany	56.01	124	22	6.58	9.34	49.43	46.07
Ireland	37.34	80	0	0.00	0.00	37.34	37.34
Italy	54.27	117	23	6.88	10.67	47.39	43.60
Japan	32.17	68	24	7.18	11.35	24.99	20.82
Netherlands	63.59	150	5	1.50	2.18	63.89	63.21
New Zealand	54.29	124	0	0.00	0.00	54.29	54.29
Norway	59.11	136	5	1.49	2.17	57.61	56.94
Sweden	59.90	141	0	0.00	0.00	59.90	59.90
Switzerland	63.21	112	0	0.00	0.00	63.24	63.24
U.K.	36.08	301	0	0.00	0.00	90.08	90.08
U.S.	78.86	170	5	1.50	2.32	77.36	76.54

The average degree of adjustment using data from the U.K. is 0.2993 per unit year of disruption. The corresponding figures for other countries range from 0.4104 for Canada to 0.4731 for Japan. My index of institutional sclerosis after adjustment for major disruptions is shown in the last two columns of table 3.3. Adjusted Index A is based on the adjustments using average degree of disruption for the U.K., while Index B makes allowance for the disruptions using each country's own average degree of disruption. The results indicate that due to a long history of industrialization, political stability, and democratic freedom of organization without much disruption, the U.K., the U.S., Canada, and Switzerland are the four countries whose institutional sclerosis is most severe. The adjusted index of institutional sclerosis is lowest in Japan, Ireland, Austria, and Finland.

Recall that a preliminary test of Olson's theory was made by using, as a rough proxy, the length of time since the consolidation of modernizing leadership. In the preceding section I mentioned an index which measures the institutional sclerosis which results from the accumulation of common-interest groups. I believe that given the assumptions used in the conceptualization and estimation, the obtained index is close to that implied by Olson's rather general theory.

The results showing the relationship between the two measures of the dependent variable—the growth rates of total and per-capita income—and the two measures of institutional sclerosis as the independent variables—Index A and Index B—are shown in table 3.4 with t-values in parentheses. To check the accuracy of the model with respect to the sample countries, some different combinations of sample countries were tried. The overall results of this cross-sectional study of advanced industrial countries seem to support strongly Olson's theory of the political economy of comparative growth. Measures of the independent variable explain about half of the variation in growth rates among eighteen countries in the sample even at

---

over the period from t_2 to t_3. Country B is also a late starter and its common-interest groups began to accumulate their power at time t_1. When we choose F for the curve along which accumulation of institutional sclerosis follows, average degree of accumulation

$$D_A = [F(t_n) - F(t_0)]/(t_n - t_0)$$

for country A and

$$D_B = [F(t_2) - F(t_1) + F(t_n) - F(t_3)]/(t_2 - t_1 + t_n - t_3)$$

for country B. The total degree of adjustment for the disruption of country B during t_2 to t_3 is $D_A(t_3 - t_2)$ with reference to country A and $D_B(t_3 - t_2)$ with its own reference.

Table 3.4. Test Results with Index of Institutional Sclerosis

I. Growth Rates of Total Income as Dependent Variable
   All Countries: n = 18
       1. Y = 8.3662 − 0.0655 Index A
              (7.87)   (3.54) R^2 = 0.44
       2. Y = 8.2849 − 0.0654 Index B
              (8.74)   (3.90) R^2 = 0.49
   Excluding Japan: n = 17
       3. Y = 6.3295 − 0.0331 Index A
              (7.62)   (2.34) R^2 = 0.27
       4. Y = 6.3836 − 0.0346 Index B
              (8.40)   (2.64) R^2 = 0.32
   Countries with No Major Disruptions: n = 8
       5. Y = 5.0022 − 0.0169 Index A
              (4.45)   (0.92) R^2 = 0.12
       6. Y = 5.0022 − 0.0169 Index B
              (4.45)   (0.92) R^2 = 0.12
   Countries with Some Major Disruptions: n = 10
       7. Y = 10.5400 − 0.0992 Index A
              (8.59)   (4.40) R^2 = 0.71
       8. Y = 10.0174 − 0.0931 Index B
              (9.30)   (4.56) R^2 = 0.72
   Largest Countries: n = 9
       9. Y = 10.8180 − 0.0949 Index A
              (12.11)   (6.51) R^2 = 0.86
      10. Y = 10.1991 − 0.9871 Index B
              (12.17)   (6.24) R^2 = 0.84
   Smallest Countries: n = 9
      11. Y = 5.1519 − 0.0180 Index A
              (4.18)   (0.78) R^2 = 0.08
      12. Y = 5.2479 − 0.0200 Index B
              (4.38)   (0.88) R^2 = 0.10

II. Growth Rates of Per-Capita Income as Dependent Variable
   All Countries: n = 18
      13. Y = 7.8599 − 0.0746 Index A
              (7.84)   (4.28) R^2 = 0.53
      14. Y = 7.7502 − 0.0743 Index B
              (8.81)   (4.78) R^2 = 0.59
   Excluding Japan: n = 17
      15. Y = 6.1359 − 0.0472 Index A
              (6.93)   (3.14) R^2 = 0.40
      16. Y = 6.1719 − 0.0487 Index B
              (7.45)   (3.54) R^2 = 0.46
   Countries with No Major Disruptions: n = 8
      17. Y = 4.3638 − 0.0259 Index A
              (4.10)   (1.49) R^2 = 0.27
      18. Y = 4.3638 − 0.0259 Index B
              (4.10)   (1.49) R^2 = 0.27

Table 3.4   (*continued*)

Countries with Some Major Disruptions: n = 10
$$19.\ Y = 9.9749\ -\ 0.1055\ \text{Index A}$$
$$(11.02)\quad (6.35)\qquad\qquad R^2 = 0.83$$
$$20.\ Y = 9.3981\ -\ 0.0985\ \text{Index B}$$
$$(11.86)\quad (6.55)\qquad\qquad R^2 = 0.84$$
Largest Countries: n = 9
$$21.\ Y = 9.6066\ -\ 0.0954\ \text{Index A}$$
$$(8.51)\quad (5.19)\qquad\qquad R^2 = 0.79$$
$$22.\ Y = 9.0512\ -\ 0.0887\ \text{Index B}$$
$$(9.12)\quad (5.37)\qquad\qquad R^2 = 0.80$$
Smallest Countries: n = 9
$$23.\ Y = 5.6298\ -\ 0.04221\ \text{Index A}$$
$$(3.68)\quad (1.47)\qquad\qquad R^2 = 0.24$$
$$24.\ Y = 5.7578\ -\ 0.0451\ \text{Index B}$$
$$(3.93)\quad (1.63)\qquad\qquad R^2 = 0.27$$

the 1 percent significance level. While countries that experienced disruption of one sort or another and countries with large populations produce surprisingly good results, counterpart countries exhibit relatively poor results. The different results for large and small countries might be due to the influence of additional factors associated with the smaller countries. The contrasting results for countries that had and had not sustained disruptions may be ascribed to the "encompassingness" of common-interest groups in a given country not being adequately accounted for in the construction of an institutional sclerosis index.

One might argue that Olson's model does not take into consideration several major factors that might have had strong effects on economic growth. According to this argument, Olson's theory is supposed to explain best the variations in growth rates that were not occasioned by direct increases in the various resources used in production. I attempt here to see what statistical light can be thrown on this issue by using the "sources of growth" data produced by Edward F. Denison, Dorothy Walters, and William K. Chung.[8] Unfortunately, the use of this data reduces our sample from eighteen countries to eleven and includes mostly the period of time from 1956 to 1962. Since except for Canada, Japan, and the United States,

8. E. F. Denison, *Why Growth Rates Differ* (Washington, D.C.: Brookings Institution, 1967); Dorothy Walters, *Canadian Growth Revisited, 1950–1967,* Staff Study No. 28 (Ottawa: Economic Council of Canada, 1970); E. F. Denison and W. K. Chung, *How Japan's Economy Grew So Fast* (Washington, D.C.: Brookings Institution, 1976).

data on the "sources of growth" are available only for the distant past, I turned for help to two recent productivity studies. Christensen, Cummings, and Jorgenson[9] provide an international comparison of postwar patterns of economic growth for the United States and eight of its major trading partners, including one developing country, Korea. Their study covers the period from 1947 to 1973 for the United States and as much of this period as is feasible for each of the eight remaining countries. Stein and Lee[10] develop and assemble indices of output, labor input, and capital stock for the years 1963–74. Again following several economists who recognize Japan as an exceptional case or an outlier, I present regression results with and without Japan in the sample. Also, in each of the following tables, there are two sets of equations: one with the growth rates of the dependent variables calculated from the total quantity of each category, and the other from the per-employee quantity of each category of the dependent variable in question.

Table 3.5 summarizes the results of simple regression equations of growth rates of national income, total and per-employee, using two alternative measures of institutional sclerosis, Index A and Index B. The results are impressive. All the estimated regression coefficients turn out to be statistically significant at the 5 percent significance level or less. The coefficients of multiple determination also indicate that the regressions provide a close fit to the data, especially since these data are cross-sectional and since the sample includes only ten or eleven countries. The results in table 3.5 indicate that the model is not sensitive to the inclusion or exclusion of Japan from our sample.

Table 3.6 is concerned with explaining growth rates of factor productivity in terms of alternative indices. The t-value and R^2 results are extremely impressive.

The importance to economic growth of technological change, whether embodied or disembodied, is commonly accepted. Empirical studies, however, have nominated many candidates to explain the "residual" in economic growth. Early empirical work often assigned the residual to technical change by default.[11] Later, as data and estimating procedure

9. L. R. Christensen, D. Cummings, and D. W. Jorgenson, "An International Comparison of Growth in Productivity, 1947–1973," Social Systems Research Institute, University of Wisconsin, SSRI Workshop Series No. 7531, 1975.

10. John P. Stein and Allen Lee, *Productivity Growth in Industrial Countries at the Sectoral Level 1963–1974* (Santa Monica: The Rand Corporation, 1977).

11. Robert M. Solow, "Technical Progress and the Aggregate Production Function," *Review of Economics and Statistics* 39 (August 1957): 312–20.

Table 3.5.   Test Results with National Income Data

I. Total Income
     All Countries: n = 11
          1. GROWTH = 9.4029 − 0.0845 Index A
                              (9.70)   (5.30) R^2 = 0.76
          2. GROWTH = 8.9185 − 0.0786 Index B
                              (10.30)   (5.40) R^2 = 0.76
     Excluding Japan: n = 10
          3. GROWTH = 8.4597 − 0.0703 Index A
                              (6.37)   (3.45) R^2 = 0.58
          4. GROWTH = 8.0602 − 0.0654 Index B
                              (6.84)   (3.35) R^2 = 0.60
II. Income per Employee
     All Countries: n = 11
          5. GROWPE = 8.6633 − 0.0895 Index A
                              (6.51)   (4.08) R^2 = 0.65
          6. GROWPE = 8.2456 − 0.0849 Index B
                              (7.19)   (4.40) R^2 = 0.68
     Excluding Japan: n = 10
          7. GROWPE = 8.6306 − 0.0889 Index A
                              (4.44)   (2.89) R^2 = 0.51
          8. GROWPE = 8.2834 − 0.0855 Index B
                              (4.97)   (3.18) R^2 = 0.56

improved, other explanations were offered, such as education, improved resource allocation, advances in knowledge, and economies of scale. It seems clear from the work of Denison and others that factor inputs (which include education) account for only about half of the growth rates, while the remainder is distributed as residual[12] among the variables mentioned above.

The above discussion is not intended to describe or characterize the residual part of the sources of growth but to indicate that even the residual sources of growth varied across nations and over time. Despite several theoretical attempts to explain the residual in terms of technical change, no empirical tests have been applied to this ignorance of our knowledge. Since Olson's model implies that institutional sclerosis retards growth disproportionately through its effect on the residual factor, I attempted to find the causal link between the residual and measures of institutional sclerosis, the results of which are shown in table 3.7. The regression results show that both independent measures appear to explain more than 70 percent of the

12. Strictly speaking, the residual in Denison's 1974 study is "advances in knowledge." Such other nonfactor input variables as economies of scale have the effect of reducing the size of the residual.

Table 3.6.   Test Results with Total Factor Productivity Data

I. Total Factor Productivity
   All Countries: n = 11
        1. RESIDU = 5.8742 − 0.0558 Index A
                  (12.27)   (7.08) $R^2 = 0.85$
        2. RESIDU = 5.5872 − 0.0524 Index B
                  (14.26)   (7.96) $R^2 = 0.88$
   Excluding Japan: n = 10
        3. RESIDU = 5.9933 − 0.0575 Index A
                  (8.61)   (5.23) $R^2 = 0.77$
        4. RESIDU = 5.7132 − 0.0544 Index B
                  (10.09)   (5.96) $R^2 = 0.82$

II. Total Factor Productivity per Employee
    All Countries: n = 11
        5. RESIPE = 6.6487 − 0.0690 Index A
                  (6.04)   (3.82) $R^2 = 0.62$
        6. RESIPE = 6.3364 − 0.0657 Index B
                  (6.67)   (4.11) $R^2 = 0.65$
    Excluding Japan: n = 10
        7. RESIPE = 7.1706 − 0.0767 Index A
                  (4.54)   (3.08) $R^2 = 0.54$
        8. RESIPE = 6.8624 − 0.0737 Index B
                  (5.08)   (3.38) $R^2 = 0.59$

variations in the growth rates of the total residual, and about half of the variations when growth rates of the residual per employee are taken as the dependent variable. As in the test with the other categories of sources of growth, results with residual data remain significant whether Japan is included in our sample or not.

Since most of the available data on sources of growth are for the 1950s and early 1960s, it is necessary to extend empirical tests to data covering more recent years. Therefore I tested my hypothesis with data on growth rates in output and factor productivity reported in two recent studies by Stein and Lee and Christensen, Cummings, and Jorgenson. Unfortunately, the data estimated are not as large as might be desirable; Stein and Lee cover only ten countries and Christensen, Cummings, and Jorgenson only nine.[13] This is, of course, a small sample. In regression results with these data, reported in table 3.8, the relationships are strongly in line with the expectations of Olson's hypothesis. The variations in growth rates in output, labor productivity, and total factor productivity are explained by the

13. From a nine-country sample (the U.S. and its eight major trading partners), one country, Korea, is not included in our analysis. It should be noted, however, that data from Korea, as well as from such other countries as Taiwan, will give good support to Olson's hypothesis.

Table 3.7. Test Results with Residual Data

I. Total Residual
    All Countries: n = 11

$$\text{OTHER} = 3.4634 - 0.0295 \text{ Index A}$$
$$\qquad\quad (9.39) \quad\ (4.86) \qquad\qquad R^2 = 0.72$$

$$\text{OTHER} = 3.3174 - 0.0278 \text{ Index B}$$
$$\qquad\quad (10.51) \quad (5.23) \qquad\qquad R^2 = 0.75$$

    Excluding Japan: n = 10

$$\text{OTHER} = 3.7989 - 0.0345 \text{ Index A}$$
$$\qquad\quad (7.46) \quad\ (4.29) \qquad\qquad R^2 = 0.70$$

$$\text{OTHER} = 3.6319 - 0.0326 \text{ Index B}$$
$$\qquad\quad (8.47) \quad\ (4.71) \qquad\qquad R^2 = 0.74$$

II. Residual per Employee
    All Countries: n = 11

$$\text{OTHEPE} = 3.1599 - 0.0292 \text{ Index A}$$
$$\qquad\qquad (6.03) \quad\ (3.39) \qquad\qquad R^2 = 0.56$$

$$\text{OTHEPE} = 3.0172 - 0.0276 \text{ Index B}$$
$$\qquad\qquad (6.54) \quad\ (3.55) \qquad\qquad R^2 = 0.58$$

    Excluding Japan: n = 10

$$\text{OTHEPE} = 3.0868 - 0.0281 \text{ Index A}$$
$$\qquad\qquad (4.04) \quad\ (2.33) \qquad\qquad R^2 = 0.40$$

$$\text{OTHEPE} = 2.9684 - 0.0268 \text{ Index B}$$
$$\qquad\qquad (4.43) \quad\ (2.48) \qquad\qquad R^2 = 0.44$$

Table 3.8. Test Results with Data from Stein and Lee and from Christensen, Cummings, and Jorgenson

I. Stein and Lee Data: n = 10
    Growth in Output

$$\text{SLOP} = 12.0112 - 0.1166 \text{ Index A}$$
$$\qquad\quad (6.14) \quad\ (3.64) \qquad\qquad R^2 = 0.62$$

$$\text{SLOP} = 11.2121 - 0.1064 \text{ Index B}$$
$$\qquad\quad (6.19) \quad\ (3.50) \qquad\qquad R^2 = 0.61$$

    Growth in Labor Productivity

$$\text{SLOPPE} = 11.5809 - 0.1249 \text{ Index A}$$
$$\qquad\qquad (6.15) \quad\ (4.05) \qquad\qquad R^2 = 0.67$$

$$\text{SLOPPE} = 10.8191 - 0.1157 \text{ Index B}$$
$$\qquad\qquad (6.35) \quad\ (4.06) \qquad\qquad R^2 = 0.67$$

II. Christensen, Cummings, and Jorgenson Data: n = 8
    Growth in Gross Private Domestic Product

$$\text{CCJAA} = 9.9797 - 0.0752 \text{ Index A}$$
$$\qquad\quad (7.15) \quad\ (3.30) \qquad\qquad R^2 = 0.64$$

$$\text{CCJAA} = 9.4748 - 0.0690 \text{ Index B}$$
$$\qquad\quad (7.39) \quad\ (3.22) \qquad\qquad R^2 = 0.63$$

    Growth in Total Factor Productivity

$$\text{CCJBB} = 10.7249 - 0.0863 \text{ Index A}$$
$$\qquad\quad (6.45) \quad\ (3.18) \qquad\qquad R^2 = 0.63$$

$$\text{CCJBB} = 10.1251 - 0.0788 \text{ Index B}$$
$$\qquad\quad (6.59) \quad\ (3.07) \qquad\qquad R^2 = 0.61$$

measures of institutional sclerosis. Though not reported in the table, the sample that excludes Japan still produces a statistically significant result with reasonably high explanatory power.

The above results indicate the explanatory power and the generality of Olson's theory in the study of cross-national data. The model is clearly satisfactory when judged for the usual criterion of overall goodness of fit as well as for the signs and significance of the estimated regression coefficients. It is also satisfactory when judged in terms of data sensitivity.

4: Notes on International Differences in Productivity Growth Rates

MOSES ABRAMOVITZ

Mancur Olson's interesting and important theory about the growth rate of productivity in relation to common-interest groups constitutes a challenge to the existing body of thought on international growth-rate differentials. Therefore, it may be useful to consider the general style of our approaches to this subject. We should then be able to understand more clearly how Olson's hypothesis complements or supplements other views and how it needs to be tested.

Whenever explanations of national growth-rate differences try to go beyond proximate growth sources, they generally follow one or two styles or combine both. (This distinction refers to rates of productivity growth, rather than to the broader questions of per-capita or aggregate growth.) One style focuses on differences in the potential for productivity growth. The other is mainly concerned with forces governing the pace at which that potential is realized. Olson's theory belongs to the second category. He holds that the pace of growth is slower in some countries than in others, according to the number, strength, and character of common-interest groups, which themselves develop slowly in the course of industrial and commercial development. Depending on their narrowness or breadth, common-interest groups impose constraints on the pace of productivity growth. To see Olson's theory in full perspective, we should consider other explanations: both those that follow the style of the first category above and a variety of possible forces that govern the pace of realized or actual potential, because they may be competitive with, or supplementary to, the common-interest-group hypothesis.

Growth Potential and International Growth-Rate Differences

"Potential for productivity growth" has two meanings in this context. First, it is the opportunity for progress that the advance of technological and organizational knowledge presents during a specific time period. Second, it is the opportunity for productivity growth that exists in a country which possesses advanced political, commercial, and financial institutions and a high degree of technical competence, but which is, nevertheless, behind the foremost country in industrial productivity. Assuming an adequate level of institutional and technical preparedness, the degree of initial backwardness of the lagging country may be a rough measure of the gap between existing and potential productivity, a potential which implies a capacity to advance during capital turnover and expansion and an accompanying economic reorganization. Contemporaneously generated technological progress, insofar as it is equally accessible to all countries, cannot help explain international differences in growth rates. On the other hand, differences among countries in initial levels of productivity can be the basis of a partial explanation, provided the several countries are sufficiently advanced in their human and institutional preparation—as Olson, indeed, recognizes.

Not only is it true that variant initial levels *can* help explain subsequent growth-rate differences; experience generally shows that they do help. Table 4.1, which presents estimates of the levels of GNP per worker in

Table 4.1. Mean Aggregate GNP per Worker of Japan, Canada, Germany, France, Italy, Netherlands, Norway, Belgium, and Denmark, 1913–1970

	1913	*1929*	*1938*	*1950*	*1955*	*1960*	*1965*	*1970*
Excluding Japan								
Mean (U.S. = 100)	65.1			51.7	53.9	59.8	62.3	70.6
Relative Variance	.053			.048	.044	.026	.017	.014
Excluding Germany								
Mean (U.S. = 100)	59.8	54.3	58.5	48.5				
Relative Variance	.102	.068	.036	.109				
All countries								
Mean (U.S. = 100)	61.2			48.4	50.8	57.0	60.1	69.8
Relative Variance	.096			.096	.078	.053	.029	.014

SOURCE: Moses Abramovitz, "Rapid Growth Potential and its Realization: The Experience of Capitalist Countries in the Postwar Period," in *Economic Growth and Resources* (Proceedings of the Fifth World Congress of the International Economic Association), ed. E. Malinvaud, vol. 1, *The Major Issues* (London: Macmillan, 1979).

NOTE: GNP figures are measured in 1965 U.S. dollars and then scaled relative to U.S. Means and variances are calculated excluding the U.S.

seven European countries, Japan, and Canada, supports this idea. The table may be interpreted as follows. By 1913, the United States had become the productivity leader of the industrialized world. This reflected its early commencement of modern economic growth, its freedom from the lingering constraints of an earlier feudal organization, its abundance of natural resources, and the rapid spread of a recently transplanted, fast-growing population. On a new continent, these factors made for relative uniformity of condition and tastes. They also provided the basis for mass markets and gave unusual scope for economies of scale. Britain apart, other countries began industrialization in later decades. Technological development did not get under way in Scandinavia, Italy, and Japan until the late nineteenth century. So, before the opening of this century, many countries were still in the earliest stages of institutional modernization: the acquisition of technical-industrial skills and experience as well as the establishment of basic transport facilities. Germany's full potential for growth was released only with its unification in 1870. Meanwhile, France suffered a serious check to its development between 1870 and 1896, a result of unfavorable crop conditions, the impact of phylloxera, and the stronger competition of New World products in both French and foreign markets.[1] These checks to rapid development in Western Europe and Japan were being overcome, however, and were disappearing between the mid-nineties and 1913. During that era a rising trend in prices replaced the deflationary tendencies and successive depressions of the last quarter of the nineteenth century.

One might, therefore, have expected that in the decades following 1913 Western Europe and Japan would have enjoyed rapid economic development, that the gap between their levels of productivity and those of the U.S. would have been significantly reduced. This expectation was not realized because of the cumulative effect of two world wars, their aftermath of political and economic turmoil, and the Great Depression. The effects of these developments varied from country to country. In the U.S. and Canada, the wars were stimuli; the other countries suffered in one degree or another. Despite a substantial recovery from World War II,[2] their productivity levels in 1950 had declined relative to that of the U.S., with

---

1. Cf. J. J. Carré, P. Dubois, and E. Malinvaud, *French Economic Growth* (Stanford, California: Stanford University Press, 1972), pp. 13–15.

2. This statement applies to Japan only with some qualification. K. Ohkawa and H. Rosovsky suggest that the initial postwar period of conversion, recovery, and rehabilitation did not end until 1952–54. See their *Japanese Economic Growth* (Stanford, California: Stanford University Press, 1973), p. 20.

the single exception of Norway's. Compared with 1913, the average decline approximated 20 percent. Although the Depression checked the growth of measured productivity, its effects on potential productivity were much less severe. The apparent recovery of productivity, relative to that of the U.S., during the thirties is largely illusory. It reflects the greater impact of the Depression on the difference between measured and potential productivity in the U.S. The decline in levels of productivity, relative to that of the U.S., between 1913 and 1950, however, was not accompanied by a retrogression in institutional and technical capabilities. On the contrary, France, Germany, Japan, Italy, and the smaller countries all gained in experience with large-scale and heavy industries and in the technological capabilities and skills of their people.

The postwar period began, therefore, with enlarged potentials for rapid growth, based upon larger gaps between levels of achieved productivity and the frontier, as represented by the United States, and on heightened institutional and technical capabilities. Subsequent developments were mainly consistent with the growth patterns that such potentials should have permitted. The Western European countries and Japan, without exception, gained relative to the U.S.[3] The average gain in the period from 1950 up to 1970 was some 37 percent. The countries which stood lowest in the 1950 ranking on the whole gained most.[4] The relative variance among the countries in productivity levels declined by five-sixths (seven-tenths, if Japan is excluded). One can also show that the proximate sources of excess productivity growth in the "follower" countries over that in the U.S., as indicated by Edward Denison's figures, were dominated by those that can be plausibly connected with growth in the course of "catching-up": the shift of labor from agriculture and petty trade to higher-productivity industry and commerce; scale-dependent technological borrowing from the U.S. as the poorer countries' consumption patterns converged toward the American pattern; and "changes in the lag in application of knowledge."[5]

3. Only Canada, of the countries represented in table 4.1, is an exception. Its relative (U.S. = 100) productivity declined from 72.2 in 1950 to 71.9 in 1970. The U.K. gain was minuscule, from 56.7 to 58.6.

4. The coefficient of rank correlation between labor productivity growth rates from 1950 to 1970 and relative levels of productivity in 1950 was -0.9 (eleven countries, including the U.S.). See my paper, "Rapid Growth Potential and Its Realization: The Experience of Capitalist Countries in the Postwar Period," in *Economic Growth and Resources* (Proceedings of the Fifth World Congress of the International Economic Association), ed. E. Malinvaud, vol. 1, *The Major Issues* (London: Macmillan, 1979), Table 2.

5. These three sources accounted for more than half, and in the cases of France, Germany, and Italy, more than three-quarters, of the excess of productivity growth over that in the U.S. See my paper,

The plausibility of the catch-up hypothesis, its general consistency with the postwar record of productivity growth-rate differentials, and the support which the character of growth sources lends to it suggest that this hypothesis contributes something substantial to our understanding of differences among countries in their growth experience.[6] Competing hypotheses, such as Olson's, should be tested jointly with the catch-up hypothesis by calculating regressions in which measures of initial levels of productivity and of the strength and breadth of common-interest groups both figure as explanatory variables.

For our purposes, we must recognize that the operational form in which Olson has cast his ideas makes it hard to distinguish clearly between the behavior predicted by his theory and by the catch-up hypothesis. This is because, in a first application of his theory, Olson proposes that we may treat the number of years preceding a given date, during which a country has been free from serious political or military turmoil, as a proxy for the strength of common-interest groups. Since it is likely that a country's productivity level is also a function of the number of years that it has enjoyed peaceful development, the growth predictions yielded by the catch-up hypothesis and by the operational form of the Olson hypothesis are likely to be similar. So far as postwar growth rates are concerned, both hypotheses suggest that the U.S., Canada, and the U.K. would grow at relatively slow rates whereas Japan, Germany, Italy, France, and the Netherlands would experience relatively rapid rates. The difference between hypotheses is that the initial levels of productivity from which the catch-up hypothesis proceeds can be measured directly. By contrast, it is difficult to measure the strength and breadth of common-interest groups in a reasonable, uniform fashion. Accordingly, it is not clear that such groups were consistently weaker or, to use Olson's term, more "encompassing," in the fast-growing countries. To get a better grip on the possible significance of Olson's hypothesis, and to distinguish it more clearly from the catch-up hypothesis, we badly need a more direct way of measuring the relevant characteristics of common-interest groups.

"Rapid Growth Potential and Its Realization," p. 15 and note 13, where I also argue that these figures may be regarded as lower bounds because they allow nothing for the support which opportunities for catch-up lent to rapid capital accumulation by supporting rates of return to capital.

6. The catch-up hypothesis does not enjoy clean-cut empirical support. In its simplest formulation, one would expect that growth processes in which catching up was a strong element would exhibit retardation. The productivity growth rates of Japan and of European countries from 1950 to 1970, however, show no consistent tendency to fall. I believe this failure can be explained (ibid., pp. 13–14) in ways which are not inconsistent with the catch-up process, but the need for such explanation does point to the fact that catching up is not the whole story.

Conditions Controlling the Rate of Realization of Potential

Although they are difficult to distinguish at present, the catch-up and Olson hypotheses really belong to different styles of explanation. The former is concerned with growth potential in the sense already explained. The latter, on the other hand, is concerned with forces governing the speed with which potential is realized. In that style of explanation, however, it does not stand alone. The following brief notes are intended to suggest other influences that are sometimes advanced to explain the pace of realization; therefore, they require testing along with the Olson hypothesis. I have written about these influences as factors that may help us understand why the postwar pace of growth in Western Europe and Japan was, in general, so much more rapid than in earlier periods of similar duration.[7] Here I consider the same theme insofar as it may bear on international growth-rate differentials. The following three headings refer to processes through which the realization of potential may be regarded as taking place.

Facilities for the Diffusion and Adaptation of Technological Advances

The practical applications of existing technology demand awareness, appraisal, commercial acquisition, and adaptation to a form compatible with a country's resources and scale of market. Technological applications must also be suited to the style of products of the markets and firms of the country in question. Several conditions may affect the speed with which firms in different countries act.

Awareness, appraisal, and adaptation depend on the numbers of available applied scientists and engineers. The way they are integrated into the commercial side of business firms is also significant. This integration improved considerably after the war in such countries as France and Italy, once they had recovered from the shock of defeat and occupation.

After the war, firms became better aware of the importance of maintaining close connections between their R and D establishments and the commercial sides of business. They also saw the value of developing similar connections with the more basic engineering and scientific work of universities. Britain moved especially slowly in this respect; Japan, Germany, and France, more rapidly.

Pressures generated by postwar liberalization of trade and the establishment of the Common Market were probably important in stimulating firms

7. Ibid., p. 20.

to modernize. A plausible speculation is that such pressures had a more profound effect on countries like France and Italy, whose industries had earlier been more thoroughly protected than had those in Britain, where trade had been somewhat freer, and which joined the Common Market late.

Conditions Facilitating Structural Change

Sectoral redistribution of output and employment is both a necessary condition and a concomitant of productivity growth. This follows from several facts: the income elasticities of consumer demand for products of various sectors are not the same; the industrial sector is the producer of capital goods, and the industrial and tertiary sectors produce the intermediate inputs on which productivity increases depend; and productivity growth brings shifts in comparative advantage, the exact nature of which is connected with countries' relative levels of industrialization and income. Sectoral shifts are also direct contributors to productivity growth: they permit countries to correct earlier misallocations of resources to low-productivity occupations (farming and petty trade); scale-dependent technological borrowing is facilitated because income growth is accompanied by a convergence of consumption and production structures, following the pattern of the country with highest industrial productivity;[8] concentrations of output, accompanying import substitution, and export expansion yield additional economies of scale. The problem is to sort out which conditions may have influenced the pace of structural change and whether they served to differentiate the experiences of one country from another in the postwar period. One can identify several conditions that may have played such a role, though the extent to which they actually did so is yet to be established.

Differences in income elasticity of demand for industry's products were reflected in the revolutionary use of consumer durables in the U.S. between the two wars. This phenomenon made a much smaller advance in Europe and a still smaller one in Japan, but the postwar growth of income eventually led to adoption of the new consumer goods. Presumably, the pace of adoption in different countries was related to their levels of income and to the persistence of traditional consumption patterns.

Income inequality and dualism were also significant conditions. With average levels of income so low in Japan and Italy, one might have ex-

8. Cf. Edward Denison, *Why Growth Rates Differ* (Washington, D.C.: The Brookings Institution, 1967), pp. 235–50.

pected that the move to expensive consumer durables would have been especially slow. The dual structure of these countries probably worked the other way. Families with a member employed in the modern sectors had incomes that soon approximated northwest European standards. As a result, the markets for complex consumer durables expanded rapidly in these countries too.

The interwar years were marked by military preparations more in some countries than in others. The heavy industries of Germany and Japan were expanded, as were to a lesser extent those in Italy. These countries, therefore, could more easily revive heavy industrial growth after the war.

Access to flexible and responsive supplies of relatively cheap labor varied from country to country. These supplies came from postwar repatriations, politically motivated migrations (of populations), labor "reserves" in agriculture and petty trade, and the flows of both permanent and temporary immigrant workers. Charles Kindleberger[9] and Denison[10] have laid stress on access to such labor because its shift from low- to high-productivity occupations raised average levels of productivity. Nicholas Kaldor[11] argued that the supply of workers who could be shifted from agriculture controlled the pace of expansion in those nonagricultural industries that were capable of yielding economies of scale or of growth. Both these arguments have merit; I should like to emphasize, however, an additional point. Granted that a large relative expansion of the non-agricultural sectors is inherent in rapid productivity growth and that further nonagricultural industries and regions are bound to grow at very different speeds: still, the pace of overall growth must depend on the prices at which the fast-growing industries and areas can obtain additional resources, especially workers. If expansion of their demand for labor drives wages up rapidly, a country's growth must be retarded. Access to large sources of cheap labor, from farming, petty trade, and from abroad, checks the rise of wages and tends to extend the duration of a spurt in growth.

These considerations suggest a possible point of relevance for the Olson hypothesis. Strong and narrow-based labor unions may resist the entry of new workers to particular industries or to the country at large; that implies, however, that there is also an underlying supply side to the story. Countries

9. Charles Kindleberger, *Europe's Postwar Growth, The Role of Labor Supply* (Cambridge, Mass.: Harvard University Press, 1967).

10. Denison, *Why Growth Rates Differ*, ch. 16.

11. Nicholas Kaldor, *Causes of the Slow Growth of the United Kingdom* (Cambridge: Cambridge University Press, 1966).

differ with respect to the availability of labor reserves in agriculture. Repatriations are not subject to the usual labor-employer conflicts over immigration policy. And, while unions might resist immigration, employer groups would likely favor it. The mode of operation and the influence of common-interest groups need clarification.

Conditions Encouraging and Sustaining Capital Investment

The several ways in which the pace of realization of growth potential may depend on the speed of capital accumulation are too well known to need recital. We should, however, recall a number of reasons why that speed might, and presumably did, differ among countries in the postwar period. Such standard savings models as the lifecycle savings model would generate hypotheses that I neglect because I have not considered the possibilities they raise. Other considerations yield suggestions more easily.

INITIAL FINANCIAL CONDITIONS. Almost all fast-growing countries entered the postwar period following episodes of serious or even drastic inflation. In Germany and Japan the preexisting debts of firms were essentially eliminated. To a lesser degree, the same was true in France and Italy. Inflation lightened the real burden of debt in the U.K., the U.S., Sweden, and Canada as well, but to a smaller extent. Insofar as one's ability to obtain finance or to accept liabilities depended on the accumulation of earlier debt, firms in the former group of countries were at an advantage. The same must have been true of households.

DIFFERENCES IN GOVERNMENT SUPPORT FOR INVESTMENT. In the early postwar years, the outlook for growth in continental Europe and in Japan was highly uncertain. There were also great needs for replacing and modernizing infrastructure, for which capital requirements were very large, but the ability and willingness of private firms to undertake investment unaided were initially limited. The volume of capital formation consequently depended greatly on direct investments by governments or on governmental aid and support to private firms. In these respects, Japan, France, and Italy went further than Germany and the U.K.; and they went a great deal further than the U.S.

DIFFERENTIAL ACCESS TO ELASTIC SUPPLIES OF RELATIVELY CHEAP LABOR. Heavy investment volume, despite a labor force of constant or nearly constant size, obviously tends to raise capital-labor ratios rapidly, driving wages up and driving rates of return down. An elastic supply of relatively cheap labor checks this process, permitting a more rapid growth of capital stock for a longer period. When a labor force grows rapidly, the ability of a given growth rate of capital stock to raise labor productivity, simply by its effect on capital-labor ratios, is reduced. Its ability to increase productivity through the introduction of more advanced forms of capital equipment, however, remains intact. Consequently, differential access to elastic supplies of relatively cheap labor is also relevant to the pace of investment.

Concluding Notes

The influence of common-interest groups in governing growth rates of productivity needs to be tested jointly with many factors: those indicated above and, presumably, still others. For that purpose, direct measures of size, strength, and character of common-interest groups need to be devised. I have already suggested why the proxy proposed by Olson (the number of years of peaceful political development) may make it difficult to separate the effects of differences in growth potential from the impacts of common-interest groups. There are other reasons why the duration of uninterrupted periods of peaceful development is likely to prove a confusing proxy:

1. How does one distinguish between political changes that are serious interruptions to peaceful development from those that are not? Was Roosevelt's New Deal a serious interruption of earlier tendencies?

2. Do all "revolutions," or political overturns, weaken common-interest groups? Why should one assume that the transitions from Louis Philippe to Napoleon III to the Third Republic were upsetting to the growth of common-interest groups? The New Deal (if that qualifies as a serious political novelty) worked to strengthen such groups.

3. Is the passage of time, alone, the dominant factor governing the strength and scope of common-interest groups? The severe military and political traumas in Japan, Germany, and Italy between 1870 and 1950 were not clearly different in orders of magnitude. The nature of the shocks had many similarities. Yet, the strength and character of common-interest groups in the three countries seem to be quite different.

These questions point up the need for more direct measures of common-interest groups. Developing consistent measures of the kind we require presupposes a great deal of knowledge about relations between the characteristics of such groups and their behavior. Besides numbers and strength,

Olson has already suggested that "encompassingness" counts. Needless to say, we still have to figure out how to measure "encompassingness." Then we must establish how much difference that quality may make to behavior. Presumably, other qualities of common-interest groupings are important and will need to be identified and studied. The Zaibatsu in Japan were, in a sense, common-interest groups, yet many students believe they had a positive effect in furthering Japanese growth during the early twentieth century. If so, what distinguished them from industry groups in other countries where they may be interpreted to have constrained growth? Further, when one considers the retarding effects of common-interest groups, one commonly thinks of them as supporting protectionist policies, and as shielding their members from competitive pressures. In the postwar period, Japan's government pursued a strongly protectionist policy, doing for industries what one might have expected a group of narrow-based industry groups to have demanded for themselves. Yet, many students think that this protectionism made for rapid progress in Japan because it was a constituent element in a broadly stimulative program of technological modernization. Evidently, there are subtleties in the operation and effects of protectionist policy. They take a great deal of study to unravel.

5: A Quasi-test of Olson's Hypotheses

FREDERIC L. PRYOR

We usually approach new writings of familiar authors with bias or prejudice. For Mancur Olson we know that no matter whether he is right or wrong, he will certainly give us an original and provocative analysis. With the essay on differential growth rates that serves as the focus of this book, he runs true to form; and this means that we will have a sufficient number of difficult theoretical and empirical questions to keep us occupied for some time.

Although my comments deal with both theoretical and empirical issues, I focus primarily on problems involved in testing Olson's hypotheses. The empirical part of Olson's paper is quite straightforward: he first discusses a number of examples illustrating his ideas that are drawn from the postwar growth experience of some major economically developed nations; and then he presents some simple econometric comparisons of growth in various subperiods of the U.S. economy. However, a number of aspects of these empirical analyses raise some serious questions.

One can object to the examples drawn from national growth experiences because they do not concern those countries whose growth experiences really need explaining: that is, there is no proof that the nations selected for study are really unusual. On this matter I provide evidence below which casts some doubt on the relevance of his examples. Further, the proposed theory may not capture the most important sources of development (or lack of development) in those economies on which they focus. On this matter I also provide some evidence which points to a quite different theory that relates growth rates to initial levels of development.

I express my thanks to Christopher Udry who served as a conscientious research assistant in collecting the data and running the regressions. For the data for Eastern Europe I am grateful also to Thad Alton, Andrew Elias, and Murray Feshbach. All are, of course, absolved of responsibilty for my errors.

With regard to the analysis of differential growth of U.S. states, three objections can be offered. First, if the regressions had been carried out for some earlier decades (say between 1900 and 1910 or between 1920 and 1930), the faster growth of the southern states might not have been obtained. Second, linking relative growth patterns between 1965 and 1974 to events occurring more than a century before, when industrialization was not far advanced in any of the states, is a dangerous procedure unless one can obtain some evidence that intervening events did not greatly influence current growth patterns. Third, current growth rates in the various U.S. states cannot be considered as independent observations of some underlying phenomenon, for such differential growth is greatly influenced by activities on the national level. Two examples can be given. The relatively greater importance of defense industries in the southern and western states (the "newer" states) had a strong impact on growth during the decade of the Vietnam War, which Olson examined. Further, given the locational pattern of committee chairmen in Congress and the federal funds flowing to the states for the construction of growth-inducing social-overhead capital, it is not unusual that the southern and western states grew faster.

Below, I outline a different test of Olson's hypotheses; it is based on an analysis of the differential growth rates of the major industrialized nations of the world plus all significant Eastern and Western European nations in the period from 1950 through 1975. I label this statistical exercise a "quasi-test" since not all of the variables that Olson specifies can be adequately quantified; further, the tests that I carry out may be too aggregative to isolate adequately the subtle phenomena with which Olson is dealing. Let me also add that it is quite possible that Olson's hypotheses can never be empirically tested in a completely satisfactory manner because of the counteracting forces specified within the model itself, for instance, the insight that although common-interest groups reduce not only static efficiency but dynamic efficiency as well, the cost of their activities to society becomes increasingly apparent so that the benefits and the incentives to society as a whole in breaking their stranglehold become stronger.

Finally, the statistical experiments described below represent only a very preliminary approach toward this fascinating topic. Although objections can be raised about particular details—indeed, I express several myself at the end of the paper—the overall results of these experiments provide illumination for the problem at hand and set up certain questions that must be answered before a completely satisfactory explanation of differential growth rates among the developed nations can be given.

Setting Up the Statistical Experiments

Dependent Variables

Specifying Olson's model forces us to focus on a number of issues which must be dealt with before the statistical tests can be carried out. First, the choice of a suitable dependent variable for testing Olson's hypotheses raises the three following major questions.

What indicator of growth should we examine? In most of his discussion Olson seems to be talking about the growth of aggregate production or income. However, differential population growth might be the major cause of differential growth of production or income, so that it might be better to examine these variables on a per-capita basis. But objections can be raised against this variable as well, for a good portion of the growth might be attributable to an increase in the labor participation ratio when more women and children enter the labor force. It might therefore be still better to use growth of production or income per economically active. In the empirical analysis below I use gross domestic product (GDP) (for the Eastern European nations I use gross national product since GDP data are not available; however this should cause little difficulty); and I present results for GDP alone, GDP per capita, and GDP per economically active. It must be noted that the reliability of the GDP per economically active leaves something to be desired for several reasons: the concept of economically active is ambiguous, especially concerning female workers in agriculture; data on the economically active at a particular time have been used in place of a proper flow variable (for instance, reduction of seasonality in the Soviet economy has meant that the series for annual hours of labor has grown faster than the series for economically active, as measured every January); and for some countries only rough estimates of the economically active were available for the years between census years. Therefore, although GDP per economically active probably is more useful than the other variables in testing Olson's ideas, it is the least reliable series.

Over what period of time should we measure growth? Olson speaks of the "current" growth rate, but he cannot mean this literally since growth rates in short time intervals are too much influenced by such factors as conjunctural forces that are unrelated to his hypothesis; and he cannot mean a very long time, for such growth rates would cover periods in which the key institutional variables on which he focuses his attention are changing. Murrell, below, uses five- and ten-year periods; Olson uses a decade interval which, as I noted above, was characterized primarily by war.

Below, I use a twenty-five- or twenty-six-year period and then divide this into subperiods of from twelve to thirteen years. If Olson's approach is valid, we should expect the high- and low-growth-rate countries to be similar in the two subperiods, since his proposed causal mechanism for economic growth depends on long-run sociological factors. To minimize the effect of the choice of end-dates in any of these experiments, I use the calculated exponential growth rates obtained by fitting such a growth curve to the data.

What units should be examined? In order to use data that are comparable, I have limited my sample to the important nations of Europe plus the other developed nations in the world (a sample that includes twenty-nine countries in all). The inclusion of so large a number of countries in the study has three justifications. First, the differences between these countries should provide sufficient variation with which to test Olson's ideas. Second, Olson mentions in his essay a number of nations having noticeably high growth rates (Japan, Germany, Sweden, Norway, and France) and several which have noticeably low growth rates (the U.K., the U.S., and Australia). It is, however, unclear if he selected these on the basis of absolute growth rates (in which case some of his case studies could be questioned) or on the basis of growth rates adjusted by some implicit *ceteris paribus* clause. By having a large sample and testing a number of *ceteris paribus* conditions, we may be able to isolate for case studies a group of suitable nations with which to test Olson's ideas. And third, by including the countries in Eastern Europe in the sample, we can test explanations of differential growth rates that are quite general and that permit transsystemic factors to be isolated. More specifically, if one believes as I do that bureaucratic politics play a key role in determining economic policies of nations with centrally administered economies, there is no reason why Olson's theory cannot apply to growth rates in these countries. The alternative theory of growth which I propose below covers these countries as well. For those who do not like including the centrally planned economies of Eastern Europe in the analysis, the regressions are also run using the Western nations alone.

Independent Variables

PER-CAPITA GDP IN A COMMON CURRENCY.   A number of economists have noted that growth among nations with a per-capita GDP above a certain critical limit appears to be inversely related to their levels of economic development and, moreover, that this phenomenon appears among countries in both East and West. As Olson has pointed out, this is because the nations with lower levels of economic development can borrow technology from the more advanced nations more easily than these latter nations can develop still more advanced technologies. He might have also added that the economically less-developed nations have a greater potential for growth by transferring their labor force from low-productivity agriculture to high-productivity industry, a source of growth not open to such nations as the U.S. or the U.K., which have only a small share of their labor force still remaining in agriculture. I use data (described in Appendix A) of per-capita GDP in 1970, and from these estimates calculate the average GDP per capita in a common currency for the six years from 1960 through 1965, which fall in the middle of the time period I am investigating. For the two subperiods, I use the per-capita GDPs in 1957 and 1970. For the period as a whole, as well as the two subperiods, we expect (and find) a strong inverse relationship between average GDP per capita and the various measures of growth which are used as the dependent variable. Further, this variable reflecting the relative levels of economic development is the only independent variable discussed in this essay that has a statistically significant relationship to the various measures of growth.

SIZE OF NATION AS REFLECTED BY POPULATION.   Olson argues that the larger the population of the nation, the less likely to be found are all-embracing common-interest groups; and, therefore, we should find a negative relationship between this variable and the growth rate. A counterargument can, however, be offered: the larger the nation, the more difficult it is for even a narrow common-interest group to form, so that we would expect a positive relationship between the population level and growth rates of production. I use the population in 1963 (the middle of the period) and have calculated the regressions with this independent variable specified both without a transformation and with a log transformation (the latter regressions are not presented). In neither form does this variable appear a very promising explanation for differential growth rates.

POLITICAL DOMINATION BY A COMMUNIST PARTY.   Those nations in Eastern Europe that have been ruled by communist parties for a quarter of a century have certainly experienced total devastation of almost all previous common-interest groups except those centered on the parties themselves. Further, the party represents an extreme form of an all-embracing common-interest group—one that is strongly committed to high rates of economic growth. If Olson's approach is correct, we would expect to find a positive relationship between this variable (specified as a dummy variable) and the growth rates; such expectations are, however, disappointed.

ETHNIC HETEROGENEITY.   Olson argues that all-embracing common-interest groups are less likely to be found if there is great ethnic or religious heterogeneity. Two indices of ethnic heterogeneity have been calculated, one by a group of Soviet social scientists on the basis of data on ethnic groups;[1] the other by Taylor and Hudson on the basis of linguistic evidence.[2] Given Olson's hypotheses, we would expect to find a negative correlation between such a variable and growth rates; but the relationship is not significant for either variable. In the regressions below, only the Soviet series—which seems to correspond more to Olson's hypothesized relationship—is presented.

RELIGIOUS HETEROGENEITY.   I have constructed a dummy variable that indicates religious heterogeneity (it is described in Appendix A). According to Olson's approach, it should have a negative relationship to the growth rates, a correspondence that is not found. Other series on religious heterogeneity can be found in the literature (for example, Banks and Textor),[3] but these variables did not seem sufficiently promising to test further.

Procedure

In order to avoid being open to the charge of massaging the data to an illegitimate degree, I adopted in the beginning and stuck by a three-step procedure. In the first step I ran a series of regressions with equations containing all of the independent variables that are specified above. In the second step I culled out those variables that were not statistically significant, reran the regressions, and determined the group of countries for which case studies would be useful. More particularly, I isolated those countries whose actual growth rates are 1 percent higher or lower than their predicted rates. In the third step I added a new set of possible explanatory variables to the regressions. These attempts represent some rather uncon-

---

1. The series appears in *Atlas narodov mira* (Moscow: N. N. Miklukho-Maklaya Institute of Ethnography, 1964).
2. Charles Lewis Taylor and Michael C. Hudson, *World Handbook of Political and Social Indicators,* 2nd ed. (New Haven: Yale University Press, 1972).
3. Arthur S. Banks and Robert B. Textor, *A Cross-Polity Survey* (Cambridge, Mass.: MIT Press, 1963).

trolled experiments of a variety of hypotheses and, since none yielded results of interest, they received only scant attention.

Results

The key regressions are presented in table 5.1, and the most important result can be easily summarized: except for those variables representing per-capita GDP, none of the proposed explanatory variables is statistically significant. Several aspects of the results should, however, be noted.

The systems variable is negative in all three experiments, which suggests that the Eastern European countries have had lower growth rates than capitalist countries, other things being equal. Part of the explanation of this surprising result is that most of the Eastern European series have a price base of 1970, which means, in turn, that for the period from 1950 to 1970 we have a Paasche index. Such a procedure often leads to lower growth rates than if the series had a set of price weights of a past year (Laspeyres index). Unfortunately, the price weights of many of the Western series are not specified so that we do not know how they are biased; I suspect, however, that most of them are chain-weighted, with the links being five or ten years in length. However, since the calculated regression coefficient is not significant, we do not need to worry about this sign.

The variable representing religious heterogeneity has the wrong sign; the variable representing ethnic heterogeneity has the correct sign and a sizeable magnitude. The population variable has the incorrect sign. Again, these results are not statistically significant.

The coefficients of determination are quite respectable. It is also noteworthy that they are highest for GDP/economically active and lowest for GNP alone, which confirms certain aspects of the comments above about the appropriateness of different dependent variables. The results for the GDP/economically active are particularly remarkable for they are for the series in which I have the least confidence.

In table 5.2 I present regression calculations for the noncommunist nations in order to avoid using the series (calculated in the West) representing growth in Eastern Europe. The results are practically the same as for the sample as a whole. In addition, I present calculations for the entire sample for two subperiods of thirteen years each. One inference we might make from Olson's analysis is that, other things being equal, growth in the latter period should be less because common-interest groups in all nations are more strongly entrenched than in the earlier period (since the nations are

Table 5.1.   Regression Equations for the Entire Sample, 1950 through 1974–75

$$1.\ \dot{GDP} = 7.486 - 0.0587^* \text{ YCAP} - 0.879 \text{ SYS} + 0.504 \text{ RELHE} - 0.314 \text{ ETHET} + 0.00209 \text{ POP} \qquad n = 29$$
$$\phantom{1.\ \dot{GDP} = 7.486}\ (0.0153) (0.518) (0.532) (1.027) (0.00436) \qquad R^2 = 0.4025$$

$$2.\ \dot{GDP} = 6.737 - 0.0434^* \text{ YCAP} \qquad n = 29$$
$$\phantom{2.\ \dot{GDP} = 6.737}\ (0.0122) \qquad R^2 = 0.3200$$

$$3.\ \frac{\dot{GDP}}{POP} = 6.869 - 0.0609^* \text{ YCAP} - 0.578 \text{ SYS} + 0.142 \text{ RELHE} - 1.148 \text{ ETHET} + 0.00239 \text{ POP} \qquad n = 29$$
$$\phantom{3.\ \frac{\dot{GDP}}{POP} = 6.869}\ (0.0148) (0.505) (0.509) (0.983) (0.00418) \qquad R^2 = 0.5163$$

$$4.\ \frac{\dot{GDP}}{POP} = 6.269 - 0.0546^* \text{ YCAP} \qquad n = 29$$
$$\phantom{4.\ \frac{\dot{GDP}}{POP} = 6.269}\ (0.0177) \qquad R^2 = 0.4469$$

$$5.\ \frac{\dot{GDP}}{ECAC} = 7.421 - 0.0701^* \text{ YCAP} - 0.821 \text{ SYS} + 0.233 \text{ RELHE} - 1.381 \text{ ETHET} + 0.00353 \text{ POP} \qquad n = 27$$
$$\phantom{5.\ \frac{\dot{GDP}}{ECAC} = 7.421}\ (0.0151) (0.514) (0.501) (0.966) (0.00410) \qquad R^2 = 0.5789$$

$$6.\ \frac{\dot{GDP}}{ECAC} = 6.491 - 0.0583^* \text{ YCAP} \qquad n = 27$$
$$\phantom{6.\ \frac{\dot{GDP}}{ECAC} = 6.491}\ (0.0123) \qquad R^2 = 0.4716$$

SYMBOLS:

$\dot{GDP}$: average annual growth rate of GDP (GNP for the Eastern European nations); 1950 through 1974–75

$\dot{GDP}/POP$: average annual growth rate of GDP (GNP for the Eastern European nations) per capita; 1950 through 1974–75

$\dot{GDP}/ECAC$: average annual growth rate of GDP (GNP for the Eastern European nations) per economically active; 1950 through 1974–75

YCAP: GDP per capita in "international dollars," average 1960 through 1965 as a percentage of GDP per capita in U.S.A. in 1970

SYS: political systems dummy variable: 1 = political domination by communist party; 0 = other types of polities

RELHE: religious heterogeneity dummy variable: 1 = religious heterogeneity; 0 = no religious heterogeneity

ETHET: ethnic heterogeneity, continuous variable: 1 = totally heterogeneous; 0 = totally homogeneous

POP: population in 1963 in millions

n: size of sample

R^2: uncorrected coefficient of determination

*: statistically significant at the .05 level

NOTE: Figures in parentheses are the standard errors. Sources of data are described in Appendix A; data of major variables are presented in Appendix B.

Table 5.2.   Other Regressions

Capitalist Nations, 1950 through 1974–75

1. $\dot{\text{GDP}}$ $= 7.102 - .0479^*$ YCAP $\qquad$ $n = 21$
$\qquad\qquad\qquad$ $(.0160)$ $\qquad\qquad$ $R^2 = 0.3195$

2. $\dfrac{\dot{\text{GDP}}}{\text{POP}} = 6.981 - .0665^*$ YCAP $\qquad$ $n = 21$
$\qquad\qquad\qquad$ $(.0147)$ $\qquad\qquad$ $R^2 = 0.5179$

3. $\dfrac{\dot{\text{GDP}}}{\text{ECAC}} = 7.439 - .0736^*$ YCAP $\qquad$ $n = 19$
$\qquad\qquad\qquad$ $(.0158)$ $\qquad\qquad$ $R^2 = 0.5594$

Entire Sample, 1950 through 1962

4. $\dot{\text{GDP}}$ $= 6.291 - .0452^*$ YCAP $\qquad$ $n = 29$
$\qquad\qquad\qquad$ $(.0157)$ $\qquad\qquad$ $R^2 = 0.2347$

5. $\dfrac{\dot{\text{GDP}}}{\text{POP}} = 5.800 - .0593^*$ YCAP $\qquad$ $n = 29$
$\qquad\qquad\qquad$ $(.0158)$ $\qquad\qquad$ $R^2 = 0.3425$

6. $\dfrac{\dot{\text{GDP}}}{\text{ECAC}} = 5.878 - .0582^*$ YCAP $\qquad$ $n = 27$
$\qquad\qquad\qquad$ $(.0139)$ $\qquad\qquad$ $R^2 = 0.4139$

Entire Sample, 1963 through 1974–75

7. $\dot{\text{GDP}}$ $= 6.449 - .0303^*$ YCAP $\qquad$ $n = 29$
$\qquad\qquad\qquad$ $(.0120)$ $\qquad\qquad$ $R^2 = 0.1905$

8. $\dfrac{\dot{\text{GDP}}}{\text{POP}} = 6.074 - .0369^*$ YCAP $\qquad$ $n = 29$
$\qquad\qquad\qquad$ $(.0116)$ $\qquad\qquad$ $R^2 = 0.2747$

9. $\dfrac{\dot{\text{GDP}}}{\text{ECAC}} = 5.940 - .0386^*$ YCAP $\qquad$ $n = 27$
$\qquad\qquad\qquad$ $(.0134)$ $\qquad\qquad$ $R^2 = 0.2478$

SYMBOLS: See Table 5.1.

NOTE: YCAP for the entire period is defined as the average GDP per capita for the years 1960 through 1965; YCAP for the regressions for the 1950–62 period is defined as the GDP per capita in 1957; and YCAP for the 1963–74 period is defined as the GDP per capita in 1970. The per-capita GDPs for all three definitions are calculated as a percentage of the per-capita GDP of the U.S.A. in 1970. Figures in parentheses are the standard errors. The data come from sources described in Appendix A.

"older"). If we determine a predicted growth rate for nations with per-capita GDPs within the range of the countries we are studying, we find that exactly the opposite is true, that the predicted average annual growth rates are slightly higher in the latter than in the former period.

Using these regression equations, I present in tables 5.3 and 5.4 a listing of those countries whose actual average annual growth rates were 1 percent above or below their predicted values. Although such a cutoff limit is arbitrary, it serves to focus our attention upon the most "unusual" cases, which should prove easiest to explain using Olson's new approach. Three aspects of these tables deserve comment:

First, although some of the examples used by Olson to illustrate countries with particularly high or low growth rates appear in the tables (for instance, Japan and West Germany have extra-high growth rates, while for

Table 5.3. Countries with Extra-High or Extra-Low Growth Rates,
1950 through 1974–75

Growth Measure	Entire Sample		Capitalist Nations	
	Extra-High	Extra-Low	Extra-High	Extra-Low
GDP	Japan	Ireland	Japan	Ireland
	West Germany	U.K.	West Germany	U.K.
		Hungary		
GDP/capita	Japan	New Zealand	Japan	New Zealand
	West Germany	Ireland	West Germany	Ireland
		Poland		U.K.
		Hungary		
		U.K.		
GDP/economically active	Japan	Poland	Japan	New Zealand
	West Germany	New Zealand	West Germany	Ireland
	Italy	Australia		Australia
	France	Hungary		U.K.

NOTE: Only those countries are listed whose actual growth rates are at least 1 percent above or below their predicted values; they are listed in order of decreasing absolute value of such differences. The formulae on which the whole sample results are based are presented in Table 5.1 and are regressions numbers 2, 4, and 6. The formulae on which the sample results of the capitalist nations are based are presented in Table 5.2 and are regressions numbers 1 through 3.

Table 5.4. Countries with Extra-High or Extra-Low Growth Rates
in Different Subperiods

Growth Measure	1950 through 1962		1963 through 1974–75	
	Extra-High	Extra-Low	Extra-High	Extra-Low
GDP	West Germany	Ireland	Japan	Hungary
	Japan	U.K.	Greece	U.K.
		Portugal	Canada	East Germany
		Belgium		Czechoslovakia
		New Zealand		Ireland
GDP/capita	West Germany	Ireland	Japan	Hungary
	East Germany	New Zealand	Portugal	U.K.
	Japan	Poland	Greece	Ireland
	Austria	Australia		New Zealand
	Italy	Portugal		Switzerland
GDP/economically active	West Germany	New Zealand	Japan	Hungary
	East Germany	Ireland	Portugal	New Zealand
	Japan	U.K.	West Germany	Portugal
	Bulgaria	Australia	Finland	Czechoslovakia
	Italy	Portugal	France	U.K.
		Poland	Netherlands	

NOTE: Only those countries are listed whose actual growth rates are at least 1 percent above or below their predicted values; they are listed in descending order of such differences. The formulae on which these results are based are presented in Table 5.2, regressions numbers 4 through 9.

some indicators the U.K. and Australia have extra-low growth rates), we also find some surprises for the period as a whole. Among the fast-growing nations, the Scandinavian countries—which have all-embracing common-interest groups—do not appear. And among the slow-growing countries we find New Zealand, Ireland, Australia, and Hungary. Since the common-interest groups in Poland and Hungary were mostly obliterated after World War II and since both Australia and New Zealand are not far removed from their frontier past, we would hardly expect from Olson's approach to find them among the slow growers.

Second, although some nations seem to appear among the fast or slow growers for whatever indicator for the entire period that we select, other nations appear only for certain indicators. Among individual subperiods, such a phenomenon is even more pronounced. Thus determination of the dependent variable is a particularly crucial aspect of Olson's theory.

Third, the countries appearing on the extra-high or extra-low growth rate lists for the two subperiods composing the twenty-six-year period are, in many cases, quite different. If the sociological factors specified by Olson have validity, we would expect to find such lists quite similar, for the underlying structure of common-interest groups should not change greatly. Of particular interest is Portugal, which appears among the slow growers in the period from 1950 through 1962 and among the fast growers in the later period, a phenomenon that cannot be explained by the replacement of Salazar since Salazar's death occurred in the early 1970s.

Taking the sample as a whole for the entire period, another set of experiments was carried out by adding some "wild variables" into the regressions. One of these variables was McClelland's famous "achievement motivation,"[4] as measured by the achievement ratings that McClelland's team derived by examining children's books from twenty-four of the twenty-nine nations in the sample. Such a variable has almost no effect on the results. I also added into the regressions a set of variables defined and calculated by Banks and Textor[5] that allegedly measure common-interest group influence. Unfortunately, no explanation was given as to how these variables were coded or, indeed, what they actually mean. Further, two of the four were collinear with other dependent variables discussed above and thus could not be used. The remaining two variables had little effect on the regressions.

4. David C. McClelland, *The Achieving Society* (Princeton: Princeton University Press, 1961).
5. Banks and Textor, *A Cross-Polity Survey*.

Interpretations and Conclusions

The regression experiments lead to several important conclusions. First, the results provide favorable evidence for the hypothesis that growth rates are inversely related to the level of economic development. Second, the results do not appear very favorable to Olson's hypotheses. In particular, the variables that he suggested would reflect certain aspects of the activities of common-interest groups did not prove to be related in a statistically significant fashion to the dependent variables; and the lists of fast- and slow-growing nations were more variable between time periods than one might suspect from the long-term sociological factors that he outlines.

Nevertheless, these statistical exercises cannot be considered to disprove completely Olson's ideas, for my procedures raise some questions as well that must be clearly recognized. Some of my data, particularly for the Eastern European nations, leave something to be desired; and although I used the best available estimates, certain anomalies in the table raise some small doubts. Further, because I am unable to obtain any proxy for the crucial explanatory variables, the relative strength of narrowly defined common-interest groups, a direct test cannot be made. Perhaps my failure to provide measures to represent directly particular aspects of the process that Olson discussed (for instance, the system of collective bargaining in the various nations) meant that the effect of the proxies I did use was masked by such omissions.

Despite these deficiencies in my own methods, I believe that their empirical results suggest that certain parts of the exposition and elaboration of Olson's ideas might well be revised and strengthened. In particular, the following aspects of his approach might require greater attention:

First, what exactly is Olson's theory trying to explain? In particular, what measure of growth is he talking about and for how long a period should this growth be measured?

Second, why do the results of the tests I have presented differ among different time periods, and, more generally, what additional factors must be introduced to explain decade-long spurts or declines of growth that act to change drastically relative growth?

Third, what types of proxy variables can be developed to measure directly the growth-retarding effects of common-interest groups, given the fact that the variables he has suggested do not appear very promising?

Fourth, how might Olson explain the empirical results obtained in my analysis of slow and fast growers for the entire sample for the entire period?

For instance, why are Poland, New Zealand, Australia, and Hungary on the bottom of the list of growth rates of GDP per economically active (a variable that I think is the most significant)? And why are the nations whose rapid growth he emphasized in his essay not on my list of fast growers?

If I may draw an analogy from religion, Olson appears to have a monotheistic view toward economic growth; and so, in their own peculiar and different way, do some orthodox Marxists. Most growth economists, if I am able to understand their theological views, are polytheists since they have been betrayed too often by premature monotheism. They might hold that although Olson's ideas may well explain the relative differences between German and British growth (as demonstrated by Murrell), they might have little relevance for other pairs of nations.

Perhaps monotheism is more correct than polytheism; and perhaps Olson is facing the same type of blind resistance that the prophets of old faced when preaching to the heathen. Nevertheless, not only would I be happier if some of the more murky parts of his doctrine were cleared up, but I would also like to see a sign—a dove flying out of a rainbow or, more mundanely, some more solid empirical evidence—before I can embrace this new faith wholeheartedly. But to the monotheistic prophets of the Bible, this type of philistine reaction was all too common—and seldom discouraging.

APPENDIX A
Sources of Data

GDP or GNP Time Series[6]

For Western nations the basic source is the OECD (n.d.); this is supplemented by data from the United Nations (n.d.) and various national sources. For the Eastern European nations excluding the USSR and Yugoslavia, the basic source is Alton [1977, 1974, 1970], supplemented

6. Thad P. Alton, "Comparative Structure and Growth in Economic Activity in Eastern Europe," in U.S., Congress, Joint Economic Committee, *East European Economies Post Helsinki* (Washington, D.C.: Government Printing Office, 1977); idem, "Economic Growth and Resource Allocation in Eastern Europe," in U.S., Congress, Joint Economic Committee, *Reorientation and Commercial Relations of the Economies of Eastern Europe* (Washington, D.C.: Government Printing Office, 1974); idem, "Economic Structure and Growth in Eastern Europe," in U.S., Congress, Joint Economic Committee, *Economic Development in Countries of Eastern Europe* (Washington, D.C.: Government Printing Office, 1970); Rush V. Greenslade, "The Real Gross National Product of the

by data from Stolper [1960], various national sources, and unpublished information obtained from Thad Alton. For the USSR the data are taken from Greenslade [1976]; and for Yugoslavia, the data come from the World Bank [1975], supplemented by other World Bank materials and estimates made on the basis of data from national sources.

Population and Labor Force[7]

For population the basic source is the United Nations *Demographic Yearbook,* supplemented by a variety of national and other sources. For the Western nations data on the economically active come primarily from the OECD [1976] and [n.d.], supplemented by estimates and data from national sources. For Eastern Europe the data come primarily from Elias [1970], Feshbach and Rapawy [1976], Myers [1974], and Rapawy [1976]. For Yugoslavia the economically active are determined by interpolating such data between census years. For Greece and Austria the data for different census years do not appear comparable and no estimates are made.

GDP in a Common Currency[8]

For the Western nations the data come from Kravis, Heston, and Summers [1978], using the data in their Table 1, supplemented by their estimate

USSR," in U.S., Congress, Joint Economic Committee, *Soviet Economy in a New Perspective* (Washington, D.C.: Government Printing Office, 1976); OECD, *National Accounts of OECD Countries: Main Aggregates 1974* (Paris: n.d.); Wolfgang F. Stolper, *The Structure of the East German Economy* (Cambridge, Mass.: Harvard University Press, 1960); United Nations, *Yearbook of National Account Statistics* (New York: annual); World Bank (International Bank for Reconstruction and Development), *Yugoslavia: Development with Decentralization* (Baltimore: Johns Hopkins University Press, 1975).

7. Andrew Elias, "Magnitude and Distribution of the Labor Force in Eastern Europe," in U.S., Congress, Joint Economic Committee, *Economic Development in Countries of Eastern Europe* (Washington, D.C.: Government Printing Office, 1970); Murray Feshbach and Stephen Rapawy, "Soviet Population and Manpower Trends and Policy," in U.S., Congress, Joint Economic Committee, *Soviet Economy in a New Perspective* (Washington, D.C.: Government Printing Office, 1976); Paul F. Myers, "Population and Labor Force in Eastern Europe," in Joint Economic Committee, *Reorientation and Commercial Relations of the Economies of Eastern Europe* (Washington, D.C.: Government Printing Office, 1974); OECD, *Labour Force Statistics, 1963–1974* (Paris, 1976); idem, *Manpower Statistics* (Paris, various years); United Nations, *Demographic Yearbook* (New York, annual); U.S., Department of Commerce, "Estimates and Projections of the Labor Force and Civilian Employment in the U.S.S.R., 1950–1990," Foreign Economic Report No. 10, prepared by Stephen Rapawy (Washington, D.C.: Government Printing Office, 1976).

8. Frederic L. Pryor, "Comparable GNP's per Capita: An Addendum," *Economic Journal* 89 (September 1979): 666–69; Irving B. Kravis, Alan Heston, and Robert Summers, "Real GDP Per Capita for More than One Hundred Countries," *Economic Journal* 88 (June 1978): 215–42.

"D" for other nations. For the Eastern European nations the data come from Pryor [1979].

Other Dependent Variables[9]

The series on religious heterogeneity is constructed from data presented by Taylor and Hudson [1972] on Christian and Islamic communities. The dummy variable representing religious heterogeneity is defined as unity if any two sects (Protestant, Catholic, other Christian, or Islamic) each included more than 25 percent of the population; otherwise the dummy variable is zero. For several countries this procedure had to be slightly modified. The variables representing ethnic heterogeneity are continuous variables ranging from 0 (complete homogeneity) to 1 (complete hetero-geneity). One of these variables was calculated by Taylor and Hudson [1972] from linguistic data of Muller [1965]. The other is based on ethnic groups per se and was originally presented in *Atlas narodov mira* [1964]; it has been modified slightly by Taylor and Hudson [1972]. From Banks and Textor [1963], the following four variables are taken: "interest articula-tion by associational groups," "interest articulation by institutional groups," "interest articulation by non-associational groups," and "in-terest articulation by anomic groups." The data on achievement moti-vation come from Russett et al. [1964], who drew the data from McClel-land

APPENDIX B
Data for the Entire Period, 1950 through 1974–75

Country	GDP	$\frac{GDP}{POP}$	$\frac{GDP}{ECAC}$	YCAP
Austria	5.07	4.14	—	37.9
Australia	4.61	2.60	2.28	54.4
Belgium	4.10	3.56	3.62	52.5
Bulgaria	5.97	5.18	5.44	26.0
Canada	4.84	2.81	2.27	63.6
Czechoslovakia	3.87	3.20	2.99	50.7

9. *Atlas narodov mira;* Banks and Textor, *A Cross-Polity Survey;* Siegfried H. Muller, *The World's Living Languages: Basic Factors of Their Structure, Kinship, Location and Number of Speakers* (New York: Ungar, 1964); Bruce M. Russett et al., *World Handbook of Political and Social Indicators* (New Haven: Yale University Press, 1964); Taylor and Hudson, *World Handbook of Political and Social Indicators,* 2d ed.; David C. McClelland, *The Achieving Society.*

Denmark	4.14	3.44	3.41	55.1
East Germany	3.94	4.25	3.98	51.0
Finland	4.82	4.20	4.24	44.2
France	5.12	4.12	4.50	51.7
Greece	6.32	5.64	—	23.5
Hungary	3.87	3.16	3.45	34.9
Ireland	3.17	3.02	3.75	32.2
Italy	5.34	4.70	5.50	35.2
Japan	9.11	8.00	7.74	30.2
Netherlands	4.92	3.68	4.05	50.1
New Zealand	3.80	1.44	1.74	55.0
Norway	4.30	3.48	3.75	51.2
Poland	4.62	3.40	3.11	27.8
Portugal	5.80	5.72	5.66	16.4
Rumania	5.70	4.66	4.54	23.4
Spain	5.96	4.98	5.11	26.3
Sweden	3.87	3.03	2.60	66.7
Switzerland	4.07	2.69	2.76	59.4
U.S.S.R.	5.18	3.78	3.90	34.4
U.K.	2.67	2.18	2.37	54.3
U.S.A.	3.42	2.04	1.89	83.1
West Germany	5.74	4.57	5.00	57.6
Yugoslavia	5.96	4.91	5.31	19.1

SYMBOLS: See Table 5.1.

NOTE: The data come from the sources described in Appendix A. YCAP is defined as the average per-capita GDP in a common currency for the period 1960–65 as a percentage of the per-capita GDP of the U.S. in 1970.

Part II: The Evidence from Selected Countries

6: The Comparative Structure of the Growth of the West German and British Manufacturing Industries

PETER MURRELL

For those who have a firm belief in the potential of economic growth for raising overall economic welfare and reducing poverty, the study of comparative growth performance is a vital area of research. However, such study has not been noted for its successes. For example, no convincing theory has been developed elucidating the sluggish economic growth of the United Kingdom relative to its European neighbors. The lack of a general theory does not imply a paucity of ad hoc explanations for the U.K.'s performance; rather there is a surfeit of such explanations. However, these explanations are not ones that economists are eager to embrace. To quote one leading exponent of modern economic growth theory:

> Every discussion of the relatively slow growth of the British economy compared with the Continental economies ends up in a blaze of amateur sociology. The difference is the bloody-mindedness of the English worker, the slowness of English management to adopt new products or new processes or new ideas, the elaborately amateur character of English business practice, the excessive variety of English goods corresponding to a finely stratified society, or the style of English education and the attitudes it imprints on graduates, or the difference is all of these in unspecified proportions. This may just be a complicated way to admit ignorance. More likely it suggests that the

I thank Chris Clague and Mancur Olson for their helpful comments and Kwang Choi for both research assistance and valuable comments. I benefited from the discussion of this essay at the Conference on the Political Economy of Comparative Growth, University of Maryland, College Park, December 1978. My research was partially supported by the University of Maryland Computer Science Center.

identifiable purely economic factors do not account for the full difference between the growth of productivity in Britain and in, say,
Germany or Sweden.[1]

The disquieting notion that an important economic problem has slipped
into the domain of "amateur sociologists" is not the only cause for dissat-
isfaction. A list of observations on the British character does not constitute
a unified theory. Moreover, the link between differences in character and
differences in rates of economic growth is supported only by casual observation rather than by formal empirical tests.

Much of the foregoing criticism of economic knowledge of comparative
growth will be made moot if Olson's challenging new theory gains acceptance. The starting point of Olson's theory is his earlier analysis of the
formation of common-interest groups;[2] using this analysis, one can make
predictions about relative growth rates:

> Associations that provide collective goods are for the most fundamen-
> tal reasons exceedingly difficult to establish, especially for larger
> groups; none will attract a significant percentage of scattered groups
> like consumers, taxpayers, the unemployed, or the poor; associations
> that can promote the common interests of some groups will be able to
> establish themselves, but only in favorable circumstances and thus
> often only long after the common interest arises; as associations with
> monopoly control or political power accumulate, they delay the inno-
> vations and reallocations of resources needed for rapid growth,
> though this need not occur if the associations encompass a substantial
> percentage of those who bear the costs of the delays.
>
> It follows that countries whose special-interest groups have been
> emasculated or abolished by totalitarian government and foreign oc-
> cupation should grow relatively quickly *after* a free and stable legal
> order is established.[3]

The theory does not focus solely on formal organizations. Rather, Olson
suggests that social norms and social behavior patterns can be viewed from
the same perspective:

1. Robert M. Solow, "Science and Ideology in Economics," *The Public Interest* 21 (Fall 1970):
102–03.
2. Mancur Olson, *The Logic of Collective Action* (Cambridge, Mass.: Harvard University Press,
1965), and "The Political Economy of Comparative Growth Rates," ch. 1, above.
3. Olson, "The Political Economy of Comparative Growth Rates," pp. 24–25.

Social incentives will not be very effective unless the group that values the collective good at issue interacts socially or is composed of subgroups that do. . . . This means that special-interest groups will tend to have socially homogeneous memberships and that they will have an interest in using some resources to preserve this homogeneity. . . . The forces that have just been mentioned, operating simultaneously in thousands of professions, crafts, clubs, and communities, could by themselves explain some degree of class consciousness and even cultural caution about the fluctuating incomes and status of the businessman and entrepreneur.[4]

Thus, the theory not only helps to explain why the U.K. has a much lower growth rate than West Germany but also unifies the observations of the amateur sociologists. The relatively poor growth performances of the U.K. are no longer related to features intrinsic in the "British character"; rather, the U.K.'s relatively slow growth rate can be explained using descriptions of normal socioeconomic behavior in nations that had contrasting experiences in the years before 1948.

My purpose here is to test the Olson hypothesis on the outstanding example of its implications: the comparative growth performances of West German and British manufacturing industries. Before the theoretical basis for the tests is developed, I will discuss a set of statistical results whose theoretical basis has as yet eluded adequate explanation. It will be shown that these results can be explained by theoretical implications of the Olson hypothesis that are developed in the ensuing pages.

The Relationship between Output Growth and Productivity Growth

A number of studies have shown that there is a strong relationship between growth of output and growth of labor productivity in manufacturing. Kaldor emphasized that this relationship could be found in intercountry comparisons.[5] Intracountry, interindustry studies for the United States and the U.K. have given similar results.[6] On the surface, the relationship between

---

4. Ibid., p. 29.
5. Nicholas Kaldor, *Causes of the Slow Rate of Growth of the United Kingdom: An Inaugural Lecture* (London: Cambridge University Press, 1966).
6. K. D. George and T. S. Ward, *The Structure of Industry in the EEC* (London: Cambridge University Press, 1975); and J. W. Kendrick, *Productivity Trends in the United States* (Princeton: Princeton University Press, 1961).

productivity growth and output growth is not surprising; one would expect that increases in productivity would lead to a fall in prices and an increase in output. The significant feature lies in the strength of the relationship between output growth and productivity growth. Kendrick's data for thirty-three industries in the United States show that

> one fourth of the variance in relative output changes may be explained by relative changes in the prices (unit values) of the products of the thirty-three groups over the long period [1899–53]; . . . one-half of the variance in relative price changes may be explained by relative changes in productivity. Yet the degree of association between relative changes in output and in productivity is greater than might be inferred from these correlations.[7]

In order to explain the strength of the relationship between changes in output and in productivity, Kaldor and Kendrick turn to the same source: economies of scale. They argue that there are significant increasing returns to scale in production so that when output increases, labor productivity will also increase. This argument implies that increases in input use cause the increase in labor productivity. Therefore, tests of the Kaldor-Kendrick economies-of-scale hypothesis should examine the relationship between changes in labor input and changes in labor productivity.

Kendrick's analysis provides only weak support for his own hypothesis. Of 35 correlation coefficients between productivity growth and increases in labor input, only 6 are statistically significant.[8] George and Ward have examined the economies of scale hypothesis using interindustry data for the U.K. and West Germany in the postwar period.[9] Their results would lead one to reject the economies-of-scale hypothesis for both countries. Moreover, they find that the relationship between growth of output and growth of labor productivity is not statistically significant for West Germany for the time period from 1953 to 1969.

Cripps and Tarling and Rowthorne have examined the economies-of-scale hypothesis by using international comparisons.[10] Cripps and Tarling obtain, at best, weak support for it; Rowthorne's results argue persuasively for the rejection of the hypothesis. By increasing the sample size and by

7. Kendrick, *Productivity Trends*, pp. 205–06.
8. Ibid., p. 216.
9. George and Ward, *The Structure of Industry*, pp. 62–63.
10. T. F. Cripps and R. J. Tarling, *Growth in Advanced Capitalist Economies: 1950–70* (London: Cambridge University Press, 1975); and R. E. Rowthorne, "What Remains of Kaldor's Law?" *Economic Journal* 85 (March 1975): pp. 10–19.

pointing out the overwhelming importance of the Japanese observation to previous results, Rowthorne shows that there is no significant relationship between employment and productivity growth rates.

One may summarize the aforementioned results as follows:

1. There is a significant relationship between growth of output and growth of labor productivity in both interindustry and intercountry analyses. This relationship is much stronger than the one which would be implied by a causal relationship leading from relative productivity increases to relative price decreases and then to output increases.
2. The relationship between growth of output and of productivity is not present in interindustry studies for West Germany.
3. The economies of scale explanation for the relationship indicated in item 1 has not been supported by statistical tests.

In the ensuing sections, I will develop implications of the Olson hypothesis which can be used to show that the preceding results are predictions of that hypothesis; they will, therefore, serve to lend credence to the Olson hypothesis.

Patterns of Industrial Growth

An immediate implication of the Olson hypothesis is that, in the postwar era, the influences of formal and informal common-interest groups, social classes, social norms, and traditionalism are much stronger in the U.K. than in West Germany. (For brevity's sake I will refer to all such growth-inhibiting forces as inertial forces or inertial influences.) Since the U.K. has experienced continuing political stability in the modern era, inertial forces will be strong in older industries in that country. In contrast, one would expect inertial forces that are industry-specific to be weaker in new industries.

The events of 1933 to 1948 destroyed many inertial forces in West Germany. As the actions that destroyed the inertial forces were unrelated to the age structure of industry, one can posit that in 1948 the strength of any industry-specific inertial forces in West Germany was independent of the age of an industry. The independence of age and strength of inertial forces in German industry would be a continuing feature of postwar development because, as Olson emphasizes, inertial forces arise very slowly. Thus, from the point of view of inertial influences, one may regard all West

German industries as "new." In contrast, the U.K. has both old and new industries. One would expect that this pattern of inertial influences would be reflected in the pattern of industrial development in the two economies.

In testing the foregoing theory, one faces a crucial question: how can one measure the age of an industry? Many variables would seem to be candidates as measures of industry age: length of time since initiation of production, age of plant and equipment, average length of time that employees have been in their present jobs, amount of stock issued in previous twenty years as a proportion of all stock issued. I have chosen to use the relative change in importance of a particular industry in overall industrial production as a variable to measure age. Thus, industry A is defined as newer than industry B at time t if the growth of output of industry A in some time period immediately preceding time t is greater than the growth of output of industry B in the same time period.[11]

At this juncture, the reader may suspect that the use of growth rates to measure industry age will impart a bias to the tests. For example, the foregoing theory predicts that in the U.K. industries that have grown relatively fast in the past will grow relatively fast in the future. While this implication is not quite tautological, it is uninteresting and is certainly explicable in terms of theories other than Olson's. However, the possible bias introduced by using growth rates as a measure of industry age will be avoided in this study by formulating all tests in comparative terms. Thus, the tests will compare the U.K. and West Germany and show that effects which are present in the U.K. are not present, or not as strong, in West Germany. Therefore, one can presume that growth rate could be replaced by a surrogate measure of industry age and the test results would not change.

The use of growth rates to measure industry age rests solely on the observation that when there has been growth of output, changes must have taken place in the industry. These changes may have occurred in management, labor force, capital stock, or, more likely, in a combination of all these elements. Thus, the higher the growth rate of output has been, the more some productive elements will have changed. Industries in which these changes have been more sizeable will have had less time in which inertial forces could have developed. Also, one can expect these changes themselves to have been destructive of inertial forces. Thus, in the U.K.,

11. It should be noted that a new industry, as defined by this measure, has not necessarily just come into existence. Rather, a new industry is one that must have gone through a large number of changes in recent years, which implies that a large proportion of the components of that industry are new.

industries that experienced higher rates of growth before 1948 would have been less subject to inertial forces after 1948.

Ideally, to apply the foregoing theory, one would require information on industrial growth rates before 1948. However, this information is difficult to obtain, especially so in a form which gives comparable statistics for West Germany and the U.K. This difficulty is not present for the postwar period to the same degree; therefore, tests will be formulated using post-1948 data. It is possible to use the post-1948 data because of an important implication of the Olson hypothesis.

The Olson hypothesis predicts that if industry A has grown faster than industry B before 1948, then, in the U.K., inertial forces will be stronger in industry B than in industry A. Thus, *ceteris paribus,* industry A will grow faster than B after 1948. A measure of industry age using post-1948 growth rates will be a surrogate measure of industry age in 1948. Reinforcing the argument for the use of post-1948 growth rates is the fact that factors which influence the structure of industrial growth rates, such as income elasticities of demand and susceptibility of industrial processes to technological change, will have similar influences both pre- and post-1948.

The foregoing reasoning provides a framework within which all the results discussed earlier can be explicated. That discussion would lead one to predict that, in countries with a stable recent history, industries that are growing fast are the ones in which inertial forces are less strong. Therefore, these industries are much more likely to be receptive to technological change and will show higher rates of productivity increase. One would expect in turn to see a strong correlation between growth of output and growth of productivity in interindustry studies for both the U.S. and the U.K. The similar correlation for West Germany would be expected to be much weaker. These are in fact the very results which were reported previously. The economies-of-scale explanation for these results, which foundered when faced with a direct test of its veracity, also could not account for the differences between the results for West Germany and the U.K.; the Olson hypothesis explains them. Thus, the results reported in the previous section are all supportive of the Olson hypothesis. In the ensuing section, much stronger tests of this hypothesis are formulated.

The United Kingdom and West Germany Compared

Let G_j^i be the growth rate of industry j in country i: i will correspond to the U.K. or West Germany (W.G.) and $j = 1, \ldots, n,$ where n is the total number of industries. Let us assume that industry j is newer than industry k in both countries. In the previous section, it was concluded that inertial forces would be stronger in old than in new industries in the U.K., whereas the strength of inertial forces would be more likely to be equal across German industries. Thus, newer industries in the U.K. would be relatively more successful in comparison with overall U.K. economic performance than would new industries in West Germany, as compared with overall German economic performance. However, because both economy-wide and industry-specific inertial forces are stronger in the U.K. than in West Germany, one would expect that $G_j^{UK} < G_j^{WG}$ and $G_k^{UK} < G_k^{WG}$. Thus, in order to test the Olson hypothesis, one must examine the performance of industry k relative to industry j in each country and test whether this relative comparison is different for both countries.

In testing the Olson hypothesis, one needs a null hypothesis that predicts the comparative structure of growth rates when inertial forces are of no significance. There is one such null hypothesis which seems intuitively the most plausible. The West German aggregate growth rate is proportionately higher than the British aggregate growth rate so that the growth rate in a particular West German industry is higher than the growth rate in the equivalent British industry by the same proportion:[12]

$$G_j^{UK} = \beta G_j^{WG}, \text{ where } \beta < 1 \text{ and } j = 1, \ldots, n. \tag{1}$$

In the next section I will examine arguments why equation 1 could be expected to be correct in the absence of inertial forces. Also in that section, possible biases in the tests that use equation 1 will be examined, and alternative but less plausible forms of the null hypothesis will be used.

Presently, I will develop implications of the Olson hypothesis on the assumption that equation 1 would be satisfied if inertial influences were of no significance. In interpreting test results, one should remember that this assumption is implicit in the construction of the tests. An evaluation of the power of the test results reported in this section relies on the acceptability of equation 1 as a null hypothesis.

In order to formulate tests, one must examine relative growth performance for industries j and k when industry j is newer than k in both countries. If equation 1 were true and inertial forces were of no significance, one would expect that

---

12. In the ensuing pages, I have omitted error terms which, if included in equations and inequalities, would represent all influences on comparative growth rates not examined in this study.

$$\frac{G_j^{UK} - G_k^{UK}}{G_A^{UK}} = \frac{G_j^{WG} - G_k^{WG}}{G_A^{WG}}, \tag{2}$$

where G_A^i is the growth rate of all industry and i corresponds to U.K. or W.G. If the comparative structure of growth rates independent of inertial forces could be described by equation 1, then those inertial forces would produce an effect such that

$$\frac{G_j^{UK} - G_k^{UK}}{G_A^{UK}} > \frac{G_j^{WG} - G_k^{WG}}{G_A^{WG}} . \tag{3}$$

Thus, in order to test the null hypothesis versus the Olson hypothesis, one must examine whether expression 2 or 3 provides the closer description of actual growth rates.

Having suggested that tests comparing expressions 2 and 3 are based on the most reasonable alternative to the Olson hypothesis, it is appropriate at this juncture to explain the intuition behind the expressions. Suppose, for the sake of explanation, that industry j has a higher rate of technological change than industry k and that West German manufacturers exploit this technological differential more fully than British manufacturers. Therefore,

$$GR_j^{WG} - GR_k^{WG} > GR_j^{UK} - GR_k^{UK},$$

even though industry j is newer than industry k. The Olson hypothesis would say that industry j in the U.K. is relatively receptive to technological change compared with industry k in the U.K., although not necessarily so compared to industry j in West Germany. Thus, in order to compare the differences between growth rates, one must adjust the differences between British industry growth rates by a factor that measures the growth performance of British industry. Differences between West German growth rates must be similarly adjusted. The use of aggregate growth rates as denominators in expressions 2 and 3 provides the appropriate adjustments.

With industry j newer than industry k, support for the Olson hypothesis is obtained if inequality 3 is correct and support for the null hypothesis is obtained if inequality 3 is incorrect. If the Olson hypothesis is incorrect and the null hypothesis adequately describes the structure of growth rates, the expected value of the number of times that inequality 3 is verified is one-half. If inertial influences are significant, the expected value of the number of times that 3 is verified is greater than one-half.

The United Nations *Yearbook of Industrial Statistics* provides the basic data for the tests. Coverage is from 1953 onwards, and indexes of industrial production provide the information to calculate growth rates.[13] In formulating tests, one must measure newness of industries. From the point of view of pure theory, one needs only measure age by looking at British growth rates; however, such a procedure would introduce a bias into the tests. Thus, industry j is defined as newer than industry k if and only if industry j has grown faster than industry k in *both* West Germany and the U.K. Tests were carried out for two different time periods. Thus, the time period for growth rates used to define industry age was either 1953–63 or 1953–68.

Once age of industry has been defined using growth rates for 1953–68 (1953–63), the foregoing theory can be tested by examining the structure of growth rates during the interval 1969–73 (1964–73). The growth rates used are those for twenty-seven manufacturing industries. For these industries comparable data from both countries are available.[14] For the test of inequality 3 versus equation 2, two sets of data are used. First, aggregate growth rates for the twenty-seven industries are tested. Second, since the United Nations has published data on the production of a wide range of industrial commodities, data on 235 commodities for the period 1969–73 could be used, where each of the 235 commodities was produced in one of the twenty-seven industries. In tests using commodity data, age of industry was defined using the 1953–68 growth rates of the industry in which the commodity was produced.[15] In the tests using the commodity production data, when industry j was defined as newer than industry $k,$ comparisons based on inequality 3 were carried out for each commodity produced in industry j versus each commodity produced in industry k.

Results of these initial tests are presented in the first three lines of table 6.1. In order to clarify the construction of this table, I will interpret the first line in it. The test described on the first line matches the null hypothesis of equation 1 against inequality 3 as the alternative hypothesis. The growth rates from 1953 to 1968 of all twenty-seven industries are used in order to

13. United Nations, Statistical Office, *Yearbook of Industrial Statistics* (New York: United Nations, annual). (Formerly *The Growth of World Industry*.)

14. The ISIC codes for the industries included in the sample are: 311, 313, 314, 321, 322, 323, 324, 331, 332, 341, 342, 351, 353, 354, 355, 356, 361, 362, 369, 371, 372, 381, 382, 383, 384, 385, and 390. For some industries the published data does not extend as far back as 1953; in such cases, the growth rate over a shorter time period is used to define industry age.

15. Commodity production growth rates before 1969 could not be used to define industry age because coverage of commodities is much less complete in the decade before 1969 than in the years after 1969.

Table 6.1. Tests of the Significance of Inertial Influences

Industries Included	Age Defined By	Data Used for Comparisons	Number of Comparisons Made	Number Supporting Olson Hypothesis	Proportion (col. 5/col. 4)	95 Percent Significance Level
All	Growth rates 1953–68 for 27 industries	Growth rates 1969–73 for 235 commodities	21,216	11,636	0.5485	0.528
All	Growth rates 1953–63 for 27 industries	Growth rates 1964–73 for 27 industries	283	182	0.6431	0.620
All	Growth rates 1953–68 for 27 industries	Growth rates 1969–73 for 27 industries	285	164	0.5754	0.620
Heavy	Growth rates 1953–68 for 15 industries	Growth rates 1969–73 for 140 commodities	7,701	4,344	0.5641	0.539
Heavy	Growth rates 1953–63 for 15 industries	Growth rates 1964–73 for 15 industries	82	67	0.8171	0.673
Heavy	Growth rates 1953–68 for 15 industries	Growth rates 1969–73 for 15 industries	88	68	0.7727	0.665

define the age of any industry relative to another. Comparisons of growth performance during the interval 1969–73 are made using data on the growth rates of production of 235 commodities. If industry j has a higher rate of growth than industry k in one country and a slower rate of growth in the other country from 1953 to 1968, then no comparisons were made between industries j and k.[16] Thus, the number of comparisons was not strictly determined by the number of commodities in the sample. The actual number of comparisons made is given in column 4. In column 5, the number of comparisons which supported the Olson hypothesis (the number for which inequality 3 was verified) is given. In column 6, this number is interpreted as a proportion of all comparisons made. The appropriate test is one in which the null hypothesis is accepted if the proportion in column 6 is not significantly greater than one-half.

In order to conduct significance tests, it is necessary to calculate the standard errors of the proportions in column 6. As an understanding of the procedure of calculation of standard errors is not necessary for interpretation of the test results, discussion of the calculation of the standard errors is relegated to an appendix. For reasons given in that appendix, the standard errors have an upward bias. Thus, the test results appear slightly less favorable to the Olson hypothesis than would be the case if unbiased standard errors were used. Employing the assumption that the proportions are normally distributed, the standard errors were used to calculate 95 percent significance levels which are given in column 7. The Olson hypothesis is accepted at the 95 percent significance level if the proportion in column 6 is greater than the proportion in column 7.

The results reported in the first three lines of table 6.1 give firm support to the hypothesis that old industries fare less well in the U.K. than do equivalent industries in West Germany. The extension of the Olson hypothesis proposed in the foregoing pages certainly provides an explanation for these results. There is some possibility that alternative explanations for the test results could exist—explanations independent of interest-group behavior. However, by examining a subset of the data, one can obtain further results that point very strongly to the conclusion that inertial forces produce the effects found in the first test results.

Industries included in the manufacturing sector are heterogeneous in character. In particular, the manufacturing sector contains both heavy and

---

16. These comparisons were excluded from the analysis in order to remove any bias that would be embodied in the tests if only British growth rates were used to define industry age.

light industry. Although the distinction between heavy and light industries is usually based on a heuristic classification, that distinction does rest on some very basic notions of the qualitative characteristics of industries. Heavy industries have high capital-labor ratios, high concentration ratios, high unionization rates, and large factories (in terms of size of workforce).[17]

The characteristics of heavy industries would make these industries more susceptible to the influence of inertial forces. Higher concentration ratios facilitate noncompetitive behavior. Higher unionization rates imply that heavy industries are more susceptible to the formation of formal and informal common-interest groups. Larger enterprise size means, in terms of employment, that an employee's social interaction is much more likely to be in social groups dominated by fellow employees. Such social interaction would tend to facilitate the cohesion of group interests and strengthen existing inertial forces present in the industry. Therefore, if inertial influences are present their effect on heavy industries is likely to be greater than on light industries. Tests on a sample of heavy industries would give stronger results than tests on all industries together.

Using International Standard Industrial Classification codes, one can divide manufacturing industry into heavy and light. Industries with codes below 350 are light industries: food processing, beverages, textiles, etc. Those with codes above 350 are heavy industries: chemicals, iron and steel, transportation equipment.[18] There are fifteen heavy industries. Lines 4 through 6 of table 6.1 contain the results for an analysis of these fifteen industries.[19]

17. See Frederic L. Pryor, *Property and Industrial Organization in Communist and Capitalist Nations* (Bloomington, Ind.: Indiana University Press, 1973), pp. 59–60, for a discussion of the characteristics of heavy and light industries. Pryor, Appendix B-7, and George and Ward, *The Structure of Industry*, ch. 3 and 4, have evidence showing which industries have the characteristics attributed to heavy industries.

18. See Pryor, *Property and Industrial Organization*, for a classification of industries into heavy and light. Pryor's classification covers only twenty industries; thus, it could not be used formally to divide the twenty-seven industries of this study into two groups. I chose the ISIC codes to classify industries because such a classification seems to fit heuristic notions of the distinction between heavy and light industries very well. Use of a strict definition based on the ISIC, rather than a looser definition, has the advantage that the definition is not framed to be favorable to any particular hypothesis. The classification based on ISIC codes conforms to Pryor's classification where they overlap.

19. One industry that would be classified as heavy has been omitted. The performance of the "petroleum and coal products sector" (the name is somewhat of a misnomer since products of petroleum refineries appear in another sector) in the tests is anomalous. In the tests summarized on lines 2 and 3 of table 6.1, only seven out of forty-seven comparisons for this sector satisfied inequality 3. Thus, both the null hypothesis and the alternative hypothesis are inadequate as interpretations of the comparative behavior of this sector. (The proportion 7/47 is significantly less than one-half.)

The reason for the anomalous performance of the petroleum and coal products sector may be

By comparing lines 1 through 3 with lines 4 through 6 of table 6.1, one can see that the proportion of comparisons supporting the existence of inertial forces is greater for the tests using only heavy industries than for the tests using all industries. This is exactly the prediction one would make using knowledge of the characteristics of heavy industries combined with the implications of Olson's hypothesis. Any competing hypothesis must explain not only why old industries fare relatively worse in the U.K. than in West Germany but also why this effect is more pronounced when only heavy industries are analyzed. The extremely strong test results of this section were obtained using the assumption that if inertial forces were of no significance equation 1 would be satisfied. I now turn to a justification of the use of that assumption.

The Null Hypothesis Considered

In this section, I assume that inertial forces are of no significance and examine the likely relationship between the growth rates of an industry in two countries that are growing at different rates. In order to conduct such an examination, one must make specific assumptions about the cause of the two countries' differing growth performances. Here, two such assumptions are used in two different analyses. In each case, one can make firm conclusions about the relationship between the growth rates of specific industries. For both cases, equation 1 describes the comparative structure of growth rates.

In the analysis which follows, strong simplifying assumptions must be made since the analysis involves comparison between two complete economic systems. Therefore, the general argument is one of analogy from these simple examples. The strength of the argument lies in the extent to which the assumptions are not contrived and are, in fact, commonly used in the economics literature. It is the ease with which equation 1 can be derived

---

explained by the effects of inertial influences. The products in this sector are produced primarily in nationalized industries in the U.K. Therefore, in the U.K., this sector was less subject to the dictates of the market than were other sectors. This sector was in absolute decline in West Germany. In old, nationalized industries, interest-group behavior may lessen the possibility that growth will be negative. Thus, the results for this sector may, in fact, reflect the power of interest groups in nationalized industries to reverse an absolute decline in the growth of that industry.

Given that the anomalous performance of this industry can be explained by reversion to the effects of inertial forces, after noting special characteristics of this industry, I have decided to omit this sector from the heavy-industry analysis.

from simple, common assumptions that is persuasive in the decision to employ it as the null hypothesis for testing the effects of inertial forces.

The strongest simplifying assumption in the following analysis is the assumption that the two countries with differing growth rates start from identical positions: identical prices, production levels, and consumption levels. To assume that the two countries are in different positions would necessitate additional assumptions on how these countries came to be in different positions: exactly the phenomenon which I am examining. In order to avoid the problem of directly assuming that which is being examined, I assume that initial production conditions are the same in both countries but that the countries are moving to different positions. The difference between the following scenarios lies in the specifications of the cause of the two countries' differing growth rates.

Scenario One

The rate of saving is higher in country A than in country B. Perfect markets exist in both countries and all industries have identical production functions. Capital is instantaneously transferable between industries so that there are no relative price changes. Hence in each country total income, total investment, and total consumption are all rising at the same rate as total output. Thus, the change in output of each industry is equal to the change in consumption due to movement along an Engel curve.

Assuming that consumers have the same preferences in both countries, one can write

$$c_j^k = c_j(w^k),$$

where c_j^k represents consumption of good j in country k and w^k represents total income in country k. Using the notation $\dfrac{dc}{dt} = \dot{c}$, one can write

$$\frac{\dot{c}_j^k}{c_j^k} = \left(\frac{\frac{\partial c_j}{\partial w^k} \cdot w^k}{c_j^k} \right) \cdot \left(\frac{\dot{w}^k}{w^k} \right).$$

Thus,

$$\frac{\dot{c}_j^A}{c_j^A} = \frac{\beta \dot{c}_j^B}{c_j^B}, \tag{4}$$

where β is the rate of growth of output in country A divided by that of country B. Equation 4 is the null hypothesis used in the previous section.

Scenario Two

Technological change produces growth. At any time, in any industry, there is a set of technological changes which are ripe for discovery. In some industries this set is larger than others, solely because of technological and scientific factors. In each industry, some technological changes will be more difficult to accomplish than others. Managers in country A are more successful in research and development than managers in country B. Thus, in a certain time period, W percent of the feasible changes in all industries are implemented in country A, while only U percent (less than W percent) are implemented in country B. Thus,

$$\dot{\Pi}_i^A = \gamma \dot{\Pi}_i^B, \text{ where } \gamma > 1 \tag{5}$$

where Π_i^k is a productivity index for industry i in country k and γ is an increasing function of W/U.

Let us assume that there are constant returns to scale in all industries and that perfect markets cause prices to fall to costs instantaneously. For each country,

$$p_i y_i = \sum_{j=1}^{n} p_j x_{ji}$$

and
$$y_i = F_i(x_{1i}, \ldots, x_{ni}, \Pi_i), \quad i = 1, \ldots, n$$

where p_i is the price of good i, y_i is the output of good i, and x_{ji} is the input of good j into the production of good i. Thus, on the assumption that there is no international trade (an assumption which will be dropped later),

$$\dot{p}_i y_i + \sum_{j=1}^{n} p_i \frac{\partial y_i}{\partial x_{ji}} \left(\sum_{k=1}^{n} \frac{\partial x_{ji}}{\partial p_k} \dot{p}_k \right) + \sum_{j=1}^{n} p_i \frac{\partial y_i}{\partial x_{ji}} \left(\sum_{k=1}^{n} \frac{\partial x_{ji}}{\partial \Pi_k} \dot{\Pi}_k \right)$$

$$= \sum_{j=1}^{n} \dot{p}_i x_{ji} + \sum_{j=1}^{n} p_j \left(\sum_{k=1}^{n} \frac{\partial x_{ji}}{\partial p_k} \dot{p}_k \right) + \sum_{j=1}^{n} p_j \left(\sum_{k=1}^{n} \frac{\partial x_{ji}}{\partial \Pi_k} \dot{\Pi}_k \right),$$

where $i = 1, \ldots, n$.

Although simplification of this equation is possible, it is not necessary. By inspection one can see that any solution of the n equations will have any single price change equal to a weighted sum of the productivity changes. The weights will be a function of the present state of the economy, not of the rate of change of any variables. Hence, the weights will be the same in both countries. Therefore, from equation 5,

$$\frac{\dot{p}_j^A}{p_j^A} = \frac{\gamma \dot{p}_j^B}{p_j^B}, j = 1, \ldots, n. \tag{6}$$

Since total amount sold is a sum of consumption plus intermediate use,

$$y_j = c_j(p_1, \ldots, p_n) + \sum_{i=1}^{n} x_{ji}$$

$$\dot{y}_j = \sum_{k=1}^{n} \frac{\partial c_j}{\partial p_k} \dot{p}_k + \sum_{k=1}^{n} \sum_{i=1}^{n} \frac{\partial x_{ji}}{\partial p_k} \dot{p}_k + \sum_{i=1}^{n} \frac{\partial x_{ji}}{\partial \Pi_i} \dot{\Pi}_i. \tag{7}$$

Assuming the same demand functions in each country and noting that the weights attached to the rates of change of prices and productivities in equation 7 are independent of rates of change, one can combine equations 5, 6, and 7 to obtain

$$\frac{\dot{y}_j^A}{y_j^A} = \frac{\gamma \dot{y}_j^B}{y_j^B}, \tag{8}$$

which is identical to equation 1, the null hypothesis.

The assumption that the economies are closed is unreasonable. When one assumes that foreign trade is possible, the foregoing analysis must be modified because all prices in country A will be declining faster than equivalent prices in country B. Thus an exchange rate adjustment will be required in order to balance trade. Let q_j^A be the price of good j in country A measured in country B's currency units. Therefore,

$$q_j^A = p_j^A s,$$

where s is the relevant exchange rate. It is known that

$$\frac{\dot{q}_j^A}{q_j^A} = \frac{\dot{p}_j^A}{p_j^A} + \dot{s}/s$$

and $\dot{s}/s > 0$. Using equation 6,

$$\frac{\dot{q}_j^A}{q_j^A} = \frac{\gamma \dot{p}_j^B}{p_j^B} + \dot{s}/s.$$

Thus, in industries in which productivity changes have induced only small price changes, the following inequalities will be satisfied:

$$\frac{\dot{q}_j^A}{q_j^A} > 0 > \frac{\dot{p}_j^B}{p_j^B}.$$

In industries in which price changes have been large,

$$\frac{\dot{q}_j^A}{q_j^A} < \frac{\dot{p}_j^B}{p_j^B} < 0.$$

Assuming that own-price effects dominate cross-effects, industries with small price changes will be those that are growing most slowly. Therefore, taking into account foreign trade transactions, one would modify equation 8 to conclude that

$$\frac{\dot{y}_j^A}{y_j^A} < \frac{\gamma \dot{y}_j^B}{y_j^B}$$

if industry j is slow growing, and

$$\frac{\dot{y}_k^A}{y_k^A} > \frac{\gamma \dot{y}_k^B}{y_k^B}$$

if industry k is fast growing.

The above inequalities can be embodied in a simple operational equation of the following form (using the notation of the previous section):

$$G_j^A + \sigma(G_A^A - G_j^A) = \gamma\, G_j^B, \quad 1 > \sigma > 0.$$

Comparing two industries,

$$(G_j^A - G_i^A)(1 - \sigma)/\gamma = G_j^B - G_i^B,$$

or

$$(G_j^A - G_i^A)/\gamma > G_j^B - G_i^B. \tag{9}$$

Inequality 9 contains the same terms as inequality 3; however, the signs are reversed. Since the process which leads to inequality 9 can be expected to operate at the same time as inertial forces, it tells us that the tests of the previous section will be biased toward acceptance of the null hypothesis.

The test in the previous section requires as evidence for the existence of inertial forces when industry j is newer than industry i

$$(G_j^A - G_i^A)/\gamma < G_j^B - G_i^B. \tag{10}$$

A better test would require as evidence for the existence of inertial forces

$$(1 - \sigma)(G_j^A - G_i^A)/\gamma < G_j^B - G_i^B. \tag{11}$$

Thus, the tests in the text assume that when equation 10 is incorrect the

Olson hypothesis is not supported, even though equation 11 may be true in such a case. Consequently, the tests using equation 1 as null hypothesis provide strong evidence for the Olson hypothesis because they are biased against acceptance of this hypothesis.

The foregoing analysis has attempted to interpret the importance of the test results by justifying the use of equation 1 as a reasonable null hypothesis. An alternative method of assessing the results is to examine their robustness by formulating different tests which, under any reasonable assumption about the structure of comparative growth rates in the absence of inertial forces, would be biased against acceptance of the Olson hypothesis. These tests would begin with the general null hypothesis

$$G_j^{WG} = \alpha + \beta G_j^{UK}, \; \alpha > 0, \; \beta > 1, \; j = 1, \ldots, n. \quad (12)$$

If α is significantly greater than zero, this hypothesis implies, for example, that an industry which is growing slowly in West Germany would be declining in the U.K. Because of such implications, equation 12 seems to be inferior to equation 1 as a candidate to describe the comparative structure of growth rates.

If inequality 11 were correct and inertial forces were of no significance, one would expect that

$$(G_j^{WG} - G_i^{WG})/\beta = G_j^{UK} - G_i^{UK}. \quad (13)$$

If industry j is newer than industry i and inertial forces were of some significance, these forces would produce an effect such that

$$(G_j^{WG} - G_i^{WG})/\beta < G_j^{UK} - G_i^{UK}. \quad (14)$$

Thus, in order to test the null hypothesis equation 12 versus the Olson hypothesis, one must examine whether 13 or 14 provides the closer description of actual growth rates.

In order to formulate such a test, one must obtain an unbiased estimate of β. However, β can only be estimated in the absence of inertial forces. If inertial forces exist, then an estimate of β which assumes an absence of inertial forces will be biased downward. If this estimate is then used in tests of equation 13 versus inequality 14, the results must be biased toward acceptance of the null hypothesis whatever the true value of β is in the absence of inertial forces.

In the test results presented in table 6.2, the estimate of β is a number that satisfies inequality 14 half the time when the data for all twenty-seven manufacturing industries are used. This estimate is then used to test the

Table 6.2. Tests of Equation 13 versus Inequality 14 Using Estimates of β Derived from Data for All Twenty-seven Manufacturing Industries

Industries Included	Age Defined By	Data Used for Comparisons	Number of Comparisons Made	Number Supporting Olson Hypothesis	Proportion (col. 5/col. 4)	95 Percent Significance Level
Heavy	Growth rates 1953–68 for 15 industries	Growth rates 1969–73 for 140 commodities	7,701	4,134	0.5368	0.539
Heavy	Growth rates 1953–68 for 15 industries	Growth rates 1969–73 for 15 industries	88	64	0.7273	0.669
Heavy	Growth rates 1953–63 for 15 industries	Growth rates 1964–73 for 15 industries	82	54	0.6585	0.672

hypothesis that inertial forces exist in heavy industry. Thus table 6.2, whose structure is identical to that of table 6.1, contains results for heavy industries only. In interpreting the results, one should remember that there are two senses in which the tests favor the null hypothesis. First, if the alternative hypothesis is true, the proportion in column 6 will be biased downward. Second, the 95 percent significance level in column 7 will be biased upward for reasons presented in the appendix. Given these biases, the fact that the proportions are all close to, or greater than, the 95 percent level of significance (the percent levels of significance are 94.0, 98.7, and 93.6) is strong evidence for the existence of inertial forces.

Conclusion

The foregoing results point strongly to the existence of significant effects due to inertial forces within British industry. Not only do the tests give significant results when the null hypothesis used is the one justified by a theoretical analysis, but significant results are also obtained when the null hypothesis used is such that the tests are biased against acceptance of the conclusion that inertial forces are significant. Moreover, in all cases, test results are much stronger for heavy industries than for all industries combined. The stronger effect of inertial forces in heavy industry is exactly the prediction one would make having assumed that inertial forces are due to group behavior.

One mark of the worth of a new theory is the ability which that theory has to explain observations which have previously eluded adequate explanation. Studies that have shown productivity growth and output growth to be strongly related in Britain and the United States constitute one set of such observations. These studies become comprehensible once one realizes that output growth is a surrogate measure of newness of industry that is positively related to productivity growth owing to the effect of inertial forces. Thus, the tests I outline can be interpreted as providing support for a theory which explains the causal mechanism underlying the results obtained by Kaldor, Kendrick, and others.

The importance of a new theory is not only in helping to explain past statistical regularities but also in providing a guide for future action. Many predictions emanate from the foregoing analysis: I will focus on one such prediction as an example. The foregoing results point to the importance of entry into an industry for the promotion of dynamic efficiency. New firms entering an industry (assuming that inertial forces which pose barriers to entry can be overcome) are less likely to be troubled by inertial forces than old, established firms. Thus, the new firms will be more likely to promote technological change and adopt aggressive growth policies than old firms. Hence, positive encouragement for new firms entering an industry would seem to be a vital element of any policy aimed at promoting growth.

In advanced industrial economies, declining industries are often the recipients of government aid. That aid often takes the form of a subsidy for research and development, given because declining industries are observed to be technologically backward relative to foreign competitors. The analysis which lies behind the choice of policy ignores the causal mechanism that produces the technological backwardness. If the backwardness is due to inertial forces, then research and development aid might have little effect unless that aid flowed toward new entrants into the industry. Olson's theory, together with the extension developed in this paper, shows not only why aid to new entrants will provide a high economic return but also why such aid will attract well-organized political opposition.

APPENDIX

One can view the amount $(G_j^{UK}/G_A^{UK}) - (G_j^{WG}/G_A^{WG})$ as an observation on the jth industry. Suppose that there are n such observations. For the moment, assume that one can order the industries by age. The tests of equation 2 versus expression 3 or 13 versus inequality 14 use every possible pairwise comparison from the n observations. The test statistic is the proportion of these comparisons for which the observation for the newer industry is greater than the observation for the older industry.

As no standard formula for the calculation of the standard errors of the test statistics could be found, a numerical procedure was adopted. All possible orderings of a set of observations were enumerated, the test statistic was calculated for each ordering, and the standard deviation of these statistics was calculated. In using this standard deviation as the standard error of the test statistic, one is assuming that all orderings of the n observations are equally likely. This assumption is equivalent to the assumption that equation 1 has an additive error term which has an expected value of zero and homoscedastic variance.

When there are n industries, $n(n - 1)/2$ comparisons are generated. However, for reasons explained in the text, not all comparisons could be made. For example, in one case (table 6.1, row 2) there were observations on twenty-seven industries, and only 283 of the possible 351 comparisons were generated. This is approximately the number of comparisons which would be generated by twenty-four industries. Thus, for this case, if the standard error for twenty-seven industries (351 comparisons) were used, one would be using a downward-biased statistic. If the standard error for 283 comparisons (twenty-four industries) were used, one would be using an upward-biased statistic (because the amount of dependence among all comparisons for twenty-four industries will be greater than the amount of dependence among 283 comparisons from twenty-seven industries). The latter option was chosen so that the tests of significance would have a conservative bias, that is, a bias toward acceptance of the null hypothesis.

A second problem arising in the calculation of the standard errors was that the number of comparisons for the commodity data was so great that computational limitations prevented the calculation of exact standard errors. However, after the exact standard errors were generated for thirty different sample sizes, estimates of the standard errors for the commodity data could be found using regression techniques. The estimated regression equation was

Standard error $= (0.469)$ (number of comparisons)$^{-0.333}$.

This equation had an R^2 of 0.99. Predictions using this equation were used to obtain the standard errors given on lines 1 and 4 of table 6.1 and line 1 of table 6.2. For reasons given in the previous paragraph, the standard errors are biased upward.

7: Divergent Growth Rates: Some Experiences of the United Kingdom and Italy

URSULA K. HICKS

Growth in the limited sense of expansion of incomes and output is never a continuous process; it differs from period to period as well as from country to country and from region within a country to region. In modern Italy periods of rapid growth seem to have been succeeded by periods of little growth; these may be due either to consolidation of gains or to stagnation. Thus, for example, rapid growth took place after World War II, but in the most recent period fundamental weaknesses that had not been fully eliminated began to show up again, as we shall see. Such a sequence is no doubt common experience; hence, in attempting to measure growth rates the period selected is vital.

A problem of great interest is to diagnose why some European Economic Community (EEC) countries and Japan have been growing much faster than other EEC countries and the United States. Parallel differences in growth rates also occur among the less-developed countries: contrast the successes of Taiwan and South Korea with the mediocre showing of the African countries and the Indian subcontinent.

In seeking any general explanation of the problem, the first necessity is to examine basic differences between countries that may be growth-promoting or growth-retarding. Of these basic differences location is one of the most important. It may affect comparative growth rates in a number of ways. If location is unfavorable from the point of view of trade or other economic activities, or if it becomes so as a result of a change in established trade routes or of the decay of natural resources (or the demand for them), the economic outlook may be permanently damaged. *Mutatis mutandis,*

I have derived much assistance in the Italian sections from Dr. Laura Castelini of Pisa, a specialist in public administration, and from Professor Francesco Forte of Turin, a participant at the Conference on the Political Economy of Comparative Growth Rates.

some of these influential factors may turn more favorable, opening up new opportunities. In either direction, the effect on growth rates can be very powerful, both nationally and regionally. Examples are so numerous throughout history that no general discussion seems called for, but a few recent experiences can throw light on the present discussion. It would seem for instance that climatic change has been an important contribution to the poor showing of Sicily and southern Italy (the Mezzogiorno)—once important grain exporting areas but now too arid for successful cultivation and consequently a notable factor in Italy's slow growth. Exhaustion of coal has been an important loss in south Wales and northeast England. The damage caused by a change in trade routes is apparent in the western ports of Britain, which declined owing to the decay of cotton trade with the U.S. and the loss of colonial trade with the West Indies and India.

Now, with the economic center of Western Europe shifted to Brussels, both the U.K. and Italy (whose former Mediterranean trade was very important) find themselves peripheral as compared with most of the original members of the EEC. Growth in France was held back in the 1950s by loss of its colonial trade, but its central European position has helped its economic recovery just as has occurred in the Netherlands and Belgium. When locational changes such as these affect a country, its economic flexibility and adaptability to changing circumstances are of first importance. It generally seems more difficult for a country with a long-established pattern of industry and trading stations to counter an unfavorable change or even to take advantage of new opportunities than it is for a country that is just making its way in the world economy, such as Taiwan or Korea or, above all, Japan. But clearly this can be no more than one factor contributing to the problem of divergent growth rates.

Economic adaptability depends on the ease with which occupational shifts can be made. The first shift required for growth is from preponderant traditional agriculture to other employments. A reduction in the agricultural labor force is necessary in order to free resources for growth occupations. In the U.K., with its early industrialization, the shift from agriculture started in the eighteenth century and has long been virtually complete. In some parts of the United States the process also started early. By 1950 the active agricultural sector (per thousand of the population) was 29 in the U.K. and 65 in the U.S. Between that date and 1970 the British figure had been reduced to half (14) and that of the United States to a third (24) of the 1950 figures. Since then, they have had little agricultural reserve on which to draw; in the U.K. it has virtually dried up. In 1970

France still had an agricultural reserve of 64, Germany and Sweden just over 40, and Japan 127.

By 1970 Italy's agricultural reserve had been substantially reduced, but it was still large (77). There was, however, an important difference in Italy as compared with most advanced countries. In the latter the growth of industrial and other sectors has greatly exceeded the flight from agriculture. In Italy this is much less true. In the U.K. and Sweden the industrial sector actually lost workers between 1950 and 1970, but this was compensated by the expansion of other activities. In the U.S. the relative growth of the industrial labor force was moderate but positive; it was matched, however, by a very large expansion in other activities. In Japan the growth of both the industrial labor force and other activities was very large indeed, the latter actually being the next highest after the U.S. and above that of the U.K. and Sweden.

The key problem in determining growth rates is the content of the "other" category. This sector is expanding fast in almost every country, but its possible content is so varied that without disaggregation (which the statistics do not allow) the extent to which the various items promote or retard growth cannot be judged. In any case productivity in other activities is largely unmeasurable, so that improvement will scarcely show up in the statistics. Yet a time must come when expansion in the industrial sector cannot be absorbed by the home market without an expansion of some of the other activities. The apparent failure to increase productivity must then slow down the *recorded* rate of overall growth, irrespective of the actual rate.

A basic shift of labor from agriculture is necessary for growth; this is, however, far from being all that is required. Repeated shifts between industries and between industry and other activities as circumstances change is necessary for sustained growth. There is no end to this process in a rapidly changing world. Hence the factors promoting or retarding shifts are of vital importance. Of first importance among these are population problems.

Growth rates may be substantially influenced by changes in population, either in numbers or in quality and social outlook. Shifting is obviously easier where population is expanding, so that it can be achieved largely by new entry. In the U.K., population has become almost stationary, as it has been in the U.S. since large-scale immigration ceased. Populations in the other EEC countries are still growing, although, especially in Germany, only slowly. But in Germany and France it has been possible to supplement the labor reserve with short-period immigration from the poorer Mediterranean countries. In Japan, population is still expanding fairly rapidly, and, as we have seen, the agricultural labor reserve is still ample. Here then we have one cause of difficulty for the U.S. and the U.K. in relation to other advanced countries.

A society's educational system is extremely influential in suiting the population for the labor force, especially where it affects traditional socialization. Besides imparting knowledge and broadening minds, education is a discipline, and this may be vital for growth. Japan has had universal primary education since 1872, only two years after the U.K. and well before most other countries. Soviet policy also made universal literacy a top priority. But the content of education (especially after the primary stage) is also most important for growth. Major religious influence in education may be seriously retarding. This was discovered by the Moslems in northern Nigeria when they came to compete with Christian southerners who had had a much wider education than that offered by Koranic learning. By attempting to maintain the status quo, traditional Roman Catholic schools may have had a retarding effect, in, for example, the poorer parts of Ireland, Italy, and Spain. The Japanese curriculum is narrow, being short on languages and history; it contains no religious teaching but is very strong in mathematics and in moral training and discipline. Its effect on Japanese society is undoubtedly growth-promoting.

Similar retardation may be caused by traditional social outlooks and social stratification. The most serious example of this is the caste system of India, which is only slowly breaking down. It has often been asserted that the British social outlook and education also suffer from status stratification. The elite ''public'' schools and the older universities (it is suggested) have established a bias in favor of a literary, antiscientific, and hence, by implication, antigrowth training.

These class differences are often exaggerated. The purpose of the public schools was to train boys for the civil service, the army, management, and the professions. However, as we shall see, the British education system is now undergoing a substantial change both in organization and curricula; it remains to be seen whether the new system is better for growth.

Where the U.K. and the U.S. differ from other advanced countries is in their long and proud experience of peaceful democracy. There is no inherent reason why this should retard growth, but it has been asserted that revolution, asset destruction, and the break with former social and industrial practices and inhibitions caused by war may promote growth and may account for the recent success of, for instance, Japan and Germany as well as for the relative sluggishness of the U.K. and U.S. economies. This argument cannot reasonably be carried very far, since countries react very differently to war experience, both socially and politically. The postwar British economy has been neither stagnant nor sterile in ideas: the automobile industry was thriving for many years, and such important inventions as the jet engine were made. But the resources necessary for sustained development and growth were not available, and that had to be left to others, especially to the U.S. It has been demonstrated that growth in the British economy in the postwar period was faster than at any other period of its history (Phelps Brown, 1977), but other countries were growing faster. In the U.K. the most immediate need after the war seemed to be the building of homes for the labor force, bomb damage having been much greater in residential areas than in industrial areas. It was felt that this could be most effectively achieved by an extension of the local Council House policy inaugurated after the first war, more especially as this was regarded as an important welfare service. At a later stage I shall examine the effects of this policy on growth.

Probably the biggest difference between the prewar and postwar years has been the expansion of public sectors relative to the rest of the economy. This is so universal and well-documented a change that it is unnecessary to discuss it in detail. My concern is simply to explore how far its various aspects have accelerated or retarded growth rates. The established democracies have all been affected to varying degrees by the new status of public sectors. The change has also conspicuously influenced the emergent countries, many of which started independence with parliamentary institutions but are gradually becoming one-party states, frequently dominated by the military.

Generally speaking, the national government sector has grown most conspicuously, although (especially recently) there has been a parallel movement of growth and consolidation of subnational governments on a regional basis. They seek more autonomy by way of devolution, which would also imply more control over the lives of their citizens. These new assumptions of power have greatly accelerated since the energy crisis, which seemed to require additional controls of various types. The new situation that has emerged is a kind of ''socialism''; but this concept itself is undergoing change. The orthodox nineteenth-century form of socialism was typified by the nationalization of basic industries and services on the one hand and by the development of social services on the other. Its objective was to overcome the claimed inefficiencies and inequities of the market system and the capitalistic organization of production.

In many countries the railways, communications, and other basic industries have been nationalized, and social services have been introduced and expanded, especially pensions and welfare measures. But in the U.K. and Italy the tenets of the welfare state have been pressed most fully, with social assistance, family allowances, compensation for unemployment, and retirement pensions available at what must now be considered an unnaturally early age. Both countries in principle offer free education, right through the tertiary stage, and largely free health services. But the greater experience of British administration results in better performance.

An implicit long-term objective of the welfare state is the total abolition of the private sector; but this is still a distant goal. Nevertheless, the position has been reached in both the U.K. and Italy in which only a small sector of the economy remains completely independent of government policy (if we except the necessity for paying taxes, which in Italy can often be avoided, and the effect on private sector decision making of externalities arising from government activities). All other sectors are highly dependent on government decisions, be they in relation to wages and employment, conditions of work, or projects undertaken on government orders. In all this the U.K. and Italy are in very similar positions.

But public relations never stand still. The welfare state, especially in its industrial features, was a development of a very important aspect of nineteenth-century socialism, which has now changed substantially. The recent striking modification in the objectives of socialism, which can be dated from the late 1960s or early 1970s, can be seen most clearly in respect of labor policy and of the government's attitude toward employment. When not in the depths of depression, government seems to have shifted emphasis from maintaining employment to preserving individual rights. What is claimed is not just the right to work, but the right to work at one's own job in one's established environment. It is consequently the duty of employers to continue to provide this work, if necessary with help from subsidies, even if they are unable to make profits. While this policy is not necessarily antigrowth if the trouble is short-term, its effects on flexibility can be disastrous. Both the U.K. and Italy have followed this line. If anything, Italy was the first to adopt it, with subsidies to ailing firms, penalties for dismissals, and compensation for workers made redundant.

Is it possible to say how far the welfare state and its recent manifestations explain lagging growth? Generalization is difficult because of deep differences between countries in social aspirations. Growth is not a primary objective of the welfare state; people are much more interested in living well. This is not inherently antigrowth. If the nationalized industries are as efficient as their predecessors in the private sector they need not retard growth. The benefits of the welfare state are generally very welcome to the public, even if they call for heavy taxation. The embarrassment to the budget is not perceived, even by many Members of Parliament. A good example is the universally popular British National Health Service, whose costs are unbalancing national finances. The most growth-retarding aspects of the welfare state not only deter shifting and adjustment to change but actually promote rigidity in such areas as wages and employment and, more serious, the building of homes for workers by public authorities.

A brief examination of certain aspects of U.K. policy will serve to illustrate these points. Consider direct government expenditure (purchase of goods and services on both current and capital account, including debt service) and indirect government expenditure by way of subsidy to the nationalized industries, to private-sector firms, to local government, and to the public. Tax and borrowing policy largely follow and complement expenditure, consistent with such long-term fundamental policies as the greater equalization of income and wealth, which cannot overtly be set aside. Nevertheless, some of the largely ad hoc policies that are adopted may conflict with these basic aims. They may also be inconsistent with each other to the extent that they retard growth more than the capitalist/ market economy they are designed to improve.

These various potentially retarding aspects can conveniently be discussed under the following heads: (1) incomes, employment, and social services, (2) government relations to private-sector firms, (3) the nationalized sector, (4) local government and housing, and (5) administrative costs and financial control. The potential growth retardants in the U.K. are for the most part long lived and traditional, but in some circumstances (for instance, under the Labour Government of Sir Harold Wilson and Mr. Callaghan) they have operated at a high degree of intensity. Under the Conservative Government of Mrs. Thatcher there have been a number of attempts at relaxation and even at a return to a free-market economy, but it is evident that a major change of direction is impossible and that long-term factors must inevitably reassert themselves to a substantial degree. Since conscription would be unthinkable, the failure or success of financial control is of first importance.

Incomes, Employment, and Social Services

By and large, wages in the U.K. have not for a long time been determined by market forces but are "administered" as a result of prolonged discussion between the trade union leaders and the government department most closely concerned. So far as possible wage levels are fixed partly as a consequence of the government's overall policy and partly with an eye on the relative rates of pay in the public and private enterprise sectors. There exists a strong (charitable or paternalistic) urge to increase differentially the wages of the lower-paid workers and of those who have unpleasant jobs; decisions along these lines reduce grade differentials. Inevitably, the higher-paid, more skilled workers subsequently attempt to regain their status. There is a risk that this process will be repeated up the income scale, leading to strikes and, perhaps, inflation; it may well be a retardant on growth.

An important factor in determining wage policy in the U.K. has long been the dread of general unemployment. This implies that policy followed in respect of industrial expansion or contraction and of acceptance of new projects tends to be decided with reference to effect on employment, not economic merit. Hence it may well be more sensible for a firm to hang on to labor that it does not want (notwithstanding the embarrassments of overmanning and its effects on productivity) than to dismiss workers and face consequent heavy redundancy costs. Under the Labour Government assistance to small firms in difficulty was fairly freely given, especially where the high international value of sterling could be shown to be increasing the difficulty of exporting. Conservative policy is tougher, but for nationally important firms such as British Leyland and Rolls Royce the Conservatives have been constrained to follow a broadly similar policy, though with much greater emphasis on cost reduction and rationalization. In respect of the nationalized sector the difference in policy between the two parties is very substantial: under Labour an easy cost policy and accumulation of deficits and debts; under the Conservatives a policy of setting prices not merely high enough to cover a deficit, but in some services (postal, railways, electricity) high enough to make a net profit. The basic Conservative objective has been to eliminate waste and to increase efficiency. This policy has clearly made life very difficult for many consumers and some firms and has led to an increase in unemployment. In the short period, the effect has clearly been anti-growth. But in the longer run (perhaps five years), it may well satisfactorily promote growth.

In spite of all the efforts of governments, especially the Labour Government, wages have inevitably risen sharply; but payments derived from the welfare state have risen even more sharply for much of the labor force. To the lower-paid workers in particular, welfare receipts are of immense importance. It is widely accepted social policy that if the chief wage earner is out of work (either because he is on strike or because he has lost his job) his dependents should not suffer but should be enabled to maintain their accustomed standard of living. (Indeed if this were not done deprivation would probably be very heavy since their furniture, kitchen equipment, TV, car, and house are all purchased on the installment plan.) In addition to unemployment payments, there are available retirement pensions, social security, and supplementary assistance; but the Conservatives have tried to insist on substantial cuts in education and the National Health Service.

Clearly any discussion of wage and employment policy cannot avoid the problem of the trade unions. A striking change in the postwar world in all advanced countries (including Japan) has been their increasing importance. It has been asserted that this phenomenon has especially been a feature of such stable democracies as the U.K. and the U.S. But the phenomenon is far too widespread to provide more than a very partial explanation of lagging growth. Nevertheless, it is clear that the basic objective of trade unions is to improve the position of their own members without thought as to the effect their activities (strikes or prolonged working to rule) may have on the health of the economy. Both Italy and the U.K. have been particularly plagued by union activity in both public- and private-sector employment. It has been claimed that where trade unions are bigger and more embracing (as in Sweden), they are more conscious of the effects of their actions on the economy, and so are less obstructive; but recent troubles in Sweden do not support this view. In any case, small groups of key workers are able deliberately to affect—and temporarily disrupt—the whole working of the economy.

Steps to improve the position of one's own group require the maintenance of the closed shop in order not to waste any benefits on free riders, and they also include the maintenance or recovery of grade differentials. Successive British governments have attempted to rationalize and moderate these aims and the wage demands arising from them. They have had some success so far as the trade union leaders are concerned and sometimes with the rank and file, but the shop stewards tend to be much more intransigent. The task of the British government is made more difficult by the socially accepted principle that a worker's family must not suffer because he is on strike. This clearly encourages strikes and discourages job changing. Retraining schemes have been introduced to combat overmanning, but they are of limited effectiveness.

It has traditionally been British policy to keep the prices of basic foods low, both on welfare grounds and in order to mitigate demands for higher wages. Entry into the EEC has made this policy more difficult, but at least there are no taxes (VAT) on basic foods in Britain as there are in several EEC countries.

Probably the two most damaging results of trade union action for British industry are the uncertainty of delivery dates that ensues, to the damage of British tenders for foreign investments, and the difficulty of persuading workers to operate new technical improvements, which interfere with their customary regime.

Italy has a system of welfare provisions that is very similar to the British scheme. Indeed, in respect of pensions it seems to be even more generous, although any retirement earnings discovered are deducted from the pension (in the U.K. they are much more likely really to be deducted). In both countries the work force, as a percentage of known employment, declines very sharply when the pensionable age is reached. In Italy there is a gradual decline in participation of the 55–59 age group (76 percent). In the 60–64 age group it falls to 42 percent, and above 65 to 10 percent. The comparable figures in the U.K. show a decline from 95 percent to 87 percent and 20 percent, respectively. The low level of all measurable participation rates in Italy is very striking.

The opposite side of the welfare benefits coin reveals the high taxes and social security contributions that have to be imposed to finance them. In Italy these have traditionally weighed more heavily on the lower-paid workers than in the U.K., because the greater part of Italian tax revenue has been derived from taxes on outlay, including food and other basic needs. The British tradition is very different, being overweighted with taxes on income. Since 1974 very important changes have been introduced into the Italian tax structure. There is now a highly progressive personal income tax with current withholding for all employed workers. Others are required to make a comprehensive return of income from all sources for the previous year (but this is badly checked). As a result of these changes Italian direct taxes, which previously represented some 7 percent of GNP, have soared to some 14 percent. This is certainly due to some extent to better administration, but an unknown amount is due to inflation, which at an earlier stage was only noticeable in respect of VAT.

Social security in Italy has traditionally been financed by a very heavy payroll tax; its rates have been slightly eased, but it is no longer fully indexed. In addition there is a property or, more strictly, capital gains tax, which can be very severe in urban conditions. There is also a local government income tax. Value-added taxes are quite widely applied, and there are also such minor levies as an inheritance tax and stamp duties on legal transactions; all these taxes accrue directly to the national government. The regions and provinces have virtually no autonomous tax rights and must rely wholly on annual transfers from the government, broadly awarded on a population basis.

In both countries the effect of heavy social security contributions from workers is to cause an unknown but significant number of workers to disappear from the labor market (and, hence, from the statistics). They are not necessarily unemployed; they merely change to hidden work in the private sector, no doubt less well paid, but free of taxes and social contributions. It is by its very nature impossible to measure the extent of this underground labor, although something can be learned from sample enquiries. Estimates for Italy in 1971 and 1974 claim that to a recorded labor force of over nineteen million should be added a hidden labor force of over two million. There is reason to believe that there has recently been a considerable increase in underground labor because technical advances in such major industries as steel, textiles, and electronics enable small but vital parts to be made at home, where the labor is undetectable. In the U.K. it is estimated that some £12 million of income tax revenue are lost annually to similar practices. Concealed work is encouraged in two ways: the marginal rate of tax on entering the income tax range is high, and the system of deduction from the pay envelope includes a record of income from the main job only, since the taxpayer need file no return unless he has substantial taxable property. Most of the unrecorded labor in the U.K. is in services.

In Italy not only is there much unrecorded and untaxed work, but the total disappearance of workers is on a large scale. Official wage rates have been set very high (perhaps with the idea of keeping up with other EEC countries). Not much of the labor force can really qualify for employment at these rates, and in any case small firms cannot afford them. Hence there is strong incentive for collusion between small employers and the underground labor force. A good deal of the large discrepancy between the shrinkage of the agricultural labor force and the known expansion of labor in the industrial sector may well be due to this factor. The available statistics do indeed support this contention to some extent, but they are not reliable enough to merit much faith. Italian industry is still predominantly on a small scale. In 1961, when employment opportunities were relatively good, 27 percent of the labor force worked in firms employing fewer than ten workers and 25 percent were in factories of between 100 and 999 workers. In the U.K. the comparable figures were 2 percent and 45 percent.

Another aspect to be considered is the way in which the wage structure by age groups in both the U.K. and Italy (and a number of other countries) retards growth, unlike the wage structures of some other countries, notably Japan. In Japan, wages for those who do not finish school are set very low, so that there is competition to employ them, and the problem of juvenile unemployment that afflicts so many countries is completely bypassed. In Japan wage rates rise gradually over life, and there is a premium for remaining in the same firm. However, Japanese old-age pensions are quite inadequate, so that the incentive for personal saving is very high, which is certainly not true in the welfare state. In Italy 70 percent of the unemployed are young. In the U.K. (and indeed in most other countries) this proportion is also alarmingly high.

Relations with Private-Sector Firms

Turning from the attitude of governments to the worker/taxpayer and his relations with his employer, I will now discuss direct government policy in respect of firms in the private sector. Both Italy and the U.K. operate a variety of industrial controls that may distort the decision making of firms and so give rise to some rigidity. In the first place, in both countries industrial location has long been greatly influenced if not actually dictated by government agencies. Italian firms are under strong pressure to set up new plants in the south, where labor, although plentiful, is largely untrained, the standard of education low, and both markets and communications inferior. A powerful firm such as Olivetti is probably in a position (although unwillingly) to offset its losses in the south by profits from the north and may be able to adjust its tax liability favorably; but a new venture may well go under.

In the U.K. formerly strict rules of industrial location have been loosened by the impact of the depression, but change of location is still difficult.

Strong dividend limitation was enforced in the U.K. under the Labour Government, so that it was difficult for a firm to attract funds for expansion. This policy has been reversed by the Conservatives, but owing to the depression expansion is still poor. Moreover, under the Location of Industry legislation (a relic of wartime scarcities) firms making good profits in prosperous areas have not been permitted to expand there but must locate in "assisted" areas with high unemployment, however inconvenient this may be for their markets. Even if a firm is willing to open up in a new locality and is eligible to receive permission to do so, it will find it very difficult to provide adequate accommodation for the workers. It will probably have trouble persuading its labor force to upset domestic arrangements by moving.

The Labour Government initiated two special organizations for dealing with rising unemployment: the Public Enterprise Board and the Jobs Creation Programme. The latter was an unfortunate affair. It started in 1975 with a budget grant of £30 million; by 1977 it had spent £166 million with no appreciable effect on unemployment and very poor monitoring. The (Parliamentary) Public Accounts Committee was very soon at its throat, and it vanished. It is not, however, impossible that the Conservative Government may be constrained to try some sort of substitute to meet the (now much worse) unemployment situation.

The National Development Board has been and is a much more substantial project. It functions as a sort of development bank, making loans and taking up equity issues of large firms that are in difficulties. It is thus out for profits of its own, as well as helping to restore them to its protégés. For the purpose of rescue, a reorganized corporation, more or less under government control, has been launched (as British Leyland developed out of the private-sector firm of Leyland Motors). The sums negotiated have been very large: it claims to have had some successful ventures, but its profits are largely phony because it uses purely historical cost accounting for depreciation and replacement. The Conservatives were at first opposed to the whole organization but seem now to be prepared to tolerate its continuance and even to undertake some important new ventures.

The Nationalized Sector

The nationalized industries and services have plenty of problems of their own, and backdoor nationalization of the types we have been discussing does not make them any simpler. The problems are related especially to wages, employment levels, and grading—both within the industries themselves and in comparison to similar employment in the private sector—and to the planned output of goods and services and their prices. It is convenient to distinguish between the deliberately nationalized industries and services (many of these came into existence under the Attlee government immediately after the war; others were established later) and the piecemeal takeovers of large firms, at first largely as rescue operations but with a steady policy of expansion on ideological grounds. In the last days of the Labour Government this category expanded extremely rapidly and at very high cost; but it does not suit Conservative attitudes.

The deliberately nationalized industries had various origins: some were taken over en bloc from the private sector as natural monopolies, considered to be harmful in private hands; some were transferred from the administration and control of the local authorities (electricity, gas, health, and assistance); and some were more recent transfers to new fringe organizations, such as aerospace, atomic energy, North Sea oil, ports, and shipbuilding. Whatever their origin all nationalized industries and services have to struggle with similar problems. Many of the industries that were taken over, especially the railways and coal mining, were already in financial embarrassment and were subsidized from the start. Even those that were not in immediate need have since required assistance. So, by and large, the entire nationalized sector has been receiving subsidies, clearly a most substantial weight on the budget.

Up to about 1956 state subsidies to industry increased steadily but at a fairly modest rate; but in 1957 there was a sharp upward surge. For a few years they remained fairly stable at the higher level, but then in 1973 they again leaped upward. Subsidies to the public sector were at a lower level than subsidies given to the private sector: in respect of some of the nationalized industries, policy has recently been modified. Prices were raised irrespective of the effect on sales, with the result that identifiable profits have been made, for instance in telecommunications, railways, electricity, gas, and water supply. But by and large subsidization still continues. It is difficult to say whether this change of policy promotes or retards growth: it reduces the burden on the budget, but it adds to the costs and inconveniences of industry and the public, so probably it tends at least to reduce flexibility in the economy.

Wages and employment policy have all along been a headache for the nationalized sector. Great efforts have been made by both political parties to keep down the wages and salaries of state workers. Since these wages and salaries were more under government control than were wages in the rest of the economy, it was felt that they should set an example of an anti-inflation policy. After a good deal of bitter experience it became clear that such a policy was not acceptable and would lead only to strikes and break-downs. In spite of the so-called social contract, any attempt at confrontation tended to end in capitulation by the government in order to avoid the spectre of unemployment.

From about 1965 wages in the public sector have tended to swing ahead of those in the private sector, but, oddly, productivity in the public sector has been conspicuously rising while employment has been falling. Thus it has been possible for enterprises to raise the wages of those actually employed without increasing their deficits. The explanation would seem to be that since, for the nationalized industries, the cost of borrowing is not a consideration (for approved activities they can have virtually what they want) they have been able to substitute cheap capital for dear labor, thus indirectly adding to the level of unemployment and the degree of overmanning.

In spite of the recent limited adventure into high-cost sales it has been the general policy of nationalized industries and services to dispose of their output below cost. The result of this (social) policy is that either every additional output increases the deficit and the need for subsidy or queueing develops. A prime example of the first alternative is the Concorde, for which additional flights do not even cover running costs; and of the second alternative, the National Health Service (NHS), where queueing is notorious.

The NHS has special problems of its own for which no solution is yet in sight. One of the most intractable of these is the enormous cost of drugs and technical improvements that have revolutionized the medical treatment of many diseases. These changes could not have been foreseen when the NHS was inaugurated; but once the discoveries had been made they could hardly be ignored. As a result governments are unwilling to pay sufficient wages and salaries to the personnel required for full functioning of the service. Queues lengthen and wards are closed down. (In 1977 the cost of the NHS was estimated at £6,000 million, three times more in real terms than in 1949.) Costs are further increased through the policy of endeavoring to reduce if not to eliminate the number of private patients in NHS hospitals. Unquestionably, standards are sagging. This provides an obvious stimulus to the establishment of private hospitals outside the NHS; but this would reintroduce the class differences it was hoped to avoid.

It is difficult to judge the extent to which the great experiment of the NHS promotes or retards growth (apart from its very real burden on the budget). By their nature the services are difficult to monitor. It cannot be denied that there are wastes, too-high administrative costs, and perhaps a tendency for overprescribing, if only to try out new drugs. Undoubtedly the nation's health has improved, and the anxiety that results when a member of a family falls ill and treatment cannot be afforded has been removed. The monopoly power and restriction of entry into the medical profession, which is so notorious (for instance in the United States), has almost completely been eliminated. But inevitably by far the largest element in the outlay goes to those who cannot work fully because of some disablement or weakness. More particularly it goes to the steadily rising volume of old-age pensioners, who will in any case fail to undertake normal paid work because of the deduction of pension from their earnings.

Before leaving the discussion of the public sector at the national end I must discuss two very large services that are of great importance for growth or antigrowth: namely, education and housing. In these services British policy has been mainly (and increasingly) determined at the national level, but execution is very largely the business of the local authorities, except that in respect of the conduct of tertiary education (universities and technical colleges) these authorities have very little say. In respect of housing, the building of new towns and subsidies to private housing associations are the business of the national government. Private sector provision in both services is still active although left-wingers would like to bring them wholly into the public sector in the name of equalization (egalitarianism).

I argued above that the established British educational system, although perhaps peculiar, is by no means growth-retardant or unfitted for the modern world. At the moment, though, it is in a state of flux and transition, the final outcome of which in respect of either educational results or growth promotion cannot yet be foreseen. Broadly, the new system of the Labour Government aims (as an exact parallel to the NHS) at a totally state-run provision of primary and secondary education, which is to be conducted in large "comprehensive" schools. The independent public schools would not presently be disturbed; but "direct grant" grammar schools, which are independent of the local authorities, would cease to exist: either they must (if they can afford it) become independent public schools, or they must come wholly into the state system.

Our concern here is not to judge the educational merits of the change, but rather to note the immense costs that the transition involves: need for much new school building, loss of the endowments and income of the direct grant schools, and the inevitable readjustment of curricula. All this has hit the national resources at a most difficult moment. The ideology of the educational reorganization is exactly parallel to that of the NHS: identical free treatment for all, with curbs placed on private effort and greater centralization of powers and policy decisions. As in respect of the NHS there is also the same, though unmeasurable, danger that in attempting universality, decline and dilution of standards will be serious, especially as there is no agreement concerning the desirable courses for the new system.

Local Government: Housing and New Towns

Finally we come to what is probably the most serious obstacle in the path of flexibility and shiftability in the British economy; it is also the least understood. The public building of good working-class housing started soon after the end of World War I. It was a response to the realization on wartime call-up of the bad conditions and poor health with which a large section of the populace had to struggle. The actual estate planning and house building was allocated to the local authorities, who were considered to know best what the local needs were. From the first the service was heavily subsidized. The policy of "council" housing was continued throughout the interwar period with a good deal of enthusiasm by both political parties, although with a slight difference of emphasis: the Conservatives preferring a "sanitary" policy of concentrating on the worst conditions and Labour encouraging as much building of new houses as possible so as to create a national asset (Bowley, 1945). Council house building received its real boost after World War II through the need to restore bombed areas. Owing to a tough policy of rent control the supply of rented houses in the private sector shrank drastically. Also, the building of new houses in the private sector became almost impossible. Thus there was no means by which an expanding firm or one locating in a new neighborhood could provide accommodation for its employees. At one point 43 percent of the nation was housed in state-provided homes.

The greater part of British council housing is in individual houses with gardens, although more recently experiments have been made of large blocks and high rises of flats (more beloved by the town planners than by the tenants). The rents of all publicly provided accommodation were set very low and only gradually increased as prices rose. Nevertheless, they were too high for the very poor. Their real appeal was to the trade union level, both manual and clerical. The rent bonus to council house tenants was very large, and since the allocation of houses was the monopoly of each little housing authority it would be extremely risky for a family to give up the house it had and try its luck in a new locality where it had no roots and must go to the end of the queue. Given the generous standard of unemployment pay it would often be preferable to keep the house even if work prospects were poor. Two effects of British housing policy thus stand out: extreme difficulty for employers to provide adequate accommodation where they need it for expansion or relocation and strong disincentive to move on the part of workers. It is easy to see that this has been a prime cause of loss of flexibility in the British economy.

There is a further aspect of British housing policy to consider. Rent policy landed the local authority property owners in continuing and mounting losses. The situation was aggravated by the general failure, in the anxiety to build more and more houses, to provide adequate maintenance and repair services; houses built fifteen or twenty years ago were already lapsing into slum conditions. This raised an outcry among social workers, which can hardly be ignored. But meantime the costs of repair and rehabilitation rose astronomically; thus an awkward dilemma has arisen. The Conservatives urge local authorities to sell or even give away what houses they can. Economically this is entirely sensible; it would put a stop to the mounting drain on local resources and probably be agreeable to most of the tenants. Labour demands the production of an even greater "public asset." The dilemma persists.

The root of the trouble has been the continuance of local responsibility for a much-enlarged service. National responsibility would at least have made it possible to restore flexibility by building houses where they were wanted on economic grounds. But the government's policy in respect of new towns or of its subsidies to housing associations (the two fields in which national authority is responsible) do not suggest that the improvement would necessarily have been achieved.

The idea behind the new towns movement was to reduce urban congestion, especially in London, which had proved an easy target for German bombing. In order to minimize commuting, the new towns were planned as balanced communities, including industry and services as well as residential areas. They were also regarded as an accommodation for the expected mass immigration to the southeast, which in fact did not occur. More recently, new towns have been established in depressed areas as a boost to morale and economic advance; the results are not very encouraging.

Some of the new towns have been rather successful; but on the whole their problems have been the opposite of those of the local authorities. Highly sophisticated town planning and house building are wasted because not enough people want to go to live in them. The industrial opportunities offered do not fit in with economic and population trends. Finally, as a result of decongestion, the cities (especially London) are becoming short of labor and their tax bases are shrinking. The latest twist of policy is to tempt people to return to London—at considerable cost.

Administrative Costs and Financial Control

Although education and housing are local activities, they fall largely outside the general relationship of the subnational governments to the center. On the expenditure side the British local authorities are a very important element in the public sector. On the revenue side, with only one autonomous tax (the local rate on the occupation of buildings) they depend heavily on government grants to carry out their statutory duties. In general, local outlay has been noticeably rising, especially from about 1965. At that time expansion was encouraged by the ministries concerned with their various services; but notwithstanding a very large rise in property values, the rate base has scarcely expanded. This was due partly to the continuance of some remnants of rent control, partly to the failure of the national government to implement its statutory duty of quinquennial property valuations. Before the war it had been hoped to get the rate contribution to local revenue up to 50 percent; by 1965 it had fallen to 39 percent on the average and by 1977 to 27 percent. Local expenditure growth was a clear contribution to inflation, and, warned by the International Monetary Fund (IMF), the government began to reduce the total of grants, leaving the local authorities to finance what they could not abandon by higher rate poundages, which were ill received by the public.

The earnings of all grades of local government servants grew steadily but not very rapidly until about 1965. From that point, like a number of other elements in the British economy, they began to soar. The greater freedom of the then grants system (as contrasted with specific grants) enabled the authorities to pay higher wages rather than to expand or perhaps even maintain their existing services. In addition, there occurred a very heavy growth in the numbers of local employees, partly but by no means wholly due to a basic reorganization of jurisdictions, which like the education changes occurred at a most awkward moment for the economy.

The worst effects of this reorganization should be no more than temporary, although it contributed to inflation. In other respects there is little reason to believe that British local government retards growth. Politically it is a very useful and well-tried field of training for government service.

In Italy, local government and finance are also very important, but the authorities are less experienced and responsible than in the U.K. Elections tend to follow national party lines even more closely than in the U.K. A generalization in respect of Italian local government is that cities that elect a communist council can look forward to active local government, promotion of social services, and, in particular, large programs of development and low-income housing. But the new complexes are all on the outskirts of the cities and are accompanied by neglect of building and street maintenance in the inner city, where there is commonly insufficient police and security provision.

It is interesting that in Italy as well as in the U.K. there has recently been a substantial change in the organization of subnational government. The provinces have ceased to have any individual importance. Instead they have been grouped into twenty regular regions plus four frontier regions (Sicily, Val d'Aosta, Tridentino, Sardegna). The latter have somewhat wider independent powers of decision making but no fiscal advantages. Neither the provinces nor the regions have any autonomous tax powers beyond dog licensing! Each unit receives an annual transfer, which it must not exceed, based broadly on population and borrows locally insofar as it can do so. Budgetary control is poor, but spending is not inhibited by the fear of default, because units are convinced that the government will sooner or later rescue them.

It remains to discuss the effect of the new status of public sectors in relation to growth. Italian budgetary and financial control has all along been somewhat primitive and disorderly, in spite of good intentions, compared with the careful and orderly system that the U.K. inherited from the nineteenth century. It is worth glancing briefly at the latter in order to contrast it with the decay and disintegration of the system that has recently been occurring, even in the U.K., largely as a result of the changed status of the public sector. This is not inevitably to decry recent practices, because in some sense they can perhaps be regarded as a transition stage to a less rigid but still orderly system. But present policy concentrates largely on short-term measures, and on this account it may retard long-term growth.

Under the traditional British budgetary system, detailed estimates of the cost of each service are set out and are matched exactly by appropriation accounts when the expenditure has taken place. Discrepancies between the two accounts are carefully examined by the auditor general and, on his advice, by the Public Accounts Committee (PAC). This body consists of members of Parliament, their party distribution echoing that in Commons, and is chaired by a member of the Opposition. Unforeseeable (or unforeseen) additional expenditure is financed out of a limited contingencies fund and must be covered by a parliamentary appropriation. Capital account and the fiscal aspect of demand management were not so well controlled, and only recently have performance aspects been tackled. But a powerful and active expenditure committee (paralleling the PAC), working through a number of subcommittees, has been investigating administrative practices with a good deal of thoroughness. A third major committee looks after the nationalized industries. Of recent years a large number of specialized parliamentary committees have also been established.

The arrangement and classification of the estimates (''votes'') have been modified in several minor ways to take account of the postwar situation, with its enlarged public sector, and the practice of Keynesian demand management. Owing to these the budgetary structure continued to stand up to a steady moderate inflation. Since the U.K. had no previous experience of high inflation (a spectre that still haunts German policy), it had developed no defenses against it, so that when high inflation set in, the traditional system began to disintegrate. For a controlled ''balance,'' which would include any (limited) deficit necessary for demand management, there came to be substituted a ''borrowing requirement,'' which varied through the year (sometimes giving rise to multiple budgets) as circumstances changed.

It was discovered that the borrowing requirement could be covered with surprising ease: for the greater part by internal loans on which investors (especially institutional investors) were virtually captive because of exchange controls. Foreigners were also ready to invest in British government securities, since they still had complete confidence that the British government would honor its obligations even at the very high interest rates offered. For a time local governments were also encouraged to borrow abroad in order to ease the balance of payments (an extraordinarily short-term policy that overlooked the accumulating cost of debt service). Hence a new market in local bonds sprang into existence and is now of considerable importance.

It has plausibly been argued that British policy, at least from about 1970, has had a built-in risk of inflation, essentially because it seemed to provide an easy solution of policy inconsistencies. The nationalized industries found it an agreeable way through their obligations to sell below cost and to include social as well as economic purposes. The trade unions (both in the public and private sectors) felt that in respect of remuneration it was their duty to lead and to demand higher wages, even in the face of unemployment. Finally, some regard has to be paid to the necessity of allowing taxpayers some reward for their labors. All could be given at least nominal prizes through inflation. If the alternatives offered to the public were (1) setting profit ceilings, high wages, and sufficient means of livelihood with low prices or (2) letting prices rise and containing wages, the first alternative would certainly be preferred. Yet it does not lead to efficiency. The connection between the first alternative and inflation was not easily perceived, certainly not by many MPs. Moreover even if the policy did not produce efficiency, it seemed to lead to the sort of social optimum that most people desired.

But this apparently easy way out has its own risks. Foreign lenders may lose confidence (the OPEC nations withdrew their balances). Devaluation of sterling could be only a partial solution, owing to the necessity of paying more for imports, especially food, raw materials, and components. Hence policy turned to control of the money base, spurred on by the IMF and the monetarists. The monetary base in a country like the U.K. is largely dependent on external conditions, which can be controlled only partially by open-market operations on the internal market. Further, by and large, expansion of the base follows the expansion of outlay and not the other way round. The result is an increasing current deficit and a mounting burden of debt service. It is not surprising that in 1975 a large increase in the deficit took place. Even if the needs of debt repayment were evenly spread, which they are not, serious trouble could occur if the government should cease to be able to borrow freely abroad. Fortunately this is not yet a pressing problem. In 1975 it successfully floated a term loan of £4,659 million; this was not far short of all government bond sales from 1954 to 1974. The Conservative policy of high interest rates largely eliminates the problem.

Acquiescence to deficit finance appeared to be the most agreeable way of covering the growth of expenditure, both direct on current and capital account (including debt service) and indirect on contributions (subsidies) to the nationalized sector, to the local authorities, and to the private sector. Direct expenditure expanded throughout the years I have been examining, notwithstanding the efforts of the Conservative Government to contain it.

But from 1964 the fastest growth was in subsidies. From 1967 subsidies and loans exceeded direct expenditure; by 1975 the gap had widened and subsidies and loans exceeded direct outlay by £3,000 million. The main causes of this I have examined, but why should direct expenditure have grown so fast? By far the largest item in this outlay is wages and salaries, and, apart from forced fluctuations, by and large these rose faster in the public than in the private sector.

An additional factor was that workers in different industries, particularly in parts of the public sector, were receiving lower wages than workers in similar occupations elsewhere. A committee was set up under Professor Hugh Clegg to examine comparabilities. This policy inevitably led to higher wages somewhere. In practice any particular wage structure depends on so many imponderables that true comparability is a will o' the wisp. The committee is now clinically dead and efforts are being made to obliterate its memory.

From about 1974 another strong-growing element appeared in the adoption of new types of expenditure by the Labour Government. An important aspect of this policy was the proliferation of projects designed specifically to preserve and stimulate employment, without much thought being given to their economic viability. Finance for these was supplied without delay out of the contingency fund without waiting for parliamentary approval. As the policy matured it has often been questionable whether Parliament would have agreed to an appropriation, but the pass had been already sold. Another source of growing expenditure has been the multiplication of committees and commissions to examine particular problems. These bodies have been manned by businessmen and academics on a part-time basis. The members have received handsome personal allowances if not also some direct remuneration. In fact the members have become quasi public servants and have been dubbed "quangos." An academic who has been a success at this sort of work might sit on six or more of these committees and, if he was lucky, be rewarded by a life peerage. (The Conservative Government is trying to get rid of these quangos as fast as possible.) It is not that these new lines of expenditure were extremely costly. More significantly such innovations greatly increase the power of the executive at the expense of parliamentary control. Up to the change of government these additional expenditures continued to accelerate, the consequent inescapable economies falling on the local authorities and on the maintenance of fixed assets, especially of the railways. But both the expenditure committee and the Conservative party are anxious to bring them fully under control.

Enough has probably been said to account for the present lagging growth of the U.K. and also of Italy, although it is not possible to quantify the relative importance of the different causes. Both countries exhibit a strong desire for social services and approve of government pressure on industrialists. Both countries experienced a euphoric investment boom in the late 1960s and early 1970s (in this they were not unique), but the boom has deposited a legacy of inflation, unemployment, and overmanning to conceal the failure of demand. Both countries have borrowed heavily abroad but have not sufficiently recovered, at least in their short-term positions, to repay some of their debts. There the comparison breaks down.

Italy is essentially only a partially developed or partially advanced country. I refer not only to the much-advertised problem of the south of Italy, parts of which are probably undevelopable. That task is almost certainly beyond the fine but limited capacity of the north to finance. Because success has been small it is a mistake to conclude that the south has been neglected. Successive governments have poured money into it, establishing large factories that have little economic success. Housing and roads have been improved. But as a whole the area just did not take off. The best opportunities for the local labor force are abroad, especially in Germany. Their remittances are a useful source of revenue, and their factory training and discipline will prove real assets when they come back, as they certainly hope to do eventually. The south is not the only underdeveloped part of Italy, yet successive governments have sought to jack up half-developed Italy to full standards (for instance, by fixing official wage rates at advanced country levels, although they cannot be afforded). It has been suggested by Fuà (1977, 1978), a leading Italian economist, that even if the Italian economy achieves the best possible growth rate policy and is helped by relatively slow growth in the advanced EEC countries, it would take some twenty-six years for it to catch up with the standard EEC level.

The situation of the U.K. is in many ways just the opposite. It was once the pioneer of rapid economic growth. Now it has become what is probably the pioneer of the slower growth that is overtaking the advanced countries. Large parts of the U.S. are also in this condition and similar writing on the wall can be discerned in Germany and France. The U.K. has been suffering from many ill-thought-out microschemes to combat depression and unemployment (which are also apparent to some extent in most parts of the world). In the U.K. it is becoming apparent that many of these new devices are no more than short-term palliatives or deviations from elementary economic sense. On the return of world prosperity many of them should be quickly abandoned, whatever faction (except the extreme Left) is in power. The long-term situation contains elements of risk and danger, but it certainly is not desperate.

REFERENCES

Brown, Sir Henry Phelps, "What is the British Predicament?" *Three Banks Review*, December 1977.

Fuà, Georgio. "Employment and Productive Capacity in Italy." In *Banco Nazionale del Lavoro Quarterly Review*, September 1977.

_____ "Lagged Development and Economic Growth." In *Banco Nazionale del Lavoro Quarterly Review*, June 1978.

Bowley, M. E. A. *Housing and the State*. London: Allen and Unwin, 1945.

Baseri, G.; Onofri, P.; and Tantazzi, G. "Italian Stabilisation Policies under Social Pressures and International Shocks." Bologna, August 1978.

8: Economic Growth and Interest Groups: The French Experience

J.-C. ASSELAIN and C. MORRISSON

As there have been many comments or interpretations, more or less divergent, about the comparatively slow growth of the French economy between 1871 and 1945, Olson's hypothesis deserves special attention from French economists. This note will first offer some general comments about Olson's views and then confront these views with the economic, social, and political history of France of the last two centuries.

General Comment

Before we consider how to generalize this theory, we shall mention three major criticisms: first, the lack of a clear distinction between different types of changes as regards the duration of their effects throws some confusion both on theoretical analysis and on empirical tests; second, there are many cases of a reverse relationship (a recession or crisis may be the cause of groups' formation, rather than a consequence); third, there are historical counterexamples to Olson's theory.

It is difficult, on reading Olson's essay, to know precisely what period is under consideration, because the argument sometimes concerns a short period (from a historical point of view) of about twenty years, and sometimes a much longer period—several centuries in some cases. For instance, Olson refers to the social stability of England since the Middle Ages; in the United States, the length of time since statehood varies between sixty and 200 years; regarding Germany and Japan, we are concerned with the consequences of World War II over about thirty years. It seems necessary to distinguish among economic, social, and political changes according to the duration of their effects. Three types of changes might be distinguished:

a. Replacement by newcomers of the whole political and trade unions staff and of main businessmen. For some historical reason, the heads of different interest groups, of administration, and of political parties in one country are all, or nearly all, thrown away at the same time. The consequences of such an event surely cannot go beyond twenty or thirty years, for after that time the same phenomenon of aging and sclerosis will reappear as before. We could mention also the casual destruction, by war, for instance, of trade unions and cartels, without any major change in the laws regulating them. Some time, of course, is necessary to reorganize such groups, but, after twenty or thirty years, perhaps less, they could very well recover the same importance as before.

b. Institutional changes limiting the formation of interest groups and their means and powers. For instance, the closed shop is ruled out: trade unions' influence is not completely suppressed thereby, but it is nevertheless reduced for a long time, because the context is less favorable; the effect, if not permanent, will at least be long lasting (more than twenty or thirty years).

c. Institutional changes forbidding once and for all the action of some interest groups. When some country becomes a member of a regional union or common market, an industry or segment of it may be deprived of all protection against its neighbor countries' competitors, if this country is a member of the same union. As long as these economies remain integrated, the interest of this sector can no longer be protected (at least if we suppose there are no derogatory clauses and no international cartels). It would be the same if an office system, like that in France for notaries and auctioneers, were abolished, thus permitting free entrance into a profession previously ruled by a system of *numerus clausus.*

Each of these three types of changes has a different effect on growth according to Olson's theory: type *a* is favorable to growth for fifteen or twenty years, but it no longer has any influence after that time; type *b* has some favorable effect for between twenty and forty or fifty years, perhaps more, but it might be checked thereafter if the concerned groups succeed in making up their strength again in spite of the new arrangements; type *c* has a favorable effect as long as it is not cancelled.

Changes of the first type surely cannot explain growth rate differentials for more than twenty or thirty years; so the very strong changes in France during the period from 1789 to 1815 and in Germany and Japan from 1940 to 1945 cannot explain growth rates respectively in France during the interval 1840–60 or in Germany and Japan after the period 1965–70.

As for England, changes of the second type account for an apparent contradiction in Olson's argument. For he refers at once to the institutional stability since the Middle Ages and to the open nature of the English society during the eighteenth century. As a matter of fact, the situation during the eighteenth century was the result of abandoning, since the seventeenth century and the beginning of the eighteenth, many customs that impeded innovations and their diffusion. Conversely, many new laws and practices had been shaping, for about a century, a more and more unfavorable environment to growth by gradually strengthening the means and powers of interest groups. Today's environment has not been produced by centuries of institutional stability, but rather by developments new in the previous century that have benefited some social groups, an effect they had because of the political and social stability England has enjoyed for a century.

Among changes of the third type we may mention the abolition of interregional customs in France after 1789. This decision, together with the building of canals and, later, railways, made possible the creation of a national market and so had a permanent, favorable effect on growth. It could explain a quicker growth in France during the first half of the nineteenth century than in Germany before the formation of the Zollverein.

Such a distinction among three types of changes is absolutely necessary for econometric tests: the lag between the period under consideration for the test and the relevant changes depends on the nature of those changes.[1]

On the other hand, this distinction leads to a more guarded statement of the relationship between political instability and growth. Of course, a revolution or a war often produces changes of type *a,* but other changes may happen in a period of political stability, as for example the creation of the European Economic Community, which is a change of type *c.* Moreover, some changes in the political regime do not affect the powers of interest groups and their meddlings, as French history between 1930 and 1950 shows. What really matter are the conditions in which the interest

---

1. Beyond this effort to distinguish periods of differing length, it would be useful to delineate the main linkages and to specify the causal relation between instability and the growth rate. For instance, instability (international or civil war) reduces or stops investments; later, the investment rate will be automatically increased during subsequent years of peace. But such an effect of instability cannot last longer than about twenty years; it corresponds to the first type of changes. Moreover, it is not really connected with interest groups and it takes place whether such groups exist or not. The following two sequences therefore have to be carefully distinguished:

Political instability, no investment, increased rate of investment to make up for the interruption, high rate of growth

Political instability, ruling out of interest groups or their leaders, no groups or weak groups during the following period.

groups grow and act rather than political stability itself, which is only a proxy variable, and sometimes a misleading one, for those conditions.

A second exception to Olson's theory is that even an observed correlation between the existence of powerful interest groups and slow growth (or between weak interest groups and swift growth) may not prove that interest groups are really the cause of slow growth. A reverse causal relation—slow growth leading to formation of interest groups—might produce the same econometric results and would not be difficult to warrant. For, when the growth rate abruptly slows down or even becomes negative, individual and enterprise anticipations about the future growth of their incomes cease to be mutually consistent; then, forming a group and meddling will be the only way for some people to achieve the growing incomes that they expect. In this case, Olson's analysis explains very well the formation of *narrow* interest groups and the damage they cause to the economy. Two successive stages may be distinguished: first, economic crisis or recession, which produces the development of interest groups; then, during a second stage, in accordance with Olson's causal scheme these groups increase the extent of the economic disease. For such groups care only for their own incomes, and their activity tends to cast on others' shoulders the consequences of crisis. According to this interpretation, crisis and not political or social stability explains the development of groups; but stability, when groups exist, increases the unfavorable effect of group activity. H. Willgerodt[2] and W. Eltis,[3] studying the opposite cases of Germany and England, interpret trade unions' behavior, open-minded in one case, uncompromising in the other, partly as a consequence of economic difficulties, which in turn are increased by groups' actions. Conversely, during periods of quick growth, it is easier to reduce interest-group influence, because growth generates benefits for all, which make up within a short time for the losses of a given group's members. Olson mentions the possibility that a society could overcome in a democratic way the resistance of groups to encroachment on their privileges. We should add that this possibility depends on the national growth rate, even though groups receive a compensation as Olson suggests.

2. H. Willgerodt, "Some Comments on the Rate of Growth in the Federal Republic of Germany" (Paper delivered at the Conference on the Political Economy of Comparative Growth Rates, College Park, Md., December 1978), p. 2.

3. W. Eltis, "Does the Comparatively Low Defense Spending of the Losers of the Second World War Help to Explain the Comparatively Slow Growth of the Winners?" (Paper delivered at the Conference on the Political Economy of Comparative Growth Rates, College Park, Md., December 1978), p. 10.

Our third comment will contest the generalization of Olson's scheme to all countries. French history, as we will show, offers several counterexamples. The remarkable stability of the reign of Louis XV (1715–75) did not prevent the speeding up of growth toward the end of his reign. Conversely, the conspicuous instability between 1789 and 1815 was followed by very slow growth between 1815 and 1835. Last, the most prosperous decade of the period 1871–1914 under the Third Republic was 1903–13, after thirty years of stability, when many groups (agricultural interests, trade unions, industrial cartels) that did not exist in 1871, or were much weaker, had reached a very high development.

On the other hand, although Olson does explain the sustained growth in Sweden and Norway in spite of secular stability by adducing the comprehensive nature of interest groups in the two countries, the same explanation is not suitable for Switzerland. The confederal political system of this country and its ethnic and political pluralism did not favor the formation of national groups. Many groups remained confined to one canton or ethnic group until recent years; but this did not prevent Switzerland, which is, moreover, a typical example of political and social stability, from reaching one of the highest growth rates in Europe during the period 1870–1970.

German history also casts some doubt on the theory. Growth accelerated in the German Empire after 1871, when traditional interest groups were extremely strong and trade unions commenced to develop.

Take-off in backward, ''stuck'' societies also offers a set of counterexamples. Such societies often have stratified economies in which some ethnic or social groups enjoy privileges or rental revenues. The acceleration of growth in Spain under Franco between 1960 and 1975 provides the best example. Spanish society had been stable since 1939, the place devoted to the various economic and professional groups had not changed since 1939; nevertheless, some sort of economic ''starting up'' could be observed. The society remained stuck, while its economic conformation changed. We could also mention several African countries under European rule[4] which enjoyed a quick growth after 1945—not *after* but *before* becoming politically independent and experiencing all social and juridical changes and developments consecutive to independence. This growth was not accompanied by significant changes in the colonial or protectorate system that was still in force.

As for the catch-up hypothesis, it would probably be possible with a

4. For instance, Angola from 1960 to 1978, or Morocco from 1948 to 1953.

simple test to impute the respective shares of this hypothesis and of Olson's in growth rate differentials. Different economies should be selected that show the same ratio, at the beginning of a certain period, of their GNP per capita as that of the most developed country in the world, but that have very different institutional conditions (very favorable to groups in some countries, very unfavorable in others). Such a set of economies would allow an easy test of Olson's hypothesis, since the influence of the variable "difference of GNP per capita" would not be *ex hypothesis*. Conversely, we could select a set of countries with different ratios of GNP per capita, but with the same institutional conditions, to estimate the influence of this variable. By adding other countries with different institutional conditions, we could determine the supplementary share of growth rate differentials that is explained by Olson's hypothesis. Proceeding this way, so as to estimate separately the influence of each variable, would produce more significant results than would comparing countries, for which comparison both hypotheses would be called forth jointly.[5]

The most important point, however, is the extension of Olson's theory to socialist or developing economies. All his examples are chosen from among capitalist industrialized countries, either from recent history or from the nineteenth century. Olson's interpretation would be, however, perhaps best suited to Third World countries. In these countries, the industrial sector, which, as Olson mentions, is the least subject to meddling of all interest groups, is generally much less important than in developed countries. Moreover, industrial producers usually enjoy high tariff protection. So, most activities, industrial as well as nonindustrial, are not exposed to international competition. On the other hand, these societies are often much more heterogeneous than in capitalist developed countries; regional, ethnic, religious, and economic differences initially create very strong solidarities, and the formation of interest groups is all the more easy. For instance, if there is a very strong feeling of ethnic solidarity among one ethnic group in a black African country, and if most craftsmen or trades-

5. If some country has been drawn back by political circumstances (as were Germany and Japan in 1945), this hypothesis could explain not only its higher growth rates during the period when such a country catches up with the average income of countries that were on the same level as itself before the retarding events, but also higher growth rates during following years. People who have been accustomed to rapidly increasing incomes anticipate the same progression for the future. On the other hand, to this end they have accepted suffering some restraints (especially against developing strong interest-group action) and an intensive program of work and saving. Such restraints and efforts are probably not difficult to bear, as people are accustomed to them; whereas an abrupt slowing down in income growth would be heavily resented. So a supplementary variable should be added for testing the catch-up hypothesis: the rate of growth during the catch-up period or for the preceding years.

men belong to this ethnic group, craftsmen and tradesmen of the same origin will easily form groups able to weed out any competitor belonging to another ethnic group or to control entry into their profession from their own ethnic group. In other cases, various activities will have been reserved for centuries to members of some ethnic groups, so that professional status is completely identified with family origin. On the other hand, income and wealth distribution is nearly always more concentrated in Third World than in developed countries, and there is less social mobility. Solidarities among rich families are traditionally strong, either among landlords or among merchants and lenders. Interest groups are easily formed under such conditions within these hereditary oligarchies. Last, as opposed to developed countries, the military personnel, and especially officers, who have a strong esprit de corps because of their education and activity, often hold political power and, consequently, economic power.

Third World countries may offer the conditions most favorable to the formation of interest groups. Of course, they experience at the same time much more unstable political conditions than capitalist developed countries, but what really matters here is the influence of political changes on interest groups. In most cases, these changes have a small effect in comparison with those Olson chooses as examples for developed countries, for instance those of 1933–48 in Germany. It would be interesting to compare growth rates of different developing countries, excluding two categories of countries: those that are able to finance considerable investments with means derived from such natural resource exploitation as oil production; and those in which natural conditions are especially adverse to any development, as for instance some countries of the Sahel. A consequent step then would be to measure the respective strengths of groups in different countries since political instability can no longer be considered as a fully reliable criterion. We tentatively suggest measuring the share in GNP of permanently controlled activities.[6]

One of the most radical changes such countries may experience is, of course, to be converted to a Marxist-socialist system. In this case, all existing interest groups are effectively suppressed, and political change *is* a significant variable. A growth rate higher than in capitalist developing countries, where group interests prevail, should result from such a change, but such is often not the case. One should then examine more closely

6. Activities where entry has been limited in favor of the same individuals for more than ten or fifteen years.

whether interest groups really do not exist within such systems. Communist party and state propose to develop a consistent policy preventing the reconstitution of economic as well as noneconomic groups; but this deliberate policy to atomize society rests itself on the formation of an omnipotent group—the party—or, more precisely, of a cluster of groups within the party, because party heads have to be distinguished from ordinary members, technicians from politicians, civilians from military, and so on. These groups monopolize various economic responsibilities and fight for a common interest, and their membership remains highly stable.[7] Occasions in which reforms that could increase the efficiency of these economies are consistently refused might be interpreted, according to Olson's hypothesis, as defenses by ruling groups inside the party of their own interests. Such reforms would question or reduce the elements of vested interests of the ruling groups (for example, political and economic power, prestige, a privileged way of life, special liberties, access to goods and services not for sale in ordinary shops, or higher incomes).[8] Such interest groups, owing to the comprehensive powers of the state in these countries, and to the identification of party with state, are probably the most powerful interest groups now existing in developed countries.

In conclusion, these examples suggest an inquiry into the possible relationships between the growth rate and what might be called excess income. Whatever the system, capitalist or socialist, and irrespective of the level of economic development, it is clear that the common aim of any interest group is to obtain for its members some advantage[9] beyond what they would have gotten acting alone. One relationship not considered by Olson is the share of these excess incomes devoted to saving and to domestic productive investment. It is possible that the use of these excess incomes leads to secondary effects unfavorable to growth. For instance, if a group of tradesmen monopolizes export and import of a commodity and obtains excess income that is either consumed or invested abroad, there is a negative secondary effect compared with a situation in which additional incomes obtained by exporters and importers (or households and enterprises, if this monopoly were abolished) would be used for domestic productive investment. It is the same if this group succeeds in increasing their rents

7. Such periods as the Stalinist period in the USSR, or the Maoist period in China, when the party weeded out mostly its own members, must be considered as exceptional. Normally, in other periods or countries, membership of the ruling groups remains very stable.

8. The last element is only a minor one among the various interests of Marxist-socialist groups, as opposed to its status among groups in capitalist countries.

9. "Level of satisfaction" would be a more suitable general term (see note 8).

thanks to import duties or export subsidies beneficial to their products, and if it uses its excess income for luxury consumption or usury at the expense of industrial enterprises that have to finance the subsidies by paying taxes and higher wages (if real wages are to be maintained), so that their means for investment are reduced. Such a negative effect on growth is not always observed, and it would be possible to find cases in which suppressing a group's action would not increase, and would even reduce, the volume of domestic productive investment. Nevertheless, the possibility of increasing incomes through collusion, bribery, and political meddling is probably less favorable to saving and investment than is a socioeconomic system in which investment represents for a given work effort the only way of increasing future incomes.

How Does Olson's Hypothesis Fit the Economic, Social, and Political History of France since the Eighteenth Century?

French growth during the eighteenth century seems to result from stability, not from instability. The French economy obtained its best results since the end of the sixteenth century only after more than thirty years of political, economic (the effects of foreign wars between 1715 and 1750 on the French economy are marginal), and monetary stability. In a preindustrial economy, mostly dominated by agriculture, neither civil wars nor foreign invasions could have had the favorable effects described by Olson. Such disturbances always entail destruction, desertion of part of tilled land, losses and decreases in population, and a heavier fiscal burden for peasants. All this would ruin agriculture; and a decrease in agricultural production would induce a reduction of income in all other sectors. At this stage of economic development, political stability appears as a *sine qua non* for growth.

This does not mean that the Olson hypothesis has no role to play in understanding French growth in the eighteenth century. The core of his theory is the formation and functioning of interest groups and the ways in which these groups reduce the rate of growth. Political instability plays only an indirect part by creating an environment that is unfavorable to groups. If instability as an explanatory factor must be left aside for the eighteenth century, until 1789, can we hold interest groups partly responsible for economic development?

In the *société d'ordres* of the Ancien Régime, common-interest groups benefited from a particularly favorable environment. Vetoes put to every fiscal reform that was intended to decrease the burden on low-income people and increase the taxes on the rich bear clear evidence to this. Each of these planned reforms quickly triggered protests by churchmen, parliamentarians, and nobles,[10] precisely because these people were members of institutional groups. We know the fiscal system of the Ancien Régime to have had a substantial adverse effect on the growth rate. On the other hand, in trade and industry, the state had itself helped the formation of interest groups. Since Colbert, it had enacted laws on manufacturing, which were regularly enforced, it had maintained corporations, and it had given to some groups of tradesmen the monopoly of a foreign or domestic market for trade, insurance, or sea transportation. This policy, intended to stimulate growth, had in fact led to the multiplication of groups, each one enjoying the monopoly of some precisely delineated activity in a town, a province, or even colonies or foreign countries. Thus the state gave to each group what according to Olson is the most important power: that is, the power of limiting entry into industries and occupations under its control. We think that part of the increasing gap between the French and English or Dutch economies between 1650 and 1750 can be attributed to the increasing fraction of nonagricultural production controlled by groups in France as opposed to the decreasing or stable fraction in England or the Netherlands during these years.[11] Many observers of this time thought that prices higher in France than in neighboring countries and delays in introducing new technologies and new products were due to this system of trade groups (each group being in charge of a monopoly given by the state).[12] After the 1750s, the part controlled by trade groups seemed not to increase any more and even began to decrease, owing to new licenses given to rural industries

10. "When Minister of Finance Silhouette decided to levy a new tax of a twentieth, to suspend the privileges on salt, and to tax luxury goods or services such as servants, saddle horses, coaches, gold and silver, . . . the Chambre des Comptes [Accounts Court], the Cour des Aides of Paris [a fiscal court] and the Parliament of Rouen made 'representations' against these measures asking for their suppression." P. Clément and A. Lemoine, *Monsieur de Silhouette, Bouret et les derniers fermiers généraux* (Paris: Didier, 1872), p. 76; M. Marion, *Histoire financière de la France depuis 1715*, vol. 1 (Paris: Arthur Rousseau, 1914), pp. 196–97.

11. In England, for instance, the state guaranteed free entrance to all associations involved in foreign trade and let fall unobserved the old corporate regulations. In the Netherlands, one was free to produce according to demand. See E. Heckscher, *Mercantilism*, vol. 1 (London: G. Allen, 1935), pp. 170–80.

12. S. Vauban, *Projet d'une dixme royale* (1708), pp. 31–37; J.-F. Melon, *Essai politique sur le commerce* (1734), pp. 32, 33, 203. C.-L. de Montesquieu, *L'esprit des Lois*, pt. 4, bk. 20, ch. 12 and 13 (Paris: Gallimard, 1951); the same is true of Boisguilbert and d'Argenson, according to J.-J. Spengler, *Economie et population, les doctrines françaises avant 1800, de Budé à Condorcet* (Paris: Presses Universitaires, 1954), pp. 42, 43, 44, 78.

that expanded out of and free from corporations, with the help of the government. As, following Olson, the rate of growth is reduced by the formation of new groups,[13] we can presume that such development did not occur after 1740 or 1750; this could explain, or help to explain,[14] an increase in growth rate, which in the following years compares with that in England.

Looking at the 1789–1914 period, the years 1789–1871 offer a clear example of instability, with wars followed by foreign invasions at the beginning and at the end and with several great political crises and revolutions intervening. However, it seems impossible to link growth directly to this instability. First, the rate of growth attained by the French economy after 1815 is very low; from 1820 to 1830 agricultural and manufacturing production increased by 8 percent in ten years, against 48.3 percent between 1830 and 1847. True, the 1848–52 years of political upheaval were followed by some of the most prosperous in the century, but from 1871 to 1913 we see that the greatest increase in production (agricultural and manufacturing) was attained after thirty years of stability. During the next four decades, production increased as follows:

1873–1883	22.5 percent		1873–1893	22.5 percent
1883–1893	0			
1893–1903	12.6	or:	1893–1913	45.8
1903–1913	29.8[15]			

On the other hand, a link does appear to exist between rates of growth and the formation or activity of common-interest groups. Each period of stagnation (or of low rates of growth) is marked by the functioning of groups; conversely, the attempts of Napoleon III to reduce the protection of the groups' interests correspond with high rates of growth (agricultural and manufacturing production increases by 44.7 percent from 1852 to 1869), and it is during the *Restauration* of (constitutional) monarchy, a period of low rates of growth even for manufacturing production (a total increase of 20 percent from 1820 to 1830), that the manufacturers obtained high tariffs

13. M. Olson, "The Political Economy of Comparative Growth Rates" (Paper delivered at the Conference on the Political Economy of Comparative Growth Rates, College Park, Md., December 1978), p. 30.

14. Other explanatory factors must be taken into account to understand growth between 1750 and 1780. Such factors play a part in agriculture, a decisive sector, the development of which does not depend on interest-group action.

15. M. Lévy-Leboyer, "Capital Investment and Economic Growth in France, 1820–1930," in P. Mathias and M. M. Postan, eds. *Cambridge Economic History*, vol. 7, pt. 1 (Cambridge: Cambridge University Press, 1978), pp. 292–95.

to protect their products.[16] Protectionist policy expanded during the Third Republic in a comparable manner. After the fall of Napoleon III, the state lacked the will of a liberal policy; however, only twenty-one years later, in 1892, France went back to full protectionism. In 1873 Thiers proposed an important increase in tariffs, which did not pass. A new, moderate increase in duties was voted by Parliament, but in 1892 duties were substantially increased (80 percent on average above the 1881 level) owing to the collusion of agricultural and industrial interest groups and the lobbying of their associations.[17] It should be emphasized that this coalition succeeded only after a decrease of 20 percent in foreign trade between 1882 and 1886, a long stagnation of GNP (the agricultural and manufacturing production in 1892 was the same as in 1882), and a parallel move toward protectionism in many other countries. It is clear from the sequence of events that the successful lobbying of manufacturers and landlords (the increase of agricultural prices benefited the latter more than the farmers) followed rather than anticipated economic stagnation. Relying on their first advantages, the agrarian groups maintained their pressure and obtained still further advantages: higher duties on imports of corn in 1894, alleviated property taxes for small estates in 1897, a subsidy of forty million francs for agricultural loans in 1897, an increase of duties on wine and meat (1899 and 1903, respectively), and subsidies to beetroot, silk, linen, and hemp cultivation.[18] In 1903 the *bouilleurs de cru* ("farmers who distill their own crops") were in such turmoil, because their privilege to produce alcohol without paying taxes had been limited to twenty liters per farmer, that Parliament was induced to set again in 1906 the old complete exemption from taxes, regardless of the quantity produced.[19] These examples prove how the interests of each farmers' group were powerfully represented in Parliament. Such successes were partly the consequence of a swift expansion of agrarian organizations between 1884 and 1914 after a period of

16. The government wanted to establish moderate duties, but pressure from great landowners and manufacturers on representatives in Parliament (Chambre des Députés) led to very high tariffs between 1814 and 1826 on all manufactured and agricultural products. For instance, after having obtained an 80 percent duty on English iron, French producers had it put to 125 percent in 1822 because, even with an 80 percent duty, English iron was still cheaper than French. This collusion even managed to have imposed high duties on such non-French products as tea in order to help, in that case, the sale of wine.

17. Collusion between agrarians and manufacturers was sealed at the 1891 general meeting of the French Society of Farmers by a declaration from the president of the Association of French Industry. See E. Levasseur, *Questions ouvrières et industrielles en France sous la IIIe République* (Paris: Arthur Rousseau, 1907), p. 244.

18. Ibid., p. 254; P. Barral, *Les agrariens français de Méline à Pisani* (Paris: Armand Colin, 1968), p. 92.

19. P. Barral, *Les agrariens français*, p. 103.

relative individualism that had endured from the beginning of the century—a period born in the Revolution, which severed the old links of the rural communities.[20] According to Olson's thesis, the protection of farmers' interests should have hindered modernization. Although in 1913 average productivity in French agriculture was much below that in England, Germany, and the Netherlands, the formation and action of these groups were consequences of difficulties, of the agricultural crisis of the 1880s, and bear no relation to political stability.

In the manufacturing sector, the action of groups was less important if tariff policy is not taken into account. Cartelization of an industry was very rare (it happened only in steel processing and oil distribution); workers' trade unions had no exceptional power (such as the closed-shop system) and encompassed few people (5 percent to 17 percent of workers in industry in 1903, excluding coal mining).[21] On the other hand, the rate of growth of steel processing, a cartelized activity protected by high duties, was not high.[22]

A glance at the 1789–1914 period tells of the nuances which should be added to Olson's thesis. First, if instability means long wars, heavy destruction, economic disorganization, and a standstill of investment, as from 1789 to 1800, the economy needs many years to recover from it; all the more if it is in a preindustrial stage as was the French economy at the beginning of the nineteenth century. True, the Revolution brought to an end a lot of groups whose action and protection could slow down growth, but it also entailed large economic losses, which explain slow growth until

20. Ibid., pp. 104–16.
21. E. Levasseur, *Questions ouvrières et industrielles*, pp. 737–38, 771.
22. Cast iron production per capita is for the nineteenth century one of the best indicators of the relative levels of industrial development. From 1870 onwards, France lagged considerably behind Germany and the United States.

Cast Iron Production Per Capita (kilos)
(quinquennial averages)

	1840	1860	1880	1900	1910
France	12	25	46	65	100
United Kingdom	54	130	220	220	210
Germany	5	14	53	130	200
Russia	3	5	5	25	31
United States	16	25	71	190	270

When total production is considered, the evolution is even more unfavorable to France. In 1870, French production still exceeded that of Germany (1.4 versus 1.2 million tons, respectively); in 1913, it amounted hardly to a third of it (France: 5 million tons; Germany: 16.7). At the same time, Russian production of cast iron and steel nearly caught up to French production.

1830. However, the link within the Second Empire (1852–70, Napoleon III) between a new regime and a policy that was less favorable to interest groups is not a causal one. This policy originated with Napoleon III personally but was not a necessary result of the political change brought by his coming to power. We may say, according to Olson's theory, that actions of some manufacturers' groups since 1820, and of agrarian groups mainly since 1880, have reduced the rate of growth of the French economy and are partly responsible for its poor showing between 1880 and 1914, as compared with those of other countries. But we cannot assume that the formation and action of groups was delayed by political instability between 1789 and 1871. In fact, the events of the 1830s and even those of 1870–71 did very little to hinder the expansion of common-interest groups.[23] The rise of these groups is due first to the backward stage of French industry as compared to English industry (a widening gap from 1790 to 1830) and, second, to the agricultural crises of the 1880s. Social and political stability during the *Restauration* (1815–30), the July Monarchy (1830–48), and the Third Republic (1870–1940) did allow them to expand but was not the cause of their development. Such stability appears as a necessary condition, but not a sufficient one; in fact, common-interest groups were induced by the economic situation.

This conclusion is confirmed by the history of the period from 1914 to the present. We have chosen as hallmark for the beginning of each phase 1922 and 1948 because in each of them, GDP reaches its prewar level. The growth of GDP (deflated by the index of cost of living) was:

1922–1929	35.1 percent
1929–1939	0
1948–1958	65
1958–1968	67.3[24]

From these figures, we see rates of growth which were, except from 1929 to 1939, higher than ever before, a momentum never seen during the eighteenth and nineteenth centuries (when it was never higher than 35 percent in ten years). If growth rates were higher because interest groups had been cut drastically, one would expect to observe great changes between 1914 and 1921 or between 1940 and 1947 in the functioning and

23. One may even consider that political events have contributed to the development of interest groups insofar as the eviction of Napoleon III was that of a statesman who, owing to his personality and power, was free from the influence of these groups.

24. J.-J. Carré, P. Dubois, E. Malinvaud, *La croissance française* (Paris: Editions du Seuil, 1972), p. 35.

power of interest groups. In fact, the two wars and their aftermaths had little effect on the power of these groups. On the contrary, interest groups expanded quickly and increased their power between 1930 and 1939, whereas the opposite movement was observed between 1955 and 1968. Again, the successes or failures of common-interest groups are better explained by the economic situation than by sociopolitical stability or instability.

As regards duties, cartels, or favors to farmers, the situation was nearly the same in 1922 as in 1913. Laws had been passed during the war but were abrogated soon afterward. Duty levels were nearly the same after as before the war, according to the tariff law of July 27, 1919, the revised tariff by decree of August 30, 1927, and the law of March 3, 1928. In 1930, the average level of duties was 12 percent, against 9 percent in 1913. The courts had the same attitude toward cartels as they had had before the war, and prewar jurisprudence was ratified by the law of December 3, 1926.[25] Only a temporary halt can be noticed. Cartels in steel processing disappeared around 1921, to be recreated around 1925. Favors to farmers were maintained. For example, Parliament had decided during the war to abolish the privilege of *bouilleurs de cru* by suppressing the inheritance of it; but the privilege was reestablished between 1919 and 1923. The 1914–18 war consequently changed nearly nothing of the prewar advantages of the common-interest groups. We, therefore, neither impute the high rate of growth between 1922 and 1929 to a reduction in interest-group strength, nor attribute the economic crisis to the expansion of the groups before 1930; but the economy being more and more depressed, common-interest groups expanded so much and obtained so many measures in favor of their interests that, in 1939, the French economy was more dominated by them than at any time since the end of the eighteenth century. The reinforcement of protection (by decisions made in 1931, 1932, 1933, and 1934) is not a uniquely French policy since it is observed in all other countries; but this is not true of the quota system, a far more restrictive policy, since it created rents for importers who were granted licenses.[26] The main phenomenon of the thirties is that more and more activities of existing firms were protected. Farmers obtained subsidies for silk (1930 and 1931), hemp (1932), and olives (1932). A 1936 law stated that a decree will determine the saleable size of the chicory crop, no new farm being allowed to get a quota.

25. On these evolutions, see A. Sauvy, *Histoire économique de la France*, vol. 4 (Paris: Fayard, 1975), pp. 9–78.
26. Ibid., pp. 31–32.

A 1935 law forbade the creation of new mills or reopening of those closed before 1930 as well as any increase of production.[27]

In industry and services, several sectors obtained measures forbidding creation of new plants, introduction of technological change by modifying plants, and any increase in the market share of a firm. Such is the aim of a common-interest group: block access to the profession by any newcomer and maintain the current share of the market among firms. In this way, the opening of any new plant in the shoe industry, as well as any enlarging or modifying of an existing one, was forbidden in 1936. Similarly, in 1935 the creation of new firms in the sugar industry was forbidden.[28] At the same time new cartels were formed for coal (1932), azote (1934), and cement (1934). The same restrictive practice applied to services. A 1934 law created transportation cards (or rights to transport) benefiting road transporters; these saleable and inheritable cards gave a monopolistic rent to their holders. A similar practice was applied to cabs in 1937. Small retail shops were protected by other measures against circulation of new mobile bazaars (1935) and opening of new retail shops or enlarging of existing ones (1936), and fiscal restraints on department stores were reinforced.[29] Only parliamentary delays kept similar regulations from being passed for other activities. They all aimed at monopoly and market sharing for existing firms. Public opinion, whether rightist or leftist, more or less approved of such plans. When the National Economic Council asked the Conseil d'Etat about it, the answer was in favor of the *ententes* ("collusions").[30]

The labor market evolved along the same lines. The number of foreign workers grew from 1.4 million in 1919 to 2.7 million in 1931 without any objection to this inflow. On the contrary, a law easing naturalization was passed in 1927. The economic crisis altered that entirely; public opinion inclined toward holding the foreigners responsible for unemployment. A 1932 law set a quota on foreign manpower in each sector. In 1939, the 500,000 Spanish refugees in France were settled in camps and forbidden to work.[31] Other wage earners succeeded in defending their positions. For instance, civil servants vigorously protested against the 1933–35 deflation policy and contributed to the 1936 victory of the Front Populaire although

27. Ibid., vol. 2, pp. 369–70.
28. Ibid., vol. 4, p. 70.
29. Ibid., vol. 2, pp. 373–74.
30. On this advice of the Conseil d'Etat, see ibid., vol. 4, p. 76. At the same time, several plans for a professional organization were written, which were more or less akin to corporatism.
31. Ibid., vol. 2, p. 377.

their real income had increased by 15 percent between 1930 and 1935, much more quickly than that of other wage earners when their lower probability of joblessness is taken into account. In the same way, in well-protected sectors (tobacco, state-owned manufacturers, and sugar refineries), real salaries were increasing more than the average.[32] Thus, better-organized wage earners were able to lessen the effects of the crisis on their income.

We are brought to a twofold conclusion: first, the creation and action of common-interest groups allowed many workers or self-employed to avoid the consequences of the crisis at the cost of unprotected workers. The relatively stable parliamentary democracy and the weakness of executive power allowed this behavior. In turn, these policies aggravated and lengthened the crisis; from 1929 to 1939 the decrease of industrial production was greater in France than in any other industrial country.[33]

Logically, it should be expected that the events of 1939–45 would have compromised or even suppressed the advantages obtained by common-interest groups. During these six years, France went through foreign invasions, occupation, three different political regimes (Third Republic, Etat Français, and Fourth Republic) and such important structural changes as nationalization, all of which bore more weight than those of 1914–18. However, many groups maintained their advantages throughout this period, and economic liberalization took place only later, notably after 1958. True, during the German occupation, in a penurious situation, it was natural that well-organized professional or corporative associations would increase their shares in each sector; but liberalization did not follow the end of the war. Privileges acquired by some groups were maintained until the 1950s and even the 1960s; those of cabs and alcohol distillers and the protection of small retail shops against supermarkets are examples. Transporters' rights were lessened by an enlargement of quotas, but only little by little. Millers' rights were preserved. If a mill happened to have been destroyed during the war, the state would finance its reconstruction regardless of the existing capacities in the region.[34] Very soon after the end of the war the beetroot producers, thanks to their influence on newspapers and in Parliament, again received their prewar privileges regarding alcohol distillation versus sugar production. Only in 1954 did the government exam-

32. Ibid., pp. 132–34.
33. The only economic betterment observed under the Paul Reynaud government of 1938–39 is due to a liberal policy involving a loosening of price controls and the forty-hours law.
34. A. Sauvy, *Histoire économique de la France*, p. 37.

ine this right.[35] Lastly, the market situation was not modified. Price controls lasted until 1957. The law on ententes changed in 1953, but in a modest way, since the ententes commission heard only about twenty-five cases between 1955 and 1959.

This example shows that political instability does not necessarily entail the disappearance or weakening of common-interest groups. On the other hand, the quick growth of the fifties and sixties allowed a liberalization of the economy at the interest groups' expense, their particular losses being compensated for by the general benefits of this growth. In turn, liberalization contributed to growth from 1958 onwards by the same causal link that operated in the 1930s, but the other way round.

The entry of France into the European Economic Community has been a determining factor in liberalization: from 1958 onwards, there was a return to relatively free prices. Another set of price controls was decreed in 1963 but was loosened in 1966 (they disappeared only by 1979 in industry). Suppression of ententes developed in the sixties, and since 1966 some penal suits have been led by the state.[36] French industry is not more protected than the industry of other EEC countries. In the commercial sector law and tax reforms have allowed supermarkets and chain stores to develop.[37] As Carré, Dubois, and Malinvaud have shown, both labor and capital markets have become more competitive.[38] Wage structure has depended increasingly on the market law of supply and demand since about 1955, and geographic mobility continues to increase. Elsewhere, the capital market in the middle and long term, which was very narrow until 1955 and reserved to a few big firms, broadened between 1955 and 1965 with the result of increased facilities for issuing bonds and ease in getting loans from banks. Significantly, the first liberalizing measures date to 1955, some ten years after a burst of growth; and the Rueff-Armand Committee report, a study of barriers against economic expansion, clearly shows the many cases in which common-interest groups had, up until then, maintained their advantages.[39]

35. Private common-interest groups were not the only ones maintaining their advantages after 1945; the same held true in the public sector. Such high civil servants' "corps" as that of the Inspection des Finances retained or got back after the war the monopoly of some of the highest positions in the administration, in spite of the attitudes of some of their members during the war.

36. Carré et al., *La croissance française*, p. 558.

37. Ibid., p. 560.

38. Ibid., pp. 536–46.

39. The report clearly defines these advantages: "It is easily observed that some actual economic laws or regulations have the effect, even if not aiming to, of unduly protecting corporate interests which may be adverse to the general interest and particularly to the goals of expansion. Such is the case when

Thus, examples found in French economic history since the eighteenth century lead to a different interpretation of Olson's thesis, at least for France. The effects of social and political instability on common-interest groups cannot be overestimated, since these groups often manage to preserve their privileges under all except revolutionary conditions. On the other hand, the economic situation is decisive in developing (when crisis or recession comes) or weakening (when expansion is swift) these groups. This remark is quite compatible with the link put forward by Olson between the role of interest groups and the rate of growth. It leads us to suggest a growth, or stagnation, model in which common-interest groups are both a consequence and a cause of growth. Olson has identified a variable which is essential to understanding the self-sustaining nature of growth or recession.

laws or regulations have the effect of unduly blocking access to some trades or professions, maintaining unjustified privilege protecting or even encouraging obsolete forms of production or activity, crystallizing in their positions the holders of certain rights, thus giving to some parts of the French economy a structure of 'offices' which was so widely known before the Revolution'' (p. 18). The report cites flour-milling and bakeries, as well as the notaries', barristers', chemists', sea-traders', and taxi-drivers' professions among activities thus regulated to the benefit of private interests. The report goes on to propose to reinforce public action against ententes, to reduce by 40 percent the quantity of distilled beets, and to ensure equal treatment of commercial firms regardless of their size (pp. 40–66). These proposals show that many common-interest groups had partly or even totally retained, in 1960, advantages obtained before the war—some dating back to the nineteenth century.

9: The Political Economy of Comparative Growth Rates: The Case of France

JEAN-FRANÇOIS HENNART

In contrast to other developed countries such as England or the United States, whose patterns of growth have been relatively continuous, France's economic development has been characterized by alternation between rapid growth and relative stagnation. The process of growth seems always to have been arrested before it could truly become self-sustaining. Placed in an historical context, therefore, the postwar expansion appears exceptional: never before has industrial production grown at such a high rate over such an extended period of time.[1]

An analysis of the sources of this growth shows that it has been accomplished not so much by the addition of new factors of production as by the better utilization of previously underutilized capacities. Whatever obstacles had been responsible for the relative backwardness of the French economy have at least partially been lifted since the war.

What were those hindrances and what factors are responsible for their reduction? In the following pages I argue that the opening of the French economy to outside competition has been the principal determinant of its postwar performance. The resulting increase in the degree of competition in the economy, which has had cumulative effects on growth, has been fostered by external pressures for economic and political integration at a time when the internal forces that had previously resisted such pressures were relatively weak.

I thank Robert Hennart, Bernard Lentz, Georges Moquet, and Dennis Mueller for many helpful suggestions.

1. According to Jean-Jacques Carré, Paul Dubois, and Edmond Malinvaud, *La croissance française: un essai d'analyse causale de l'après guerre* (Paris: Seuil, 1972), p. 32, the average annual rate of growth of productive sectors and services was 4.7 percent over the 1949–69 period. Over the 1969–73 period, the rate stands at 6.6 percent. Between 1949 and 1969, the average annual rate of growth of productive sectors (production intérieure brute) was 5 percent. This compares with 2.5 percent for 1906–13 and 4.4 percent for 1922–29, the two other periods of rapid growth.

French Economic Growth in Historical Perspective

The historical pattern of French economic growth is particularly rich and complex. In 1800 France was the largest world producer of manufactures and handicrafts, with a production 70 percent higher than Great Britain.[2] A century later, France had lost its economic preeminence to England, Germany, and the United States.

The relative slowness of economic development in France is reflected in the growth rate of per-capita income over the 1830–1930 period. French per-capita income grew at an average annual rate of 1.1 percent, compared with 1.4 percent for Germany and 1.6 percent for the United States. The rate of economic growth in England was comparable to that of France, but England had already achieved a high level of per-capita income by 1830 and therefore ended the period with a higher level. France thus failed to capitalize on the Industrial Revolution to the same extent as England, Germany, or the United States.[3]

The average growth rate of 1.1 percent hides, however, significant differences in the pace of economic progress. From 1820 to 1870, French growth was rapid, both in the industrial and farm sectors. After 1870 and until 1896, growth slowed considerably. Agricultural production stagnated, industrial production grew slowly; France was losing its relative standing. In 1870, U.S. pig iron production was 30 percent higher than that of France and Germany. In 1896, the United States produced 3.8 times and Germany 2.4 times as much pig iron as France; but after 1896 the pace of growth in France picked up again. Between 1896 and 1929, agricultural production increased at an average rate of 0.5 percent per year, and industrial production at a 2.5 percent rate. Simultaneously, there was a marked increase in the average size of agricultural and industrial production units.[4]

The Great Depression put an end to this period of rapid growth. Domestic industrial production fell continuously until 1936. Only in 1939 was the

2. French population was about three times larger. England overtook France in per-capita income as early as 1600.
3. Carré et al., *La croissance française*, p. 20. Other authors cite slightly different figures. See M. Levy-Leboyer, "La croissance économique de la France au XIX siècle, résultats préliminaires," *Annales, Economies, Sociétés, Civilisations* 4 (July–August 1968): 788–807, and "La décélération de l'économie française dans la seconde moitié du XIX siècle," *Revue d'histoire économique et sociale* no. 4 (1971): 485–507; T. J. Markovitch, "L'industrie française de 1789 à 1964," *Cahiers de l'ISEA*, série AF, no. 7 (1966); F. Crouzet, "Essai de construction d'un indice de la production industrielle pour le XIXe siècle," *Annales* 25, no. 1 (January–February 1970):56–99; J. Marczewski, "Le produit physique de l'économie française de 1789 à 1913," *Cahiers de l'ISEA*, série AF, no. 4 (July 1965).
4. Carré et al., *La croissance française*, p. 24.

1929 production level reattained.[5] The defeat of 1940 revealed a country in full decomposition: paralyzed by internal dissensions, unable to react to outside challenges, prisoner of antiquated economic and mental structures. In 1945 most observers were pessimistic as to France's economic prospects.

Yet the economic performance of France since the war has been outstanding. Between 1950 and 1975, French GDP grew at an average annual rate of 4.7 percent, lower than Japan's 8.6 percent, Germany's 5.7 percent, and Italy's 4.8 percent, but considerably higher than the 3.3 percent of the United States, and England's 2.6 percent.[6] A careful analysis of available statistics shows that this exceptional growth cannot be attributed to a mere "catching up" of the retardation due to the Depression and the war. One would expect the immediate postwar years to be characterized by fast growth as the economy attempted to return to prewar civilian production levels, but growth has continued long after 1948, when the 1929 (and 1939) production levels were reached.[7] In fact, all available economic indicators point to an acceleration of the secular growth rate since 1945.[8]

The magnitude and the constancy of the growth rate over the 1945–73 period are in contrast with past patterns of episodic growth. The fact that growth has been self-sustaining suggests that qualitative changes have taken place. One suspects that the growth-retarding factors that have eventually slowed down every other boom have not been effective since 1945.

The characteristics of the postwar economic expansion confirm this hypothesis. In marked contrast to such countries as Germany or Italy, the main source of economic growth has not been an increase in the quantity of factors of production, but a better utilization of existing resources. The postwar expansion can thus be attributed for a large part to the realization of potentialities that previously had been neglected.

---

5. Ibid., p. 35.

6. "Check up d'un géant," *L'Expansion* (July–August 1976): 62.

7. Carré et al., *La croissance française*, p. 35, Catching up relative to the United States was also taking place. Part of the postwar growth can be attributed to the adoption of U.S. technical processes and managerial techniques. The "productivity missions" organized under the Marshall Plan played an important role in bringing French productivity closer to the U.S. level.

8. Per-capita product grew at an average rate of 3.7 percent between 1949 and 1963, compared with 1.5 percent during the 1896–1929 expansion. Labor productivity also grew at a much faster rate after the war. As early as 1950, labor productivity in agriculture had started to surpass its 1900–29 trend. The same acceleration in productivity growth has taken place in industry since 1965. See ibid., pp. 136, 142, 613.

The Sources of Postwar Growth

The traditional approach to economic growth attributes increases in national income to increases in the quantity and quality of factors of production. Such a theoretical framework has limited explanatory power when applied to French growth after World War II.

By fitting a Cobb-Douglas production function with data on industrial production and labor and capital inputs (in efficiency units), J. J. Carré et al. have tried to determine the fraction of the 1951–69 growth rate of industrial production attributable to an increase in labor and capital. The results, presented in table 9.1, show that increases in the supply of factors explain less than half of the period's 5 percent growth rate. A significant contribution is made by more efficient allocation of labor resources. Half of the overall growth rate remains unexplained.

According to the calculations of Carré et al., there was no increase in total man-hours and a slight decrease in the average number of hours worked. The quality of the workforce, however, improved significantly. That improvement was due to an increase in the educational level of the workforce and in the intensity of work per hour (a consequence of the shortening of the work week). Altogether, the net increase in the quantity and quality of labor is responsible for a 0.3 percent growth rate.

Capital's contribution was greater. A little over 1 percent was due to an

Table 9.1.   Analysis of the Growth Rate of French Industrial Production, 1951–69
(percent per year)

Production Intérieure Brute		5.0
Labor inputs	man-years	0.0
	length of work	−0.1
	quality of work[a]	0.4
	intersectoral migrations	0.6
Capital inputs	net increase	1.1
	vintage effects	0.4
Demand factors		0.1
Residual		2.5

SOURCE: J. J. Carré, P. Dubois, and E. Malinvaud, *La croissance française*, p. 275.

NOTE: This table refers to the Production Intérieure Brute, which is equal to the domestic production of productive sectors. It excludes therefore government, finance, insurance and real estate, sectors which are not considered productive in French National Accounts.
a. This category includes the effect of age structure, educational level, and intensity of work.

increase in the stock of capital, and an additional 0.4 percent to vintage effects. Altogether, less than 40 percent of the 1951–69 rate of growth can be explained by increases in factors of production.

One can draw two conclusions from this analysis. First, France's economic performance is not due to increases in its labor force nor in the workers' willingness to work. Second, improvements in the allocation of resources have made a significant contribution to the rate of growth. That such improvements have been sustained over the 1951–69 period suggests that deep structural changes have taken place in the French economy. It is these structural changes that differentiate the postwar period most from the preceding periods.

Structural Changes since the War

Since 1945, there has been a marked increase in the mobility of labor across occupations, across sectors, and across space. These three dimensions overlap, since one type of movement often implies the other two.

Geographical mobility has increased continuously during this century and was 50 percent higher in 1962 than in 1901. Between 1962 and 1968 it was 30 percent higher than over the 1954–62 period.[9]

The magnitude of intersectoral migrations has also been exceptional. The major movement of labor has been out of agriculture. France did not experience in the nineteenth century the rapid transformation of agriculture that characterized British and American economic growth.[10] No doubt the poor performance of the French economy during that century is at least in part attributable to the maintenance of excess labor in the farming sector.

By contrast, the pace of agricultural outmigration since 1949 has been brisk. The average annual rate of decrease in the share of the labor force employed in agriculture had been 1 percent over the 1896–1929 period and zero between 1929 and 1949; it increased to 3.3 percent between 1949 and 1968.[11] Between 1968 and 1974 the share of agriculture, forestry, and fishing in the total labor force declined another 5.3 percent, to a little less than 10 percent. Altogether, more than three and a half millions left farming after 1949. Over the 1954–75 period, about 340,000 small shopkeepers, 224,000 artisans, and 3,000 fisherman also left their occupations.[12]

9. Ibid., p. 538.
10. Ibid., p. 213.
11. Ibid., p. 214.
12. "En vingt ans, deux millions et demi de cadres en plus," *L'Expansion* (September 1977):41.

Carré et al. have tried to evaluate the contribution of these migrations to the 1951–69 average yearly growth rate. After correcting for differences in productivity due to differences in the age/sex ratio and differences in the level of education between agricultural migrants and the labor force as a whole, they estimated marginal productivity in agriculture to be between 30 and 45 percent of that in industry. They also estimated that the productivity of artisans and small shopkeepers doubled when they left their jobs for employment in the other sectors of the economy. Altogether, Carré et al. calculated that labor migration contributed 0.6 percent to the 5 percent annual growth rate achieved in the 1951–69 period.[13] Denison's own estimate, based on a higher evaluation of the gains in productivity due to professional migrations, is 0.9 percent.[14]

The calculations of both Carré et al. and Denison can only give a lower bound to the impact of these structural changes on the French economy, for they only take into account the static effects of the changes. Outmigration, however, has also had dynamic effects.

One of the main reasons for the relative backwardness of French agriculture was that French farms were too small to allow for the efficient use of modern farming techniques. Statistics show an acceleration in the movement toward larger production units. From 1892 to 1929, the number of farms smaller than one hectare (about three acres) decreased at an average annual rate of 0.5 percent. Between 1955 and 1967, that rate stood at 1.9 percent. The share of all tillable land in farms larger than twenty hectares increased over the same period from 61 to 69 percent.[15]

The service sector also seems to have been subject to important structural changes. The only reliable data concern the trade and hotel sectors. From 1906 to 1931, medium- and large-scale units grew. Thus, the share of the labor force in this sector employed in units of fewer than six employees decreased 20 percent over that twenty-five-year period. After 1954, the decline of small units accelerated, since the proportion of units with fewer than six employees decreased 18 percent in the twelve years between that year and 1968.[16] This decline in the relative importance of the *petit commerce,* often considered one of the most characteristic of French institutions, has continued unabated up to this day. Between 1967 and

13. Carré et al., *La croissance française,* pp. 229–32, 277.
14. Edward Denison, *Why Growth Rates Differ* (Washington: Brookings Institution, 1967), pp. 209–16.
15. Carré et al., *La croissance française,* pp. 229–32.
16. Ibid., p. 235.

1976, the share of retail sales of large retail outlets increased from 5 percent to 18 percent.[17]

Most changes in French industry between 1945 and 1966 have affected small and medium-sized firms. The available data on plant sizes (as measured by their employment) show a large decline in very small firms and a stability in the relative importance of large establishments. In 1906, 58 percent of the labor force in industry worked in plants employing fewer than ten workers. In 1936 that percentage was still nearly 40 percent, but by 1954 it had declined to 25 percent and in 1966 it was only 20 percent. Data on concentration ratios also show an increase between 1955 and 1964 in the concentration of small enterprises, with no increase in the share of sales by the largest 10 percent.[18] This reorganization of industrial production into larger units better able to take advantage of economies of scale must have had a substantial impact on the productivity of both labor and capital in the industrial sector.[19]

A tendency toward larger establishments can lead to economies of scale and to increases in productivity; but changes in the internal structure of firms, though more difficult to evaluate, can also lead to important efficiency gains.

Since 1965, there has been a marked increase in the number of mergers and in the value of the assets transferred.[20] This wave of mergers has been accompanied by an unprecedented number of company reorganizations. Between 1960 and 1970, two-thirds of the 100 largest French companies underwent a change in strategy, in structure, or in both (the percentage was 40 percent between 1950 and 1960). United States management consultants played a crucial role in these reorganizations, and during that period U.S. management techniques were rapidly assimilated. The number of students in U.S.-patterned business schools increased dramatically. As one American consultant put it, "French management acted like a power vacuum cleaner in its acquisitions of U.S. systems, techniques, and con-

17. *L'Expansion* (September 1977):171.
18. Carré et al., *La croissance française*, p. 227.
19. In the 1950s, 48 percent of French workers were employed in plants of "reasonably efficient scale," vs. 70 percent in the United States. See Joe S. Bain, *International Differences in Industrial Structure* (New Haven: Yale University Press, 1966), pp. 132, 139, 164.
20. Bernard Guibert et al., "La mutation industrielle de la France," *Les collections de l'INSEE*, series E, no. 31–32 (November 1975):93–99. One result of this wave of mergers has been the increase between 1963 and 1969 of the mean (turnover-weighted) concentration ratio in industry from 20.08 to 22.11. See F. Jenny and A. P. Weber, *Concentration et politique des structures industrielles* (Paris: Documentation Française, 1974).

cepts over the last few years.''[21] By the early seventies, modern management techniques and structures had been formally adopted in a large number of French enterprises. In many ways, however, management behavior was still lagging.[22]

There has also been a slower, but no less important, transformation in the structure of ownership. Many authors, among them David Landes, have described France as the country of family firms.[23] In such firms, ownership is tightly held by family members, outside financing is shunned for fear of losing control, and management positions are kept within the family. Conservation of the family fortune, rather than development of the business, is the goal of the enterprise. Family firms are usually most efficient when kept small, and France can offer many outstanding examples of successful family enterprises. However, because of the personalized nature of management in such firms, family control becomes inefficient as the firms grow in size. When the optimum size of the firm increases, other forms of organization must be chosen.

The persistence of family control over large enterprises that has been a characteristic of the French economy is no doubt one of the factors explaining the poor efficiency and lack of dynamism of the greater part of French industry up until the last war. In 1971, families still controlled half of the 200 largest firms. Recent data show that this situation is changing, with large family firms being taken over by foreign corporations, state-owned enterprises and financial institutions.[24]

The sixties thus saw a dramatic change in the size, structure, and management of French firms. French managers are now paying more attention to profitability and marketing, and there is a greater determination to make efficient use of the firms' resources. A crude indication of this fact is the doubling between 1957 and 1974 of the percentage of workers working multiple shifts.[25]

The recent period has thus been characterized by an acceleration of structural changes in the French economy. In thirty years the small and

21. Gareth P. Dyas and Heinz T. Thanheiser, *The Emerging European Enterprise* (London: Macmillan, 1976), pp. 189, 267.
22. David Granick, *Managerial Comparisons of Four Developed Countries: France, Britain, United States, and Russia* (Cambridge: M.I.T. Press, 1972). See also Jean-François Hennart, *A Theory of Multinational Enterprise* (Ann Arbor: University of Michigan Press, 1982), pp. 141–50.
23. David Landes, "French Business and the Businessman: A Social and Cultural Analysis," in *Modern France*, ed. E. M. Earle (Princeton: Princeton University Press, 1950), pp. 334–53.
24. François Morin, *La structure financière du capitalisme français* (Paris: Calmann-Levy, 1974), p. 220. See also "Naissance des géants tricolores," *L'Expansion* (September 1977):169–73.
25. It increased from 14.3 to 31.3 percent. *L'Expansion* (July–August 1978):84.

inefficient farms, workshops, and neighborhood stores, which had characterized the French economy, have made way for larger and more efficient units. The main force behind these changes has been the opening of the economy to outside competition.

The Cause of French Backwardness

If France was in 1945 the country of small factories, small shopkeepers, and small autarkic farmers, the responsibility lies in seventy-five years of protectionism. In 1870, France's economic prospects looked bright. The signing of the 1860 Treaty of Commerce with England led to the rapid expansion of the economy and particularly to the modernization of its steel industry;[26] but soon the liberal policies were abandoned. The rapid reduction in transportation costs after 1870 increased the competitiveness of agricultural products imported from newly settled countries. The fall in agricultural prices, joined to a series of poor harvests and the destruction of a substantial part of the French vineyards by the phylloxera epiphytotic, reduced internal demand for industrial goods. Whereas Denmark and the Netherlands adapted to the new economic conditions caused by cheap imports, France protected itself behind a tariff wall.

In 1881, but especially in 1892, tariffs on agricultural and industrial goods were raised. These protectionist policies slowed down considerably the development of French agriculture and industry.

The Great Depression led to further doses of what some French authors have called *Malthusianisme économique*. Faced with overproduction and lower prices, the French chose to organize scarcity. The average ad valorem tariff on manufactures, which had been 16 percent in 1913, was raised to 30 percent.[27] More detrimental to world trade was the generalization of quotas. These affected 65 percent of all imports in 1936. In agriculture, efforts were made to support the price of wheat and wine above the domestic market clearing price, and, to avoid overproduction, measures were taken to limit yields and acreage. Unprofitable crops—natural silk, hemp, and olives, among others—were subsidized. In industry, competition was reduced by cartels, which maintained prices at their precrisis level by limiting production. Money-losing enterprises were bought by the gov-

26. André Philip, *Histoire des faits économiques et sociaux* (Paris: Aubier-Montaigne, 1963), p. 125.
27. Lawrence Franko, *The European Multinationals* (Stamford, Conn.: Greylock Publishers, 1976), p. 85.

ernment to keep them afloat. Direct investment by foreign firms was discouraged. The search for stability and order at the cost of efficiency and progress that is characteristic of the period was also extended to the service sector. Truck transportation was subjected to licensing, and licenses were kept scarce. The establishment of modern forms of distribution was forbidden by law.[28] Immigration was also severely restricted, and in 1933 and 1934 one million foreign workers were deported.[29]

World War II did not interrupt these "Malthusianist" policies. Up until the late fifties, there was little competition in the French economy. Exchange controls, import quotas, and licenses closed off the French market from foreign competition. Raw materials were allocated by trade associations. In many important sectors, such as steel, cement, chemicals, petroleum, electrical machinery, glass, bicycles, paper, and steel tubes, professional associations fixed prices and allocated production.[30] They were helped in that task by a system of price controls with prices set at a level which would assure a precarious survival to the least efficient firms in the industry.[31]

The Impact of the Common Market

The turning point in French economic policies was the opening of the country to foreign competition with the signing in 1952 and 1957 of the treaties establishing the European Coal and Steel Community and the European Economic Community (hereinafter ECSC and EEC).

By adhering to the EEC treaty, France agreed to the abolition of tariffs and quotas between the six members of the union, to the establishment of a common tariff with third countries, to the free circulation of labor and capital within the six member countries, to the instauration of competition on European markets, to the establishment of a common agricultural policy, and to the coordination of economic, financial, and social policies with its five partners.

The potential economic advantages of the treaty to the French economy promised to be substantial. The elimination of trade barriers was expected to lead to the concentration of production into larger, more specialized

28. Alfred Sauvy, *Histoire économique de la France entre les deux guerres,* vol. 2 (Paris: Fayard, 1967), pp. 358–78, 450.

29. Charles Kindleberger, *Europe's Postwar Growth* (Cambridge: Harvard University Press, 1967), p. 179.

30. Henri Ehrmann, *La politique du patronnat français* (Paris: Armand Colin, 1959), p. 315.

31. Carré et al., *La croissance française,* p. 549.

plants that would enjoy lower costs through the capture of economies of scale. Inefficient tariff factories of suboptimal size would be closed. A greater international division of labor within Europe would increase efficiency in production. The provisions of the treaty on the free circulation of labor and capital were also expected to increase economic efficiency by transferring resources from countries where they were abundant to countries where they were scarce. Last, the antitrust provisions of the treaty would improve the allocation of resources by reducing the degree of monopoly in the economy.

The impact of the EEC on the French economy has differed significantly from these predictions. On one hand, some of the potential benefits of the treaty have been forsaken because of the uneven application of its provisions. On the other, third countries have played a major (and somewhat unsuspected) role in the process of economic integration.

The three main provisions of the Treaty of Rome have been unevenly applied. Trade liberalization was swift. By 1968, internal tariffs and quotas had been abolished and the common external tariff was in force. On the other hand, the free circulation of labor and capital within the EEC is still far from being realized; barriers to the mobility of labor remain formidable. If today the movement of capital between EEC countries is much freer than it was before 1960, direct investment and investment in real estate are still, in France, subject to controls, and national bond markets are practically closed to other EEC countries.[32] Enforcement of the treaty's provisions banning restrictive practices was negligible until 1968; since then the EEC commission has been more aggressive.[33]

This somewhat disappointing record has been compensated for by the significant contribution made by third countries (and especially the United States) to European integration. The creation of the Common Market has attracted a sizeable amount of direct investment from the United States. Between 1959 and 1972, the book value of this direct investment in the six EEC countries increased from 2.1 billion to 16.8 billion dollars. In 1964, the share of U.S. subsidiaries in the Continental market ranged from 0.3 percent in primary and fabricated metals to 7.3 percent in transportation equipment. But the impact of direct investment from the United States has been much greater than these (rather outdated) figures would suggest.

---

32. "L'intégration européenne des marchés des capitaux: Réalité, mythe ou nécéssité?," *Problèmes économiques*, no. 1538 (1977):10.
33. Franko, *The European Multinationals*, p. 152.

American firms have been much more ready than their European rivals to supply all Common Market countries from a few large, specialized plants. Conditioned by a competitive home market, they have fought aggressively for market shares. The accusations of unruly and ungentlemanly behavior that have been leveled against them by their European rivals show that they have often upset restrictive practices. It is no coincidence that industries in which market competition and interpenetration have been the greatest (transportation equipment and electrical machinery, for example) are also those in which U.S. firms have the largest market shares.[34]

National Economic Consequences

Thus while European states have generally tried to resist integration, outsiders have attempted to make the best of it. The net result of these diverging forces has been beneficial to the French economy. In a static perspective, a better allocation of resources has been attained by greater specialization and a reduction of the degree of monopoly in the economy. From a dynamic point of view, membership in the Common Market has neutralized some of the growth-retarding forces present in French society.

The establishment of the Common Market has led to major changes in the level and in the structure of French foreign trade. The share of imports in the domestic market for agricultural and industrial products increased from 9.4 percent in 1960 to 22.2 percent in 1976.[35] More importantly, there has been a dramatic shift in structure. In 1960, 30 percent of French exports were sold on the protected markets of the former colonies; today, more than half of French exports are directed to the more competitive Common Market countries.[36] There is therefore more competition on domestic and export markets than twenty years ago.

The increase in the degree of specialization of the French economy is shown by the fact that since 1963 imports and exports have grown significantly faster than domestic production. French producers have thus abandoned less competitive products to imports and have increased the produc-

34. Ibid., p. 159.
35. Yves Barou, Michel Dollé, Christian Gabet, and Erwin Wattenberg, "Les performances comparées de l'économie en France, en R.F.A., et au Royaume Uni," *Les Collections de l'INSEE*, series E, no. 69 (November 1979):266.
36. In 1952, the geographical distribution of French exports by country of destination was the following: Franc zone, 42 percent; other less-developed countries, 15 percent; Common Market countries, 15 percent; other countries, 27 percent. In 1970: Franc zone, 10 percent; other less-developed countries, 13 percent; Common Market countries, 50 percent; other countries, 27 percent. See Guibert et al., "La Mutation industrielle de la France," p. 47.

tion of goods and services in which they had a comparative advantage.[37] This is true for both agriculture and industry.

Since the opening of the Common Market in agricultural products, France has increased its specialization in cereals, sugar beets, and milk and has experienced an acceleration of agricultural outmigration.[38] This exodus has allowed an increase in the average size of farms and a substantial improvement in the land and labor productivity of agriculture.[39] There is thus no doubt that the creation of a common market in agricultural products has been an important factor in the modernization of French agriculture.

In all industrial sectors, imports have increased their market share. The surge in foreign penetration has been especially marked for equipment and consumption goods.[40] The development of trade has greatly heightened interdependence and specialization in automobiles and electrical appliances. In most other industries, the major factor in interpenetration of markets has not been trade, but foreign direct investment. Between 1959 and 1971, the sixty-nine largest Belgian, Luxembourgian, French, German, Italian, and Dutch companies entered 1,436 foreign sales and manufacturing subsidiaries in the EEC. The number of subsidiary links formed by these firms was comparable to that of their large U.S. counterparts. In some sectors, such as steel, petroleum refining, nonferrous metals, engines and turbines for power generation, and communications equipment, the creation of local subsidiaries was the result of the preference given in government contracts to locally made products and of government subsidies to local subsidiary production. In other sectors, such as food and pharmaceuticals, local subsidiary production was the only way to get around nontariff barriers set up by national governments.[41]

In many industries, the persistence of nontariff barriers prevented the realization of expected economies of scale; but, through exports or subsidiary production, the degree of competition in each national market in-

---

37. Carré et al., *La croissance française*, p. 501.

38. "L'agriculture française dans le marché commun," *Problèmes économiques*, no. 1524 (1977):11. The average yearly rate of decline of the agricultural labor force increased from 3.3 percent between 1960 and 1965 to 3.7 percent between 1965 and 1970. See "L'Europe agricole et l'élargissement du Marché Commun," *Notes et études documentaires*, no. 4061–2–3 (February 1974):37.

39. Wheat yields increased from 33.5 quintals per hectare in 1959 to 43.7 quintals per hectare in 1973. Barley and corn yields also showed significant increases. See "L'Europe agricole et l'élargissement du Marché Commun," p. 19.

40. Equipment goods include machinery and transportation equipment; consumption goods include textiles, clothing, leather, printing, and miscellaneous manufacturing. See Barou et al., "Les performances comparées," p. 266.

41. Franko, *The European Multinationals*, pp. 155–57, 134–60.

creased substantially. This is shown in the case of France by the decline in profit rates of industrial firms over the 1953–63 period. Part of that decline was due to a high rate of capital investment, but the increase in competition must have played an important role, since the decrease in profit rates was particularly strong in sectors exposed to international competition.[42]

The Impact of Common Market Membership on Common-interest Groups

Perhaps the most significant result of Common Market membership has been the neutralization of growth-retarding common-interest organizations. Two factors have been at work: first, French sovereignty over some important economic matters has been reduced. Second, the power of French organized interests has been adversely affected by the internationalization of the French economy.

In pre-Market days, common-interest organizations had only to lobby the appropriate government ministries. Today the French government's power over many economic matters is more limited. Lobbying for the defense of particular privileges has become more difficult as each interest group finds itself faced with a larger number of competitors.

One can identify three examples of this process at work. The economic basis of the 1957 treaty was the realization by France that a customs union with such major importers of agricultural products as Germany, Italy, and Belgium would provide the demand stimulus necessary to modernize its backward agriculture. In exchange, Germany was to obtain the opening of the EEC market to its industrial goods and the promises of other EEC countries to lower their external tariffs so as to increase its exports to third countries. The internal logic of the Common Market has thus forced France to accept a significant decrease in the level of protection accorded its industries, since with the signing of the Kennedy Round external industrial tariffs were lowered by an average of 40 percent. Similarly, the extension of the EEC to the United Kingdom and Denmark is now threatening the high level of support prices benefiting French wheat and sugar beet growers.

Membership in the Common Market also makes a return to the old tradition of protectionism more difficult. In 1963, when competition from U.S. subsidiaries was starting to affect French industry seriously, De

42. Carré et al., *La croissance française*, p. 384.

Gaulle attempted to restrict foreign direct investment from the United States. But that strategy proved ineffective. American firms established themselves in other EEC countries and exported to the French market. Unable to persuade other European countries to issue EEC-wide restrictions on direct investment from the United States, the French government was forced to revert to more liberal policies.

With increased competition, it is becoming more and more difficult for the French state to fulfill its traditional role of providing a stable and protected environment for industry. Protection through tariff and nontariff barriers is forbidden by the Rome treaty. The EEC Commission began in 1968 to control the granting of subsidies by member governments, and this has hindered the long-standing French policy of subsidizing failing enterprises. Moreover, it is becoming obvious that the resources spent in supporting declining industries would be better used in helping the modern industrial sector. Since the Fifth Plan (1966–70), the official policy has been to stimulate the latter. Government policy was first aimed at encouraging mergers between French competitors so as to constitute national champions that could successfully compete on international markets. More recently, the view has evolved that a competitive domestic market is the best method to teach French firms the skills necessary for survival in the international economy.[43] The Barre government enacted laws controlling industrial concentration, increasing consumer protection and information, and creating a commission charged with curbing monopolistic practices.

The Common Market, by reducing the sovereignty of the French government, has thus forced on France policies that in a purely national context would have been successfully opposed by its organized interests. Membership in the Common Market has also decreased the power of French organized groups.

The internationalization of the French economy has adversely affected the power of French trade unions in many ways. An increasing part of French production is in the hands of multinational firms, either French firms with overseas subsidiaries or foreign firms established in France. The firm that produces in a large number of countries has a much stronger bargaining position when dealing with its workers than does the purely national firm. Its ability to shift production from one country to another on relatively short notice greatly increases its bargaining power. The threat of plant

43. Dyas and Thanheiser, *The Emerging European Enterprise*, p. 180.

closings tends to moderate union demands, while the ability to move production from struck to other plants reduces the effectiveness of strikes. Multinational production, with its potential for profit manipulation, also makes it difficult for labor unions to know what the firm can afford to give in the way of wages or benefits.

Unions have experienced great difficulties in organizing structures that parallel those of the new, larger markets. In some countries unions are illegal. In Western democracies, where they often are powerful, unions have widely differing characteristics: some are organized by craft, others by industry; some are ideological, pursuing political goals, others are pragmatic with mostly narrow economic objectives; some have political links, others keep themselves jealously independent from political parties. All are generally nationalistic. Cultural and language differences compound communication problems. It is therefore not a surprise that efforts toward international unions have not been very successful. Multinational firms have thus often been able to play one union against another. As a result of their superior bargaining power, those firms have experienced strikes of shorter duration than their purely national counterparts.[44] Increased competitiveness in the French market has also reduced the propensity of French firms to buy labor peace at the expense of consumers. French unions have found themselves confronted with employers both less willing and less able to yield to their demands.

Symmetrical effects have been felt by industry groups. The increase in the size of the market has, in most industries, increased the number of competitors. Today a successful price-fixing conspiracy must involve producers in more than one country. This has made it more difficult to establish cartels. The larger the number of competitors, the harder it is to obtain agreement. Cultural and social barriers also make contacts with foreigners more difficult than with nationals. Producers located in different countries are also likely to have divergent price structures, and this makes price fixing less easy. Last of all, most French cartels have been blessed, if not organized, by the government. The relationship between industry and government in France has been one of cooperation (some say conspiracy). The continual movement of French higher civil servants between government and industry and their membership in the same social class has

---

44. P. Ramadier and J. P. Dubois, *Vers l'Europe des travailleurs,* quoted in Richard Barnet and Ronald Muller. *Global Reach* (New York: Simon and Schuster, 1974), p. 310. For a differing view, see M. Jedel and D. Kujawa, "Management and Employment Practices of Foreign Direct Investors in the United States," mimeo, Georgia State University (March 1976).

established a community of interest between big business and the state. French legislation has thus often institutionalized restrictive practices; at the least, it has tolerated them. As the locus of power shifts slowly toward Brussels, this source of support is being reduced. The traditional indulgence of national authorities toward restrictive practices is being replaced by a less favorable attitude. Since 1968, European authorities have started to prosecute some of the most obvious cartels and have, in some cases. levied substantial fines.

Thus, France has entered since 1957 a process of internationalization that has taken on a momentum of its own. The establishment of the Common Market has had destabilizing influences on organized interest groups. The multinationalization of national firms and the discipline of international markets has reduced the bargaining power of national unions. An increase in the number of competitors has made collusion more difficult, while the diffusion of political power between the EEC Commission and the present nine member countries has reduced the support that industry lobbies had previously received from the French bureaucracy.

The Position of Common-interest Groups in Postwar France

Although France's entry into the Common Market can explain the weakening of French interest groups and the resulting improvements in allocative efficiency and in economic growth, we have yet to explain why France chose in the late fifties to compete in the world economy when it had previously consistently refused to do so.

Three factors seem to explain the inability of growth-retarding interests to block France's entry into the Common Market. First, the two groups that stood to lose the most, business and labor, were relatively weak at the time decisions leading to entry were made. Second, the political atmosphere in France was ripe for such a change in policies. Third, the issues were framed in such a way as to make them most attractive to the French voters.

French unions have had little impact on the trend toward internationalization. This is due both to their particular characteristics and to historical events.

French labor organizations are relatively weak by international standards. The proportion of workers belonging to unions is smaller in France than in other developed countries. In 1974 the percentage of wage earners belonging to unions was about 75 percent in Scandinavian countries, 70 percent in the United Kingdom, 50 percent in Germany and Belgium, 25 percent in the United States, and 20 percent in France.[45] In contrast to these countries, union membership in France has been subject to wide fluctuations.[46] French unions are generally weak in industry. The only sectors in which the degree of unionization is comparable to that found in the U.S. steel or automobile industries is in printing and publishing, in the state-owned electricity monopoly, and among teachers.[47]

More important, the financial resources of French unions are much smaller than those of the above-mentioned countries. It is estimated that the two main French unions, the CGT and CFDT, receive annually in dues one fortieth of the amount received by their German counterpart, the DGB.[48] Until recently, there were no strike funds, and strikers were obliged to rely on local solidarity.

One reason for this relative weakness is probably the division of the French labor movement into confederations, each of them with a particular ideology. No union can therefore pretend to speak for all workers. In any given industry, the employers' organization is likely to be faced with at least four union representatives. The rivalry and deep ideological division of French unions has seriously weakened their bargaining power. Their dissensions play into the hands of management. Each union will try to be the first to start a strike and upstage its rivals and the last to compromise, so as to leave the responsibility of making concessions to others. The result is often poorly planned and therefore ineffective strikes.[49]

French law does not recognize the union shop or closed shop and forbids management to check off union dues. In practice, only a small minority of workers (on the docks and in some printing trades) work in closed shops. Until 1968, the union had no legal status within the firm. It could not officially bargain with management at the plant level. Union representatives enjoyed the same legal protection against summary dismissal as those given to all union members. Unions could not post notices within the plant.

45. Georges Lefranc, *Les syndicats dans le monde*, 9th ed. (Paris: Que Sais-Je, 1975), p. 86.
46. Between 1946 and 1963, union membership declined by about 50 percent. See Jean-Daniel Reynaud, *Les syndicats en France* (Paris: Armand Colin, 1963), p. 126.
47. Ibid., p. 128.
48. "Le réveil du DGB," *L'Expansion*, no. 106 (April 1979):137. A significant part of the resources of French unions consists in government-mandated time allowances for elected worker representatives (staff delegates, delegates to the Works Council and the Security and Health Commission, etc.) who are often union members, and, since 1968, for the union representatives in the plant. See Jean-Jacques Rosa, "Théorie de la firme syndicale," *Vie et sciences économiques*, no. 86 (July 1980):1–22.
49. Reynaud, *Les syndicats en France*, p. 168.

Even today, dues collection is still forbidden in work areas and during work hours.

As research in progress by Bernard Lentz and myself shows, there seem to be few incentives in France to join unions.[50] Representation of workers has been granted by statute to an elected Works Council (Comité d'Entreprise). Unions may present candidates to that council, but, once elected, councilmen speak for the entire workforce. Collective bargaining generally takes place at the industry level, and the resulting contract is applicable to all workers, union or nonunion. The contract is also often extended by the state beyond the original bargaining unit. Furthermore, many of the nonwage benefits that are negotiated in the United States between unions and management (paid vacations or health insurance, for example) have been granted to all French workers by national legislation. In France, one does not have to be in a union, or even in a strongly unionized industry, to benefit from these advantages. We would therefore expect the relative wage effect of French unions to be small.[51]

In the United States, unions provide also some private goods to their members, especially seniority and the handling of grievances. In France, unions do not control the grievance procedure. Grievances are brought to management's attention by the ''délégué du personnel,'' who is elected by workers at the plant and who is often, but not always, a union member. But if management does not settle the grievance to the satisfaction of the worker, the employee must sue in a state labor court. These courts will hear only individual grievances. Management also retains the right to decide on the order of layoffs.

For all those reasons, one would expect French unions to have limited power. There are in fact some indications that this is the case. It is generally thought that immigration of foreign workers tends to depress national wages. The foreign worker is less integrated into society and, being in a precarious condition, is content with lower wages and more docile to his employer than his national counterpart might be. It is therefore in a union's interest to oppose immigration. Until the recent depression, French unions, in spite of their opposition, did not succeed in curbing immigra-

---

50. The following approach to French unions has been developed jointly by Bernard Lentz and myself and will be expounded more fully in forthcoming work.

51. My preliminary work shows that French unions do not have any differential impact on wages. See ''L'effet des syndicats français sur les salaires,'' *Vie et sciences économiques,* no. 86 (July 1980): 23–36, and ''The Relative Wage Effect of French Unions,'' in J. J. Rosa, ed., *The Economics of Labor Unions* (Paris: Bonnel, forthcoming).

tion. In 1946, immigrant workers made up 5.1 percent of the French labor force. By 1975 that percentage had increased to 7.3 percent.[52] Only Switzerland had a higher proportion of foreign workers in its labor force.[53] Another indirect indication of the relative weakness of French unions is given by a comparative statistical study of labor markets in eighteen developed countries. The results show that the French labor market was significantly more competitive than the eighteen-country average.[54]

French unions are also relatively encompassing, and their impact has therefore had less adverse effect on growth. The relative weakness of French unions at the plant level has led them to direct their action toward the state. This is reflected in their structure and in their strategy.

French major labor confederations are relatively centralized. They represent blue and white collar workers, professionals, and middle-level managers, and they are formed along industry lines. With few exceptions, all workers belonging to one industry, whatever their craft or qualification, will be organized in one union affiliated with one of the four main confederations. Confederations have a dual structure: local unions are members in both regional and industry federations.

By contrast with the United States, the strategy of French unions has been to put more pressure on the state than on employers. This is shown by the French pattern of short, generalized strikes and by the coincidence of strike waves with political crises.[55] The goal is to persuade the government either to force employers to accede to demands or to enact legislation that grants their requests.

Because French unions direct their action at the state, they attempt to formulate demands that reflect the desires of the largest possible fraction of the French working class. When their demands are met, it is by the enacting of statutes or economy-wide labor-management agreements covering all workers (such as legislation on paid holidays in 1969 or agreements on

52. "Les incidences économiques de l'immigration," *Problèmes économiques,* no. 1583 (1978).
53. Germany's rate was comparable. See "Comment se passer d'Ahmed," *L'Expansion* (June 1975).
54. H. A. Turner and D.A.S. Jackson, "On the Stability of Wage Differences and Productivity-Based Wage Policies," *British Journal of Industrial Relations* 7, no. 1 (February 1969), quoted in Carré et al., *La croissance française,* p. 535. The authors calculated the correlation coefficient between the structures of French wages in 1956 and 1965. They also calculated the proportion of sectors in which wage increases were serially correlated. According to Turner and Jackson, in a perfectly competitive labor market the first coefficient should be high and the second low. Results show that in France's case the first coefficient is higher, and the second lower, than in the eighteen-country average.
55. Edward Shorter and Charles Tilly, *Strikes in France, 1830–1968* (Cambridge: Cambridge University Press, 1974).

supplementary pension plans in 1957, 1961, and 1971). One would therefore expect French unions to be less opposed to structural change and to
have less of a negative impact on the allocations of resources than their
British or American counterparts.

There are also historical reasons for the inability of French unions to stop
European integration. At the end of World War II, French unions were
more powerful than they had ever been, although still weak by international standards. Union leaders had played an active role in the resistance
against German occupation, and the prestige that they had thus acquired
led to a substantial increase in union membership. The CGT, which was
becoming more and more dominated by communists, was then representing about 80 percent of French union members. Labor leaders had been
given important responsibilities in the government. Under their influence,
some of their perennial demands, such as nationalization of a subtantial
part of French industry and the creation of the ''Comités d'Entreprise,''
were put into law.

In 1947, the Federation of Metalworkers and twenty other communist-
dominated CGT federations organized into a National Strike Committee and transformed a walkout that had erupted in Marseilles over an
increase in tram fares into a general strike with heavy political overtones.
The goal of the strike was to persuade the Schuman government to reject
the Marshall Plan.[56] The failure of the strike, marred by violence and
sabotage, led to a bitter split within the CGT and to an overall decline in
union membership. Noncommunist members left the CGT to create two
separate confederations, the CGT-FO and the CGSI. Some of the national
federations, such as the very powerful teachers' union, the Fédération de
l'Education Nationale, did not join any confederation, but decided to
remain autonomous.

One of the main consequences of the split was a general weakening of
union influence. The percentage of union members among nonagricultural
employees fell from 50 or 60 percent in 1946 to 23 percent in 1954 and then
to 17 percent in 1962.[57] Organized labor was no longer speaking with one
voice: the three main labor confederations, the CGT, the CGT-FO, and the
Confédération Française des Travailleurs Chrétiens (CFTC), took opposing stands on most important issues. The CGT opposed the ECSC treaty

---

56. Georges Lefranc, *Le mouvement syndical de la Libération aux événements de Mai-Juin 1968*
(Paris: Payot, 1969), pp. 56–58.
57. François Sellier, ''France,'' in *Labor in the 20th Century*, ed. John Dunlop and Walter Galen-
son (New York: Academic Press, 1978), p. 208.

because the Communist party considered the drive for European integration to be an American-led conspiracy against the Soviet Union. On the other hand, the noncommunist unions saw in the treaty the possibility of making links with their powerful ideological brethren in Germany and the Benelux countries.[58] The Soviet invasion of Hungary in 1956 rekindled the ideological opposition between the CGT and the other unions: both the CGT-FO and the CFTC supported the Treaty of Rome, while the CGT opposed it.

The relative strength of business organizations in the immediate postwar period is more difficult to assess. In many ways the war greatly increased their power and their efficiency. On the other hand they were weakened by the accusations of collaboration directed against them and by the nationalization of a substantial part of the modern industrial sector.

During the war, the Vichy government created the "Comités d'Organisation" (COs). These were established in each industry to allocate raw materials and to organize production. They were given the power to collect contributions and statistics and to set production plans. They were staffed by professional administrators rather than entrepreneurs. The COs had important consequences for organized business: they accentuated the control of large firms over their industry; they forced upon firm owners some measure of discipline; they established tightly organized cartels that remained in force long after the war; and they also provided a staff of competent administrators who found themselves at the head of the reestablished employers' association, the Conseil National du Patronat Français (CNPF).

Because of its participation in the COs, the business community was severely punished by the new regime that took power after the war. Businessmen were publicly excoriated, industry associations were purged of collaborators, and the assets of the CNPF's predecessor, the CGPF, which had been banned by Vichy, were confiscated. The nationalization of a substantial number of what were then the largest firms had an important impact on the strength of business organizations. Some of the nationalized sectors had been important contributors to the CGPF. The two newspapers that were owned by coal and steel interests and that were the voice of business were taken over by the Resistance. The business point of view was almost totally excluded from the state-owned radio.[59]

---

58. Communist opponents of the ECSC Treaty (the Schuman Plan) dubbed it "the Truman Plan." See Ernest Haas, *The Uniting of Europe* (Stanford: Stanford University Press, 1958), pp. 114, 226.

59. Henri Ehrmann, *La politique du patronat français,* pp. 102, 186–87.

The CNPF, the new peak association that was founded in 1946, was more encompassing than similar organizations in other developed countries, since it represented both industry and trade. It was a loose federation of national industry groups and of regional interindustry associations, of the Confédération Générale des Petites et Moyennes Entreprises (CGPME, an association of small businesses), and of the Conseil National du Commerce, an association of retailers. In fact, the CNPF was dominated by national industry groups and especially by those representing the steel, metal, chemical, petroleum, and textile industries. These five groups were said to have provided in the early fifties 80 percent of the CNPF's budget.[60]

Being a confederation of such diverse and heterogeneous interests, the CNPF generally has been divided on the main issues. As early as 1948, the CGPME, complaining that the CNPF was becoming too centralized, officially left the association, although many of its members kept their individual memberships in the CNPF. The opposition between large and small firms and between industries came again to the fore when Robert Schuman proposed the establishment of a coal and steel community. The CGPME was strongly opposed to the plan. The CNPF position was an uneasy compromise between the highly favorable views held by manufacturers of electrical equipment and by coal and steel users and the strong opposition of the steel industry. The CNPF accepted the plan in principle but formulated four main objections: the ECSC High Authority was too powerful; the treaty should not contain an a priori ban on cartels, but should only sanction them if they proved to be detrimental to the public welfare; the treaty maintained state intervention in the economy; and French industry, because of its high tax burden, was not ready to compete.

When the project was submitted to the government's Economic and Social Council, the CGT and the CGPME voted against it, while the CNPF abstained. The final vote was 116 for the plan, 16 against it, with 29 abstaining.[61] The bad public reputation that the steel industry had acquired by its war-mongering activities and the recent nationalization of the coal and railroad industries, which opposed the treaty, explain in part the failure of the steel industry to block the project.[62]

The adoption of the treaty weakened the influence of the steel industry on the CNPF board. The number of board members was increased to

60. Ibid., p. 137.
61. Georges Lefranc, *Les organisations patronales en France* (Paris: Payot, 1976), p. 154.
62. Jean Meynaud, *Nouvelles études sur les groupes de pression en France* (Paris: Armand Colin, 1962), p. 345.

strengthen the influence of the chemical and electrical equipment industries.[63] From then on the CNPF participated in ECSC bodies to defend its interests.

There was no greater consensus within the CNPF as to what should be the organization's position toward the EEC. The electrical equipment, automobile, chemical, and paper industries were favorable, perhaps because the high concentration of these industries in each national market made European competition easier to control. The textile industries were against joining the EEC. Eventually, the CNPF took a position for the Common Market, while the CGPME opposed it.[64]

Since 1957, the French trade associations have attempted to influence European policy by strengthening their links with their European counterparts. In 1952, the CNPF contributed to the creation of the Union des Industries de la Communauté Européenne, an association grouping European peak business associations. Many industries now are represented by a European-wide industry lobby in Brussels.

The third group that was seriously affected by the treaties were the farmers. The farmers' peak organization, the Fédération Nationale des Syndicats d'Exploitants Agricoles (FNSEA), was dominated by the sugar beet and the wheat growers' unions. These last two unions, representing the modern farming sector, had so far successfully persuaded the FNSEA to lobby the government for higher support prices. The late fifties, however, saw the development of a rival organization that regrouped medium and small farms, the Centre National des Jeunes Agriculteurs. The CNJA, which in 1956 joined with the FNSEA, later denounced the demands of the FNSEA for higher support prices as benefiting mostly the large farmers and asked for measures encouraging structural changes. Seeing that their control of the FNSEA was eroding and that their chances of obtaining continued high support prices from the French government were diminishing, sugar beet and wheat growers supported the ECSC and EEC treaties. They hoped that European integration would open new markets for their products and were confident in their ability to obtain high support prices from the Brussels authorities. In both cases, history has shown that they were right.[65]

Most observers agree, however, that neither business nor labor had

63. Lefranc, *Les organisations patronales*, p. 155.
64. Ibid., pp. 156–57.
65. Christine André and Robert Delorme, *L'évolution des dépenses publiques en longue période et le rôle de l'Etat en France, 1871–1971* (Paris: CEPREMAP, n.d.), vol. 1, pp. 282, 299.

much influence on the French decision to join the ECSC and the EEC, both decisions being influenced by broader political considerations.[66] The authors of the ECSC treaty had two objectives: to protect France from German expansionism by encouraging both countries to work together, thus making a war between the two archenemies "physically impossible and spiritually unthinkable."[67] The second objective was to further European integration as the only defense against U.S. domination and Soviet aggression. The same political goals were even more evident in the projects for a European Defense Community, rejected by French voters in 1954, and for a European Political Community, which was never brought to a vote. Since political union seemed premature, proponents of a united Europe decided then to make a new effort to build a political union on economic bases. The powerlessness of Europe to prevent the crushing of the Hungarian revolution by the Soviets and the inability of France and England to pursue an independent policy in Suez when faced with the opposition of the United States and the Soviet Union were powerful stimulants in the *relance* that led to the Treaty of Rome.[68] Political factors were thus dominant, and this made it difficult for economic interests to gain public support for their special pleadings.

Both projects were also presented so as to win widespread voter acceptance. Their global nature created divisions within organized groups. Jean Monnet disarmed right-wing and left-wing critics of the ECSC by pointing out that the treaty left open whether the ECSC High Authority would pursue liberal or interventionist policies. Advocates of ratification dissociated steel consumers from steel producers and enlisted the support of the nationalized coal and railway industries.[69] The drafters of the project for a European Economic Community were also careful to link tariff reductions to the gradual establishment of common economic policies, thus meeting a perennial demand of French business. Two of the main objections of French business groups were neutralized by reducing the degree of supranationality in EEC institutions and by intentionally leaving vague what the policy of the Commission toward cartels would be, thus considerably weakening business opposition to the project. The inclusion, in the text of

---

66. Meynaud, *Nouvelles études*, p. 391.
67. Haas, *The Uniting of Europe*, p. 243.
68. J. Szokoloczy-Syllaba, *Les organisations professionelles françaises et le Marché Commun* (Paris: Armand Colin, 1965), pp. 308–09.
69. Henri Ehrmann, *Organized Business in France* (Princeton: Princeton University Press, 1957), p. 411.

the treaty, of a common agricultural policy with Europe-wide price supports won over the farmers. This, because of the overrepresentation of the
farm vote in the French parliament, was helpful in getting the treaty
ratified.[70]

There is no doubt that common-interest groups have succeeded in slowing down the application of the treaties. One can find many examples of
successful rearguard actions by business and farm groups.[71] However, the
cumulative factors that we have described have been at work. The internationalization of the French economy has been slowed down, but it has not
been stopped.

Conclusion

The main characteristic of the remarkable period of economic growth that
France has experienced since 1945 has been a drastic improvement in the
allocation and the utilization of productive capacities. This in turn has been
brought about by the progressive abandonment of "Malthusianist" policies which had sought to protect vested interests at the expense of economic progress. The result of these policies was the maintenance of a large
number of marginal business units. With the opening of the economy,
there has been a rapid decline in the number of these redundant farmers,
artisans, and shopkeepers.

What accounts for this drastic change in policies? Some have argued that
the crucial factor has been the nationalizations. Nationalizations per se do
not guarantee technological progress or efficient management, as shown in
the U.K.[72] Furthermore, the productivity gains have been as high in the
French private sector as in the public sector.[73]

Planning has also been credited for France's postwar progress, but this
seems exaggerated. As a tool for improving the allocation of resources, the
first four plans, spanning the years from 1947 to 1965, were not very
successful: their indications of what to produce in what amounts were often

70. Szokoloczy-Syllaba, *Les organisations professionelles,* pp. 303, 308–09.

71. Agricultural interests, for example, were influential in the rejection of the Mansholt Plan, which
would have reduced support prices on some agricultural products and would have forced structural
reforms on French agriculture. See "Un bilan du Marché Commun agricole," *Problèmes économiques,* no. 1524 (1977):15.

72. Charles Kindleberger, "La renaissance de l'économie française après la guerre," in *A la
recherche de la France,* ed. Stanley Hoffmann et al., (Paris: Seuil, 1963), p. 181.

73. Carré et al., *La croissance française,* p. 615.

off the mark;[74] and their impact on nationalized industries was limited, and that on large, private firms doubtful.[75] Their main contribution has been to incite entrepreneurs to expand, but since the latter were free to decide on production levels, the impact of planning would have been slim were it not for the entrepreneurs' desire (or necessity) to increase output.

According to Kindleberger, the defeat of 1940 led to the demise of the old elites and to their replacement with new men and new ideas of innovation and efficiency.[76] It is difficult to agree with Kindleberger. Progress in productivity has been greatest among small and medium-sized firms and in sectors where small firms predominate, such as textiles and clothing, trade, and agriculture.[77] It thus resulted from the efforts of a large number of agents. The turnover of elites after the war cannot have been that generalized.

Rather than attribute the French economic renaissance to an autonomous change in attitudes, it seems more logical to assume that the change in behavior was caused by a change in the rules of the game that resulted from the opening of the French economy to outside competition. A combination of international and domestic factors made this change possible. The weak position in which Western Europe found itself after the war, caught between a dominating United States and an expansionist Soviet Union, was instrumental in persuading public opinion, in France and in other European countries, of the necessity of forming a political and economic union. Against this general pattern of support for a united Europe, those that stood to lose the most from European integration were too weak and divided. The political skill of the advocates of European unity was also a factor in taking the political options that have had such important consequences for French economic growth.

74. The first plan (1947–52) underestimated the demand for electricity and overestimated that for coal. All plans overestimated labor requirements in manufacturing and underestimated the reduction of the labor force in agriculture. See Charles Kindleberger, *Europe's Postwar Growth* (Cambridge: Harvard University Press, 1967), p. 59. Housing demand, imports and exports were also systematically underestimated. See Carré et al., *La croissance française*, p. 572. This poor record can be explained by rivalries between ministries and between departments within ministries. According to Ezra N. Suleiman, *Politics, Power, and Bureaucracy in France* (Princeton: Princeton University Press, 1974), pp. 346–47, the important and accurate information obtained by the departments from professional associations or large firms "is not made available to those who are actually responsible for planning. . . . At best, only partial information is made available to other administrative agencies, which may merely serve to distort the planning process."

75. John McArthur and Bruce Scott, *Industrial Planning in France* (Boston: Harvard Business School, 1969).

76. Kindleberger, "La renaissance," p. 184.

77. Carré et al., *La croissance française*, p. 290.

10: Pressure Politics and Economic Growth: Olson's Theory and the Swiss Experience

FRANZ LEHNER

Olson's theory is consistent with several studies that demonstrate the crucial importance of organized interest intermediation for politico-economic development in the highly industrialized democracies.[1] These studies show that the pluralist pattern of interest organization in the advanced democracies creates problems of political stability, fiscal efficiency, and public growth. They especially pinpoint—as Olson does—the significance of the breadth of interest-group organization. Olson's theory is certainly a fruitful contribution to the study of the political economy of interest-group intermediation. He considers only the structure of interest intermediation, however, and neglects the ways in which pressure groups interact among themselves and with the politico-administrative system. This results in partially erroneous conclusions.

In the following I first demonstrate my point in a brief exploration of the Swiss case and then extend my argument in a discussion of so-called liberal corporatism.

Consociational Democracy: Interest Intermediation in Switzerland

In the perspective of the Olson hypothesis, Switzerland is a deviant case, since it combines a high growth rate with a highly differentiated interest structure. The economic development of Switzerland since 1948 has been

1. See for example Samuel Brittan, "The Economic Contradictions of Democracy," *British Journal of Political Science* (1975); Léon Dion, "The Politics of Consultation," *Government and Opposition* (1973); Gerhard Lehmbruch, "Liberal Corporatism and Party Government," *Comparative Political Studies* (1977); Franz Lehner, *Grenzen des Regierens* (Königstein: Athenäum, 1979); Stanley Liberson, "An Empirical Study of Military-Industrial Linkages," *American Journal of Sociology* (1971); Claus Offe, "Politische Herrschaft und Klassenstrukturen," in *Politikwissenschaft*, ed. Gisela Kress and Dieter Senghaas (Frankfurt: Fischer, 1972); and Philippe Schmitter, "Interest Intermediation and Regime Governability in Contemporary Western Europe" (Paper delivered at the Annual Convention of the American Political Science Association, 1977).

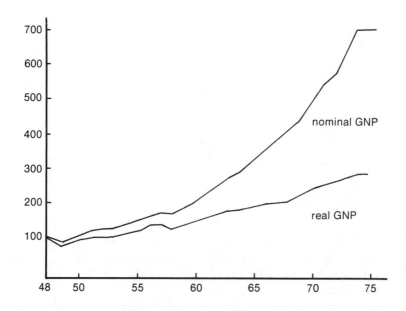

Figure 10.1.   Gross National Product of Switzerland, 1948–75 (1948 = 100)
SOURCE: S. Bieri, *Fiscal Federalism in Switzerland* (Canberra: Centre for Research on
Federal Financial Relations, 1979).

characterized by a rather high growth rate, with a setback in 1974 (figure
10.1). Although Switzerland between 1948 and 1972 never experienced an
extremely high growth rate (as, for example, Japan and West Germany
did), it always ranked well above the average of the Western countries.[2] In
terms of the Marris catch-up measures Switzerland did not perform very
well, but still registered above the mean of the countries studied.[3] Altogether, Switzerland performed economically well and experienced,
throughout the last three decades, considerable growth. Given the Olson
hypothesis, we should expect Switzerland to have a moderately differentiated structure of organized interest groups. This, however, is not true.

Switzerland has a very differentiated, pluralist structure of interest organization. This structure has neither a high degree of organizational decentralization nor a high level of associational monopoly. Philippe Schmit-

2. Stephan Bieri, *Fiscal Federalism in Switzerland* (Canberra: Centre for Research on Federal
Financial Relations, 1979).
3. Robin Marris, "Some New Results on 'Catch-Up,'" mimeographed (College Park, Md.,
1978).

ter found that Switzerland ranks low (ninth) among fifteen highly industrialized societies with respect to societal corporatism, though Switzerland ranks well above the average in decentralization of interest organization.[4] Schmitter's data only refer to interest organization on the national level and do not take into account internal fragmentation of pressure groups. The latter is high in Switzerland where the cantonal sections of most interest groups and the political parties are usually rather powerful, while the national organization resembles a more or less strong coalition. The cantonal sections of interest groups and parties, for example, often disagree with each other and with the national organization with respect to their recommendations for national referenda. Thus, interest organization in Switzerland is even more decentralized and differentiated than the Schmitter data show.

Given a rather high growth rate and a very decentralized interest organization, Switzerland seems to deviate from the pattern proposed by the Olson hypothesis. This conclusion would, however, be misleading; despite strong decentralization, interest intermediation in Switzerland is strongly integrated by consociational procedures.

Above the decentralized interest structure there is a highly encompassing coalition structure, which accommodates conflicts among interests and controls political decision making. This coalition structure provides an effective filter for the demands of pressure groups.

According to Wilson, political organizations rarely form lasting coalitions, but rather build, at best, coalitions that are limited in time and issue space.[5] Federalism and direct democracy in Switzerland create a condition that forces interest groups and parties to form highly encompassing, long-term coalitions.

Swiss federalism can be characterized by division of the nation into territorially small political subsystems (twenty-six autonomous cantons and semicantons), with a high degree of decentralization of political decision making. In recent years the federal government has gained in power, but the cantonal governments still control a considerable part of their socioeconomic development. The high degree of decentralization is paralleled by significant disparities in the socioeconomic conditions of the cantons. For example, in 1975 the national per-capita income was 19,036 Swiss Francs, but ranged as high as 32,831 Sfr. in the canton of Basel-

---

4. Schmitter, "Interest Intermediation."
5. James Q. Wilson, *Political Organizations* (New York: Basic Books, 1973).

Stadt, 27,128 Sfr. in Geneva, and 23,245 Sfr. in Zurich, and as low as 13,102 Sfr. in Schwyz, 11,739 Sfr. in Obwalden, and 11,398 Sfr. in Appenzell-Innerrhoden. Similar differences could be observed for the economic structure and provision of public goods in the cantons.[6]

This federalist structure and its socioeconomic fragmentation affects, of course, the organized interests and the party system. Both interest groups and parties are generally fragmented along cantonal borders and have strong cantonal sections with often heterogeneous interests. This fragmentation is often enforced by the cultural diversity of Switzerland. The political, social, and economic fragmentation of Switzerland creates difficult conditions for policy making: the costs of coalition formation are generally very high. It is a difficult task to reach sufficient consensus for national policymaking, since parties and interest organizations have to reach agreement within and between themselves. This presupposes a complex bargaining process. Given this situation, we might expect small and unstable majorities in national decision making. In reality, however, Switzerland is governed by overwhelming majorities. The cause of this pattern of coalition formation is the importance of direct democracy in Switzerland.

In Switzerland, legislative decisions are subject to mandatory or petition referenda. Furthermore, a constitutional right of popular initiative exists and is often an effective instrument for influencing policy, since the Swiss constitution contains detailed determinations as to the power and obligations of the national government.

Direct democracy forces, as Neidhart stresses, the formation of overwhelming majorities.[7] The formation of some type of minimal winning or minimal range coalitions would involve the high risk that excluded parties and groups would challenge decisions by means of a referendum or would attempt to influence policy making by means of an initiative. Popular votes are usually difficult to predict, especially so given the generally low turnout that typifies such voting in Switzerland. Direct democracy thus constitutes a risky environment for coalition formation. Given this state of affairs, minimal winning coalitions are unlikely to appear. To the contrary: any coalition with a predictable and safe chance of winning parliamentary *and* popular votes has to include all parties and interest organizations that

6. Bieri, *Fiscal Federalism;* see also Benno Homann, "Vorstudie zum Problem Parteiensystem und Föderalismus" (Ph.D. thesis, University of Mannheim, 1978); Franz Lehner, "Consociational Democracy in Switzerland: A Politico-Economic Explanation," mimeographed (1979); Jürg Steiner, *Amicable Agreement versus Majority Rule* (Chapel Hill: The University of North Carolina Press, 1974).

7. Leonhard Neidhart, *Plebiszit und pluralitäre Demokratie* (Bern: Francke, 1970).

may be capable of calling for a successful referendum or initiative. Given the highly differentiated, fragmented interest structure of Switzerland and the resulting multiplicity of possible coalitions, direct democracy forces parties and groups to engage in extensive and inclusive collusion. They have to accept a consociational rather than a competitive pattern of conflict management and policymaking.[8]

Swiss consociational democracy is institutionalized through an elaborate system of hearing and bargaining procedures, an extensive system of committees, and a large amount of formal and informal consultation. This system allows for much participation of interest groups, parties, and cantons in national policymaking. It also creates an extensive input of different and diverging demands into the decision-making process. This input has to be accommodated to reach consensus.

The accommodation of a variety of interests obviously requires large-scale compromise. Consensus can only be reached if the participating groups and parties are willing to accept minimal rather than maximal solutions: bargaining does not permit solutions that deviate much from Pareto optimality. For each group and party, this limits the chance to get what it demands. It will generally be difficult to obtain public goods and services that political organizations attempt to win from the state. On an aggregate level, we can assume that under the conditions of Swiss consociational democracy, the provision of public goods and services that benefit special-interest groups will be lower than in a competitive democracy. This is indicated by the fact that the share of the public sector in Switzerland's GNP is about 25 percent, while in most Western countries it exceeds 35 or 40 percent.

Summarizing our argument thus far, we can state that Switzerland has a highly decentralized and pluralist array of interests which, however, is framed by a highly encompassing coalition structure. This coalition structure reduces those effects that are associated, according to Olson's theory, with pluralist interest organization. The relatively high growth rate of Switzerland can, then, be explained if we consider not only the structure of interest organization, but also the interactions of interest groups in the policy-making process.

Considering its tight but encompassing bargaining system of consociational democracy, Switzerland deviates much less from the pattern of the

8. Ibid.; see also Lehner, "Consociational Democracy"; and Jürg Steiner, "Coalition Formation in Switzerland," in *Coalition Formation in the Western World*, ed. E. C. Browne and T. Dreijmanis (New Haven: Yale University Press, 1978).

Olson hypothesis than might appear at first glance. Yet, it still does not fit neatly: according to Olson's theory we should, in cases of highly encompassing interest intermediation, expect a high growth rate. The Swiss rate, however, is moderate. This points to an important difference between the situation of an encompassing interest organization and that of a decentralized and differentiated interest organization overarched by an encompassing bargaining system. To understand this difference we have to discuss briefly the state's role in economic growth and its ability to perform this role.

It can hardly be denied that state interventions into the economy often create inefficiencies and inhibit growth. This is especially true for the various regulations that protect firms and whole branches of industry from competition. State intervention, however, often fulfills a positive function for economic growth: the supply of an adequate infrastructure or programs for economic stability, for example, is of crucial importance for growth. This raises the following question: Under what conditions is state policy likely to produce growth-inhibiting regulations and programs, and under what conditions will it tend to produce growth-stimulating programs and regulations?

In the perspective of the Olson hypothesis, the answer to this question is simple. The more encompassing the interest organization in a political system, the more likely state economic policy will favor growth. Similarly, the more decentralized the interest organization, the more state interventions will tend to inhibit growth. This may well be true if we consider only the basic structure of interest organization. But the case becomes more difficult if we consider overarching bargaining structures.

These structures, if they are as encompassing as in the Swiss case, certainly reduce the production of regulations and programs that both benefit special interests and inhibit growth; but they reduce the supply of public goods and services in general and, hence, also reduce the provision of growth-promoting programs and regulations. The reason for this is the extremely high transaction costs of overarching bargaining systems. It is obvious that it takes much time and effort to form an overwhelming majority from a multiplicity of interests. It is also obvious that the resulting programs are generally not very innovative but strongly reflect the status quo. A good example is anti-inflation policy in Switzerland. For many years, attempts have been made to bring about legislation that enables the federal government to fight inflation efficiently and stabilize the economy, but so far no law has passed parliament. Instead, federal economic policy has to be based on so-called urgent federal acts—parliamentary decisions of limited scope that are valid for a year only and are exempted from the referendum. The federal government thus has only very limited ability to influence economic development.[9] Similar problems occur regularly in almost every important policy matter. Consociational democracy produces a considerable inertia in political decision making. This inertia lowers the amount of growth-inhibiting (as well as of growth-promoting) policy, and generally permits only limited intervention of the state into the economy. This may well explain why the Swiss growth rate is moderate but not low. The institutionalized inertia of the Swiss consociational democracy has its roots in the underlying bargaining structure; this structural analysis is applicable to states other than Switzerland. In several industrialized democracies, attempts are being made to integrate organized interests in some overarching bargaining structure.

Liberal Corporatism: A New Style of Conflict Management in the Western Democracies

In the highly industrialized democracies a new style of conflict management and decision making can often be observed: governments engage in institutionalized bargaining with established interest groups. In the United Kingdom and Sweden, for example, several tripartite commissions are at work to coordinate the demands and activities of unions, employers, and government to reach some consensus on government economic policy. Similarly, in France, the Commissariat Général du Plan (the central planning office) is engaged in preventive and extraparliamentary conflict management with companies and interest groups. In the Federal Republic of Germany, the government institutionalized "concerted action"—an informal committee of top representatives of unions, employers, and the federal government—to determine consensually activities and measures to safeguard continuous growth and employment with moderate inflation. A more established system of interest accommodation exists in Austria where a tripartite committee strongly influences prices and wages and actually determines a large part of economic policy. These bargaining structures form the nucleus of what is often called "liberal corporatism."[10]

9. Henner Kleinewefers, *Inflation und Inflationsbekämpfung in der Schweiz* (Frauenfeld: Huber, 1976).

10. Cf. Klaus von Beyme and Ghitta Ionescu, "The Politics of Employment Policy in Germany and Great Britain," *Government and Opposition* (1977); Wyn Grant and David Marsh, "Tripartism: Reality or Myth?" *Government and Opposition* (1977); Lehmbruch, "Liberal Corporatism."

The growth of liberal corporatism marks an increasing institutional recognition of the importance of organized interests in policymaking. For
many years, a large part of policy has been determined by the interactions
of interest groups and state bureaucracy. The role of these groups, however, has not been adequately represented in the institutional structure of the
political system. While the institutionally legitimated policy-making process relied on parties and parliament, interest groups played no formal role.
Group influence had not been bound and controlled by institutionalized
procedures. Quite clearly, liberal corporatism has not, so far, provided a
constitutionally determined structure for the integration of groups into the
policy process, but it does offer some opportunities for institutionalized
and controlled participation of interest groups in policy making. The bargaining structures of liberal corporatism are still weakly formalized, and
there is yet no democratic control of these structures; but, at least, pressure
groups that have become imbedded in some structurally regulated bargaining rarely compete. [11]

In the recent literature of political science it is often said that the modern
welfare state is becoming ungovernable. [12] While such an argument is often
empirically poorly substantiated and consists of extrapolations of short-
term trends and disturbances, there does remain a real problem of governability. According to Schmitter, a large part of this problem is created by
the pluralist interest intermediation of modern democracies and the lack of
competition among pressure groups. [13] From this point of view, an integration of interest groups into some overarching bargaining structure, as is
provided by liberal corporatism, may contribute to an increase in governmental capacity. It may, furthermore, be an effective means of reducing
the influence of particular interests on policy decisions and of providing a
filter for special demands that, according to the Olson hypothesis, lead to
growth-inhibiting policy.

There is little empirical knowledge as to the impact of liberal corporatism on policy formation. Schmitter's pilot study indicates, however, that
corporatist structures have a positive effect on such problems as citizen

---

11. Louis Galambos, *Competition and Cooperation* (Baltimore: Johns Hopkins University Press,
1966); Lehner, *Grenzen des Regierens;* Schmitter, "Interest Intermediation."
12. Cf. Samuel Brittan, "The Economic Contradictions of Democracy"; Michel Crozier, Samuel
P. Huntington, and Joji Watanuki, *The Crisis of Democracy* (New York: New York University Press,
1975); Anthony King, "Overload: Problems of Governing in the 1970s," *Political Studies* (1975);
Richard Rose, "Overloaded Government: The Problem Outlined," *European Studies Newsletter* 5
(1975).
13. Schmitter, "Interest Intermediation."

Table 10.1.   Liberal Corporatism and Economic Growth

Country	Ranking in Corporatism	Increase in GDP 1953–73 (percent)
Austria	1	61.4
Norway	2	95.3
Denmark	4	102.9
Finland	4	145.6
Netherlands	6	108.6
Belgium	7	105.2
Germany	8	160.2
Canada	11	64.9
U.S.	11	65.6
France	13	140.0
Italy	15	140.7

Correlation between the variables $R = 0.24$

SOURCES: Corporatism rankings taken from Philippe Schmitter, "Interest Intermediation and Regime Governability in Contemporary Western Europe," mimeographed, 1977; GDP increase calculated from Robin Marris, "Some New Results on 'Catch-Up,'" mimeographed, 1978.

unruliness and fiscal ineffectiveness. Countries with corporatist structures seem to have fewer collective protests, internal wars, and strikes than do less corporatist countries. With increasing corporatism, there is also a smaller increase in taxation and governmental borrowing. Liberal corporatism is, thus, an interesting device for dealing with some of the problems surrounding governmental effectiveness and efficiency.[14] The case looks different if we consider the impact of liberal corporatism on economic growth. A preliminary and very rough empirical test of this relationship, using data from Schmitter and Marris, did not result in any significant correlation. Countries with a high rank on corporatism did not necessarily have a high growth of GDP per capita (see table 10.1). This result is not surprising if we take into account that liberal corporatism only integrates a few major interest groups, while most of the others remain outside the bargaining. Liberal corporatism does not provide an overarching bargaining system similar to Swiss consociationalism, but rather a very limited and partial integration of organized interests. It is, on the basis of the Olson hypothesis, quite clear that liberal corporatism could be an effective means of preventing or reducing growth-inhibiting demands only to the extent that it is an encompassing structure. As long as it includes only a few major groups, the pressure for protectionist special-interest policy will not be

14. Ibid.

drastically reduced. Furthermore, the establishment of an exclusive bargaining structure, as represented by liberal corporatism, provokes increasing conflicts with excluded groups. This implies that liberal corporatism will be an effective solution to the problems described by Olson only if it becomes an inclusive structure. Such a structure, however, faces extremely high bargaining costs and a large amount of institutional inertia. Under these conditions it is unlikely that liberal corporatism can develop into an encompassing bargaining structure: organized interests that act rationally will hardly be willing to engage voluntarily in bargaining that involves high costs and offers, for each group, only a low payoff. Indeed, we can observe in most modern democracies that the existing structures of liberal corporatism are unstable.[15] Nevertheless, one should not underestimate the functional importance of liberal corporatism.

In an interesting elaboration of Olson's *Logic of Collective Action,* Widmaier demonstrated that an increasing division of labor in the highly industrialized democracies creates an increasing organization of interests. An increasing division of labor results in a continuing decomposition of society into comparatively small groups, each with a highly specialized function in economic production. These groups can, owing to their specialization and size, be rather easily organized. They also can obtain considerable political power since they "control" specialized functions in production. The consequence of this development is a high degree of organized special interest and a large load of organized demands on the political system.[16] This great load of organized demands can hardly be satisfied by the limited resources and limited capacity to increase taxation available to the government. This leads, according to Widmaier, to increasing conflicts over the distribution of governmental resources. However, these conflicts rarely take the form of direct confrontation between organized interests, but rather are carried out between interest groups and the government, or between different governmental agencies. As Presthus shows, the reason for this is that organized interests seldom compete with each other. Demands of organized interests are rarely mediated in a competitive manner but are, as a rule, forwarded through exclusive channels with particular governmental agencies and bureaus.[17] Under these conditions, an integra-

15. See Lehner, *Grenzen des Regierens.*

16. Ulrich Widmaier, *Politische Gewaltanwendung als Problem der Organisation von Interessen* (Meisenheim: Hain, 1978).

17. Robert Presthus, "Toward a Post-Pluralist Theory of Democratic Stability" (Paper delivered at the Tenth IPSA World Congress, 1976). See also Donald R. Hall, *Cooperative Lobbying—The Power*

tion of organized-interest intermediation through corporative structures is, partial though it may be, a potentially effective means of establishing competitive bargaining and reducing organized demand. Thus far, however, liberal corporatism for the most part includes only vested interests that are already part of competitive bargaining: namely, unions and employers. It is quite obvious that the problems created by massive organized interest intermediation can be solved only to the extent that competitive bargaining can be introduced in a more encompassing manner.

Conclusions

In this essay, I have attempted to demonstrate, using the examples of Swiss consociational democracy and liberal corporatism, the importance of an interactive structure of organized-interest intermediation for policymaking. The relationship between organized-interest intermediation and economic growth can, to my mind, only be understood if the analysis includes the patterns of interaction both among groups and between groups and the government. The neglect of such patterns reduces the empirical precision and validity of Olson's theory.

The patterns I have discussed are certainly not the only relevant ones. If we consider the French case, where highly specialized and decentralized interest groups can be associated with a comparatively high growth rate, we are pointed to the relevance of bureaucratic structures. France has a highly centralized and professionally integrated bureaucracy, and we reasonably may conjecture that the French bureaucratic structure overarches organized-interest intermediation in a way that is favorable to growth. Similarly, we may find that in federalist countries with a high degree of intergovernmental cooperation and bargaining, the load of organized demands on government can be reduced as cooperation and bargaining provide an effective restriction on the success of organized-interest intermediation.[18] The inclusion of such structures into the Olson hypothesis will certainly increase its empirical content. This is not the only argument for such an inclusion; a pragmatic argument may be just as important. It is

of Pressure (Tucson: The University of Arizona Press, 1969); Lehner, *Grenzen des Regierens;* Liberson, "An Empirical Study"; Offe, "Politische Herrschaft"; Robert Presthus, *Elites in the Policy Process* (New York: Random House, 1974); Fritz W. Scharpf, *Politische Durchsetzbarkeit innerer Reformen* (Göttingen: Schwartz, 1974).

18. Fritz W. Scharpf, "Theorie der Politikverflechtung," in *Politikverflechtung,* ed. Fritz W. Scharpf, Bernd Reissert, and Fritz Schnabel (Kronberg: Scriptor, 1976).

quite clear that organized-interest intermediation creates some of the most pressing problems for the modern welfare state and its economic development, yet a solution for these problems is hardly in view. Political scientists and economists can offer little advice. To find realistic solutions to these problems one has to analyze the impacts of different structures of interest intermediation and the integration of these into the political machinery.

Part III: Two Alternative Views of the Evidence

11: Between Two Worlds: Interest Groups, Class Structure, and Capitalist Growth

SAMUEL BOWLES and JOHN EATWELL

Mancur Olson's essay, "The Political Economy of Comparative Growth Rates," has much to recommend it; his distinction between causes of growth and sources of growth is an invitation to move beyond mere growth accounting to a causal or structural understanding. Helpful also is his insistence that the retardants to growth may be rooted in social institutions, rather than in technology, preferences, or resource endowments. Moreover, the urgency that some feel for just such an analysis can hardly be doubted, as the past decade has witnessed an apparently persistent decline in the economic growth of most advanced capitalist nations.

There is nothing bashful or modest about Olson's attempt. We refer not so much to the grand scope of the project as to its methodological chutzpah. The unlikely analytical tools Olson has deployed are part of a conceptual framework that not only has eschewed the analysis of dynamic structural change in favor of static or comparative static allocational questions, but also has found it convenient (if not always particularly insightful) to abstract from the static analysis of social relations that could not be fully represented as contractual or contract-like. This second characteristic of neoclassical economic theory has not troubled most economists, who have been content to invoke an interdisciplinary division of labor in the interests of developing the formal economic theory and, not incidentally, banishing the awkward question of power. "The solution is essentially the transformation of a conflict from a political problem to an economic transaction," wrote Abba Lerner. "An economic problem is a solved political problem. Economics has gained the title of queen of the social sciences by choosing solved political problems as its domain."[1] But the development of the in-

---

1. A. Lerner, "The Politics and Economics of Consumer Sovereignty," *AEA Papers and Proceedings*, 1972.

terventionist state has made it increasingly difficult for economists to quarantine the question of power. Recent history has shaken our confidence in the separability of economic and political questions. Neoclassical economists have not, however, developed conceptual tools adequate to the task of understanding the complex interaction of political and economic structures that characterize the present evolution of the advanced capitalist societies. The resulting theoretical lacunae, we shall argue, are amply exhibited in Olson's paper.

Olson's question is, of course, not new. Speculation on the relationship between liberal political institutions and capitalist economic structures has preoccupied social theorists since Adam Smith. Indeed, the erstwhile compelling claim that the capitalist economy facilitates both the rapid expansion of economic well-being and the perpetuation and extension of democratic institutions has been a major basis for the substantial political and ideological force of liberalism.[2] The optimism of the liberal tradition has not been universally shared, however. Prominent among the doubters have been those who questioned the long-term compatibility of a political system that confers considerable, if circumscribed, political power on the many and an economic system in which the many work for and support the few.[3]

Olson's essay must be placed squarely within the tradition of the doubters in questioning the viability of liberalism's grand dual project, but the substance of Olson's argument marks a significant departure. The doubters' elaboration of democratic theory—commonly called the theory of democratic elitism—has stressed the salutory, even essential, role of interest groups in mediating the relationship between a nearly universal electorate and state policy.[4] Olson's paper is thus doubly ingenuous, for in unwittingly etching the epitaph for liberalism's grand dual project, he identifies the fateful malady as those very interest groups that other doubters had hoped might render democracy safe for capitalism.

A central feature of Olson's analysis is his tendency to depoliticize economic relations and to abstract from or trivialize the economic basis of political relations. Three substantial shortcomings result.

2. E. Halevy, *The Growth of Philosophic Radicalism* (Boston: Beacon Press, 1955).

3. See, for example, S. Huntington et al., *The Crisis of Democracy* (New York: New York University Press, 1975); J. Schumpeter, *Capitalism, Socialism and Democracy* (London: Allen and Unwin, 1941); and W. Struve, *Elites against Democracy: Leadership Ideals in Bourgeois Political Thought in Germany, 1890–1930* (Princeton: Princeton University Press, 1973).

4. See J. Madison et al., *The Federalist Papers* (New York: Anchor Books, 1961); and D. Truman, *The Governmental Process* (New York: Alfred A. Knopf, 1951).

First, Olson ignores the always problematic nature of the reproduction of class structure and other aspects of the institutional basis of society. Thus in assessing the negative growth effects of interest groups in the capitalist economy Olson implicitly posits an absurd counterfactual: a society without political organization except for the ideal liberal state, distributionally neutral and Pareto-optimal. The national government itself, when not influenced by lobbying groups, has an incentive to promote efficiency and growth. Olson here skirts the problematic nature of reproducing the domination of labor by capital and the integral role played by the representative state in this process.[5] Contrary to the thrust of Olson's argument, liberal democratic institutions have been essential to stable growth in the advanced capitalist countries. Not only have these institutions legitimized an exploitative economic system, they have provided a political arena which served to heighten the salience of a plurality of immediate distributional interests as opposed to more fundamental class interests. In many of the advanced capitalist nations, the alternative to interest-group formation on the terrain of liberal democracy is not, as Olson would have it, the neutral Pareto-efficient state, but an intensification of class conflict almost certain to have negative, perhaps terminal, effects on capitalist growth, far overshadowing the interest-group-induced Pareto distortions that Olson considers decisive.

Second, Olson reduces the question of growth to a matter of allocative efficiency. The scope of Olson's economics is thus at least as limited as his political analysis; this may be clarified by the following simple accounting framework. Setting aside difficult problems of measurement, we can express the level of actual output Y, as the product of three terms: potential output P, determined by the full and efficient utilization of available resources; capacity utilization C, measuring the fraction of total available resources actually put to use; and efficiency E, measuring the degree of efficiency of the resources actually in use. Thus, we can write as an identity

$$Y \equiv PCE. \qquad (1)$$

Transforming the expression to logarithms and differentiating with respect to time:

$$\dot{y} \equiv \dot{p} + \dot{c} + \dot{e}. \qquad (2)$$

The rate of growth of actual output $\dot{y}$ is thus the sum of the rates of change

5. R. Miliband, *The State in Capitalist Society* (London: Weidenfeld, 1969).

of potential output, capacity utilization, and efficiency. Olson's analysis focuses on efficiency; little attention is given to the obviously central question of growth in potential output and changes in capacity utilization. Nor is this peculiar narrowness of vision unimportant, for contrary to Olson's exegesis, the most important negative economic effects of democratic political practices on growth are manifested not in non-Pareto-optimal static resource allocations, but rather in redistributions of the total product and restrictions on production and markets, which, while not substantially inconsistent with efficient resource allocation, nonetheless militate against high levels of investment and capacity utilization within the institutional arrangements of capitalism. By focusing on political effects on the levels of efficiency, Olson abstracts from the complex and probably more important political components in the determination of the growth of potential output and capacity utilization.

One may note in passing that a theory of growth (of $\dot{y}$ rather than of Y) requires an analysis of *changes* in efficiency levels ($\dot{e}$, not E). Much of Olson's work, including the supporting econometric work by Choi and others, appears to have overlooked this point.

Third, and as a result of the above two points, the contradiction which Olson's analysis points to is not, as he would have it "between the desire for stability and peace and the desire to realize our full economic potential." The diligent reader discovers that Olson, carefully distancing himself from Marx, is willing (in a footnote) to concede that the conflict between democracy and growth is a "contradiction of capitalism." Indeed, liberal democratic capitalism is contradictory precisely because the reproduction of the institutional structure of capitalist production requires the systematic domination by capital of the vast majority of producers, while at the same time, reproduction of the system of political relations in the liberal democratic state promises, even requires, a modicum of popular power. In the advanced capitalist societies the promise can neither be reneged nor made good. It is the capitalist institution—historical and malleable—not the "nature of things" in all its impervious inertia that renders expanded affluence and the extension of democratic rights contradictory.

These three shortcomings of Olson's perspective motivate the analyses which follow: first, of Olson's model; second, of the relation between economic growth and "institutional" development in a capitalist economy; and, finally, of the particular circumstances of the U.K. economy.

Olson's Model

Olson's model consists of two entirely separate elements: the neoclassical model of resource allocation, and his model of "interest group" formation and behavior, which itself is based on concepts derived from neoclassical theory. The separation is an essential part of his analysis: interest groups may impose upon or intervene in the market and inhibit its allocative efficiency, but they do not alter in any way the nature of the economic mechanism. If they are removed the mechanism reverts to its natural and eternal state. There is thus no organic relationship between economic and political organization; economic phenomena are not constituted by and embedded in a complex social structure. Rather, they are part of an entirely separately constituted system that may only adjust to exogenous political shocks. The political system, for Olson, is superimposed upon the economy like a photographic overlay. One is immediately reminded of the shortcomings of physiocratic treatment of taxation, of Ricardo's treatment of the Corn Laws, and of J. S. Mill's unfortunate distinction between the historico-political process of distribution and the technical process of production.

Olson's economic analysis is fundamentally contradictory. While attempting to analyze the growth experience of modern capitalism he utilizes a static allocation model, a model that, even in its intertemporal form, is entirely inappropriate to the problem of growth, as one of its leading exponents has pointed out.[6] Moreover, Olson appears to be unconcerned with the wide range of crucial weaknesses in the competitive allocation model, ranging from second-best problems to the simple point that a Pareto optimum is not necessarily a social optimum. The only analytical point made by Olson that is relevant to the problem at hand concerns the relationship between the speed of innovation and entry. His point is entirely ad hoc and quite unrelated to any analytical framework within which its relevance for growth might be evaluated. In terms of the usual theories of investment that lay stress on problems of risk, expected returns through time, and so on, it is clearly wrong: patents, for example, promote growth by *limiting* entry.

Even the rather limited growth models of the fifties and sixties recog-

6. Frank Hahn's arguments for the irrelevance of neoclassical theory to real problems are now well known. A spirited sample may be found in his articles "The Winter of Our Discontent," *Economica* (1973), and "Back to Square One," *Cambridge Review* (1974).

nized that the growth process must encompass at least two elements: the technological conditions of expanded reproduction[7] and the effective demand condition that ensures that accumulated capacity is utilized.[8] Olson, as we have shown, ignores both these elements, except to pay lip service to the growth-accounting literature. Nor is his silence here innocent, for Olson knows that attempts to build a specifically neoclassical analogue to von Neumann's growth model that would be based on the aggregate production function came to grief more than a decade ago.[9]

Olson's adherence to neoclassical economic theory affects more than his economics; it is the fundamental reason why he can do no more than superimpose politics upon economics. Critical here is his failure to acknowledge the central relationship of a capitalist economy, that between capital and labor. This essentially antagonistic relationship, occluded by the contractual veil of the free market, is manifest not only in the sale and purchase of labor power, but also in the political structure of the workplace and in the other institutional forms characteristic of capitalist societies. Olson's depoliticized characterization of economic phenomena thus severely constrains his ability to develop an even partially adequate social analysis; for the structure of neoclassical theory can comprehend institutions only as external influences on the economic model. Hence, his social analysis is a mirror image of his inadequate economic analysis. Social institutions are portrayed simply as collections of individuals (which they obviously are) operating under constraints that are reduced to the contractual relations of the market and the institutional relations of the liberal state. The analysis of class relations is ruled out, and partly for this reason the analysis of the state is trivialized, all consideration of the characteristics and requirements of specifically capitalist accumulation being excluded.[10] Similarly, he fails to acknowledge that markets and market forms—free trade, the international monetary system, corporate financial organization—are not ordained by a Pareto-omniscient God and the engineers, but are themselves social institutions, deriving their peculiar characteristics

7. J. von Neumann, "A Model of General Economic Equilibrium," *Review of Economic Studies* (1945).

8. R. F. Harrod, *Toward a Dynamic Economics* (London: Macmillan, 1974).

9. The issues are outlined by P. Samuelson, "A Summing-Up," *Quarterly Journal of Economics* (1966); and P. Garegnani, "Heterogeneous Capital, the Production Function and the Theory of Distribution," *Review of Economic Studies* (1970).

10. Compare Olson's image of the state with the arguments surveyed by T. Jessop, "Recent Theories of the Capitalist State," *Cambridge Journal of Economics* (1977).

and their quite substantial political and social effects from their particular places in the history of capitalist development.

A Framework for the Analysis of Growth

What is presented here is merely a sketch of what we would regard as an adequate framework for an analysis of the institutional context of the growth experience of the capitalist system. However, the essential content of our approach will, perhaps, be made clear in our discussion of the British case. The fundamental premises of our analysis derive from the peculiar characteristics of capitalism as a mode of production: it is a system in which production and distribution are organized through a generalized process of exchange; in which the means of production are owned and controlled by a few, with the social organization of production being centered around the sale and purchase of the labor power of the many; and for which the competitive imperative to accumulate provides the force for change.

The bases of capitalist accumulation may be found in the continuous creation, realization, and investment of surplus (that is, of production in excess of the requirements of social reproduction, which is defined as the production directly and indirectly required to maintain capacity and the customary standard of living of those who sell their labor power to capital). These three elements depend upon the economic possibilities for expansion inherent in technology, distribution, and the level of effective demand but are *determined* by the social organization of the economy. The interaction between the material and social conditions of reproduction and accumulation will be manifest in particular institutional forms ranging from the organization of the state, the organization of the labor process, and the framework of law and the monetary system to the forms of trading relations (domestic and international) and to the particular interest groups that represent economic (and other) forces on a narrower or wider scale.

For accumulation to take place it is essential that institutions be developed that facilitate accumulation, ensure the reproduction of the material and social conditions of accumulation, and legitimize the social forms of the production and distribution processes. The history of capitalist development may be interpreted as a continuous process of institutional adaptation aimed at the subjugation of ever-widening spheres of economic and social life to the characteristics and requirements of the capitalist system.

The modern corporation, for example, has developed in such a way as to increase the mobility, and hence growth potential, of capital. From this perspective modern capitalism may be seen to be more competitive to-day—in the sense of mobility and entry—than ever before, quite contrary to what Olson apparently believes.[11]

Institutional development is not necessarily geared to the needs of capitalist expansion but, on the contrary, may be the result of powerful challenges to capitalist hegemony. Institutions arising from these challenges include the organization of labor unions, the extension of suffrage, and the interventionist state. Such institutions may appear to the superficial observer to limit the rate of growth, but without them continued *capitalist* growth would not, in many cases, take place at all. Even such institutions as labor unions, the activities of which might be regarded as antithetical to capitalistic accumulation, in many instances foster and preserve such accumulation. The development of hierarchy in the labor market and within the capitalist firm was undoubtedly an essential ingredient in the success of capital's attempt to establish control over the labor process, but it was largely generated and strongly ratified through the power of trade unions.[12]

This latter point introduces an important element into our analysis: institutions may both be necessary to capitalist development and inhibit such development. Our example of the effects of labor unions in structuring and disciplining the labor market is suggestive of this duality; but perhaps of more importance is the historical evolution of institutional forms that may, in one epoch, be the very stuff of successful and rapid accumulation and in another be powerful retarding elements. The entrenchment of institutional forms, of social norms, and of forms of discourse by their very historical success implies that the recreation and modification of institutional conditions are difficult and often painful.

The ossification of institutional structures is thus a fundamental problem of the growth process. Olson is quite right to stress the potentially liberating effect of the institutional conflagration which may accompany domestic revolution or foreign occupation. But he fails to locate such changes within the context of the economic and social imperatives that initiate and direct them. His approach would, for example, conflate the achievements

---

11. On the competitive role of modern corporative organization see J. Clifton, "Competition and the Evolution of the Capitalist Mode of Production," *Cambridge Journal of Economics* (1977).

12. S. Bowles and H. Gintis, "The Marxian Theory of Value and Heterogeneous Labor: A Critique and Reformation," *Cambridge Journal of Economics* (1977); J. Rubery, "Structured Labor Markets, Worker Organization and Low Pay," *Cambridge Journal of Economics* (1978).

of the British Labour government of 1945–51 with the economic effects of Gaullism.

In liberal democratic society, maintaining a growth-supporting institutional context has typically required the frequent creation of new political alliances with both the power and the will to institute appropriate measures; the political coalition emerging out of the New Deal years is an example. Yet these alliances are difficult to form and even more difficult to maintain in the absence of quick success and substantial payoffs.

The difficulties in creating dynamic conditions in any particular country are compounded by the nature of capitalist accumulation on its modern world scale. The imperatives of competition are such that regions or countries in a position of relative disadvantage tend to be caught in a depressing cycle of low effective demand, low investment, low productivity growth, and increasing competitive disadvantage. This cumulative process,[13] when viewed in the context of the modern system of trading and monetary relationships in the capitalist world, reinforces the decline of relatively unsuccessful countries. Parenthetically it may be noted that the failure to relate capitalist accumulation on a world scale to the *particular* experiences of individual countries is a further weakness of Olson's analysis.

What we have argued above should also serve as a warning against the construction of ''models'' that reduce the explanation of the role of institutional structures in the accumulation process to a single parameter: in Olson's case, the period of democratic stability. Within the broad framework we have outlined, each nation-state will tend to have its own political dynamic, which distinguishes the form, history, and effects of its institutional structure. A satisfactory theory should then be able to comprehend the complexity of national and historical phenomena within its explanatory categories, without monocausal reductionism.

The Case of the United Kingdom

The economic history of the United Kingdom has, perhaps, commanded more attention than that of any other country, and we cannot expect within the scope of this short essay to add anything other than a perspective to the enormous weight of existing interpretation. Our perspective will concen-

13. Outlined by G. Myrdal, *Economic Theory and Underdeveloped Regions* (London: Duckworth, 1957).

'rate on the institutional aspects of British development and on the interaction of institutional development and material expansion.

The Industrial Revolution was accompanied by—indeed, it may be characterized by—dramatic institutional reform. Not only did it see domestically the establishment of a labor market, joint-stock companies, an increasingly sophisticated financial system, and factory production in general (with the accompanying creation of a proletariat), but also internationally the consolidation of empire in an era of free-trade imperialism[14] and the development of an international financial system and an outward-looking capitalist class. In the early period, growth in other countries took a form that Sayers has described as "complementary";[15] that is, growth overseas stimulated demand for British goods and was, indeed, a vital component of total demand. In the period 1836–53 net exports of British manufactures (the difference between exports and imports) grew in constant prices at 5.7 percent per year.

However, after 1850 industrialization overseas became competitive with British industry, and the growth rate of net exports fell from 2.9 percent in the period 1853–73 to 1.5 percent in the period 1873–1907.[16] The remarkable turnaround in Britain's fortunes after 1870 marked the beginning of a century of relative decline. Explanations for this phenomenon, and in particular for the failure of British industry to respond to the competitive challenges emanating from the U.S. and Germany, have been many and varied, but perhaps the most persuasive locates that failure within the institutional structure which was built up in the period of success. This comprised a domestic structure that eschewed any political or economic institution capable of controlling the economy as a structural whole, and hence of carrying out fundamental reform, and an external structure wedded to the Empire and "free trade":

> In essence, what happened, therefore, was that Britain exported her immense accumulated historic advantages in the underdeveloped world, as the greatest commercial power, and the greatest source of international loan capital. . . . When faced with a challenge, it was

14. See D. Winch, *Classical Political Economy and the Colonies* (Cambridge, Mass.: Harvard University Press, 1965); and B. Semmel, *The Rise of Free Trade Imperialism* (Cambridge: Cambridge University Press, 1970).

15. R. S. Sayers, *The Vicissitudes of an Export Economy: Britain Since 1880* (Sydney: University of Sydney Press, 1965).

16. W. A. Lewis, "The Deceleration of British Growth, 1873–1913," mimeographed (Princeton, 1967).

easier and cheaper to retreat into an as yet unexploited part of one of these favoured zones, rather than to meet competition face to face.[17]

So the institutions that had been the foundations of British success proved to be the very institutions that contributed to its failure to reform and laid the framework for ultimate decline.

The continued influence of the free-trade and free-convertibility lobby, identified increasingly with the City of London and its worldwide financial empire, led to the disastrous return to gold in 1925,[18] which crippled reconstruction in the twenties—a situation only partially relieved by the protectionist period from 1931 to World War II, during which rapid growth of new industries—electronics, automobiles, chemicals—redressed some of the competitive imbalance accumulated in the preceding half-century. The post–World War II period from 1945 to 1951 did, however, herald a truly significant change; not only was growth in foreign countries once again essentially complementary, but also there existed a class alignment, represented by the newly elected Labour government, with the will and power to restore the structural conditions for rapid growth. Undoubtedly, major and lasting beneficial reform was enacted in this period, but two factors militated against a complete change of course: first, much effort was focused on reform of Britain's archaic social institutions with less direct effort being lavished on economic reconstruction; second, economic reconstruction was itself limited by the need to export capital goods (to the detriment of domestic investment) to repay foreign debt.[19] The failure to achieve a major payoff in economic well-being and the international political imperatives of the 1950s led to the reestablishment of free-trade policies, the relaxation of domestic controls, and the beginning of the stop-go cycle of cumulative decline and "de-industrialisation."[20]

For our purpose the significant element in this narrative is the manner in which those institutions that were identified with the success of British industrialization—free trade, domestic laissez-faire (with the consequent lack of any organizational formation comparable to the German banks, the giant Japanese companies, or the French Commissariat du Plan), the City

17. E. Hobsbawm, *Industry and Empire* (Harmondsworth: Penguin, 1969), p. 191.
18. D. E. Moggridge, *The Return to Gold, 1925* (Cambridge: Cambridge University Press, 1969).
19. R. Nurkse, "The Relation between Home Investment and External Balance in the Light of British Experience," *Review of Economics and Statistics* (1956).
20. A. Singh, "U.K. Industry and the World Economy: A Case of Deindustrialisation?" *Cambridge Journal of Economics* (1977); F. Blackaby, ed., *De-industrialisation* (London: Heinemann, 1978).

of London and its financial empire, and outward-looking, internationally mobile corporations—have become just those institutions that have contributed to Britain's industrial decline and that inhibit any fundamental change. This has led a number of writers to call for a radical revision of Britain's trading relationships and, in particular, for abandonment of the general commitment to free trade and its replacement by widespread protection to reduce Britain's propensity to import and to release the British economy from its pervasive balance-of-payments constraint.[21] However, while there can be little doubt that an abandonment of free trade is a necessary precondition for the successful revitalization of British industry, it is clearly not sufficient.[22] For such a revitalization will necessarily include a major reform of industrial and social structures, and it is not at all evident that the political alignment exists to undertake such a task.

The fundamental characteristic of British political life today is stalemate. The failure of successive governments to initiate the requisite reforms has eroded the possibility of establishing the coalition of social forces that is the prior condition for change. Although it has been argued convincingly that the power of the trade unions has been developed and used defensively,[23] it seems likely that this power closed one potential avenue for the restoration of profitability and rapid growth: a massive transfer of real resources from labor to capital. Yet the trade unions have not proved sufficiently powerful to enact the structural reforms necessary to provide an alternative institutional apparatus capable of promoting rapid growth. Hence the stalemate. We see here an essential contradiction of liberal democratic capitalism: that while it provides an arena within which a certain range of conflicts may be worked out, it tends to inhibit the

21. This argument is not affected by the fact that North Sea oil will temporarily place the British balance of payments in surplus, since there is nothing intrinsic to the oil surplus that will strengthen the competitive position of the industrial sector—if anything, quite the contrary.

22. Olson has completely misinterpreted Eatwell's remarks concerning "hospitalization" of the British economy; not only has he ignored the dynamic implications of operating the economy at a high level of effective demand, but he has also forgotten that hospitalization can seldom be a cure without the administration of some form of treatment, be it medication or surgery. See Cambridge Economic Policy Group, *Economic Policy Review* (annual, 1975–80); F. Cripps and W. Godley, "Control of Imports as Means to Full Employment and the Expansion of World Trade: the U.K.'s Case," *Cambridge Journal of Economics* (1978); A. Singh, "North Sea Oil and the Reconstruction of the British Economy," in *De-industrialisation*, ed. F. Blackaby (London: Heinemann, 1978); M. Ellman, "Report from Holland: The Economics of North Sea Hydrocarbons," *Cambridge Journal of Economics* (1977).

23. J. Robinson and F. Wilkinson, "What Has Become of Full-Employment Policy?" *Cambridge Journal of Economics* (1977); R. Tarling and F. Wilkinson, "The Social Contract: Post-War Incomes Policies and their Inflationary Impact," *Cambridge Journal of Economics* (1977).

construction of a new set of growth-inducing institutions for an economy in decline.

Conclusions

What do we learn from the example of the United Kingdom? Most important, this: the analysis of the political aspects of the growth process of advanced capitalism requires a conceptual framework that treats the development of institutional and economic phenomena as an organic whole and, hence, that extends the specification of the institutional context beyond market relations and the liberal democratic constitution to include both class relations and the other social forces that contribute to the perpetuation of class dominance.

Moreover, all interest groups are not equal. As Olson recognizes, some are more powerful than others; and they differ in their effects as well. The programs of some groups are more nearly consistent with the objective of a rapid increase in economic welfare than are others. Thus in the British case, which has seen organized labor pitted against the City of London and large capital, labor has by and large supported programs that would contribute directly or indirectly to the effective use of resources: full employment, national health insurance, expanded educational opportunity, and the like. Conversely, the City and its allies have quite consistently favored an overvalued pound and government budget cutting, to the detriment of full employment, and have opposed egalitarian social programs that would have enhanced labor skills.

What Olson fails to recognize is this: the pursuit of their interests by the capitalist and working classes is hardly symmetrical in its effects on the growth rate. The interests of the dominant group must necessarily include the preservation of the institutions that support their dominance. This defense will be consistent with growth optimization only if the conditions of institutional reproduction are either entirely separable from the conditions of rapid growth or coincident with them.

Within the context of a capitalist economy, the pursuit of workers' interests may well be growth-retarding insofar as it reduces after-tax profits or creates a climate that discourages profit-seeking investment, but these effects can hardly be represented as *allocational* distortions. Indeed, the working class—by far the most ''encompassing'' of all potential interest groups—may well be the only vehicle for the construction of a social and economic system, the reproduction of which does not precipitate that fateful contradiction which is becoming increasingly characteristic of the capitalist world system—the contradiction between the pursuit of rapid growth and the quest for a democratic society.

Like neoclassical "political" economy, liberal democratic capitalist societies recall Matthew Arnold's lines from "Stanzas from the Grande Chartreuse":

> Wandering between two worlds, one dead,
> the other powerless to be born.

12: Polyarchy and Economic Growth

JAMES W. DEAN

This essay deals with the forces for and against growth under *polyarchy*, defined in this context as government in response to interest groups. It is inspired by Mancur Olson's thesis that (*a*) narrowly based interest groups proliferate as democracies mature uninterrupted by war or similar crises; and that (*b*) such interest groups inhibit economic growth.[1] Examples of such groups might be craft unions in Britain, and a counter example might be labor/management "codetermination" in the Federal Republic of Germany.

I submit that Olson's thesis, though extremely useful, is seriously incomplete. Because he has ignored both the political elements and the form of economic organization unique to polyarchy, he misses a political dynamic that is critical to economic growth. The fundamental political characteristics of polyarchy, liberalism and popular participation, work in opposition because of the basic economic characteristic of polyarchy— free enterprise. Liberalism under free enterprise accords a dominant role to a growth-oriented interest group—business—a role that Olson's thesis fails to capture. Popular participation militates against this dominant role and therefore to some extent against growth.

The first part of my essay deals with pluralist ideology, citing the U.S. Constitution as an archetype and arguing that strong liberal elements are embodied therein. The second part establishes a connection between contemporary pluralist theory and the concept of polyarchy. The third part analyzes idealized polyarchy for its ability to meet a *democratic criterion:* the articulation and realization of collective goals in accordance with popu-

I am indebted for comments to Heribert Adam, Scott Gordon, Stephen Holmes, Lawrence Pinfield, Nelson Polsby, John Richards, Richard Schwindt, and Mark Wexler.
1. Mancur Olson, "The Political Economy of Comparative Growth Rates," chapter 1, this volume, above.

lar wishes. The fourth part suggests that, in practice, polyarchy's ability to meet our democratic criterion is seriously flawed. The fifth part argues that, paradoxically, polyarchy evolves from free enterprise yet works to undermine it. The sixth and final part elaborates an alternative to the Olson thesis, cites some anecdotal evidence, and suggests avenues for further research.

Pluralist Ideology and the U.S. Constitution

Pluralist political theory has been formalized only in recent decades. The modern theorists have been predominantly Americans, who both describe and idealize elements of democratic government that apply particularly to the United States. The government of the United States was pluralist in its conception, and in many ways the Constitution is archetypical.

In 1787, when the U.S. Constitution was drafted, American society was already exceptionally heterogeneous ethnically, religiously, and regionally. The founding fathers were aware of this and were also familiar with the major seventeenth- and eighteenth-century political philosophers: John Locke, Edmund Burke, Jean-Jacques Rousseau, and Charles Louis Montesquieu. Locke propounded individualistic liberalism; Burke, social conservatism; and Rousseau, participatory democracy. The trick was to realize Locke's liberalism and Rousseau's popular inclusiveness while retaining sufficient hegemony of interests to ensure Burkian continuity in political and social life.

Of these three principles, liberalism—meaning diffusion of power—was granted a relative strength in the Constitution that was unparalleled among governments of the time, and probably remains so. Popular inclusiveness in the form of universal suffrage came much later and only gradually, and Burkian political hegemony was neglected to an extent that resulted ultimately in civil war.

Constitutional liberalism, that is, restrictions on government to protect and enlarge the interests of other groups, had been evolving in Britain for centuries, long before eighteenth-century notions of popular rule. In the thirteenth century, the Magna Carta was designed to protect the interests of nobles; the Puritan and Glorious revolutions in the seventeenth century were backed by an emerging merchant class. Similarly, both the American and French revolutions were directed less to popular control than to the "rights of man" vis à vis the government.

The uniqueness of the Constitution lies in its codification of liberalism.

First, its version of threefold separation of powers between legislature, executive, and judiciary, though modelled on Montesquieu's study of British government, formalizes and enlarges the separation. In contrast with the tradition in the British parliament, the U.S. executive branch can (with qualifications) veto the legislature, and vice versa. Also, since legislative committees typically hammer out the content of important bills, great power resides with certain individuals—for example, those with seniority.[2] Thus checks and balances, as well as the committee system, uniquely curtail the hegemonic power of U.S. government, enhance the power of individuals, and render government susceptible to special-interest lobbies. The latter can be particularly effective in blocking legislation, via minority groups of elected representatives that can constitutionally exercise vetoes, but they can also strongly modify or even initiate legislation by influencing committee members or other key officials.

A second way in which liberalism is constitutionally codified in U.S. government is through the Bill of Rights, drafted in 1789 as the first nine amendments to the Constitution. These amendments, which provided unprecedented formal guarantees of individual liberties, have proved enormously potent in serving not only the purposes for which they were designed, but also as impediments to the course of American justice. Witness the extent to which organized crime, an Olsonian interest group if ever there was one, relies on the famous Fifth Amendment to withhold self-prejudicial information. An inherent defect in liberalism, as we shall elaborate later, is its susceptibility to abuse by interest groups that accumulate extraordinary power, influence, or money.

Finally, the Constitution's stipulation of states' rights in the context of federal government conceded, in the spirit of liberalism, so much to regional interests that it led to civil war and very nearly proved self-destructive. States' rights are constitutionally underwritten by the Tenth Amendment, which states, "The powers not delegated to the United States by the Constitution, nor prohibited by it to the States, are reserved to the States respectively, or to the people." It was this assignment of residual rights that was used by eleven southern states from 1860 to 1861 to justify their secession.

In practice, states' rights continue to manifest themselves in three ways. Most obviously, they are embodied in state governments. They are also

2. Legislators with seniority come almost by definition from "safe" districts, which tend in turn to be rural and conservative.

enhanced via the Senate, composed as it is of two senators from each state irrespective of population. Lastly, states' rights are indirectly enhanced via special-interest lobbies that have coalesced around intrastate concerns and established themselves in Washington, often with encouragement from state governments.[3]

Thus, the Constitution responded to a society that was at the time exceptionally heterogeneous and became much more so. Conversely, the Constitutional framework has in three ways encouraged the evolution of pluralism, as formally expressed in interest groups, particularly their political manifestation as lobbies. The exceptional separation of government powers enhanced the political efficacy of lobbies and encouraged their ensconcement in Washington; the Bill of Rights underwrote interest groups that emphasized individual liberties;[4] federalism formally involved the states as interest groups and indirectly encouraged regionally based lobbies. Finally, the last fifty years have seen an enormous proliferation of government departments, bureaus, and agencies, each of which pursues bureaucratic goals distinct from those of the body politic and most of which are vulnerable to interest-group pressure.

American constitutional reinforcement of interest-group politics is underwritten by a prevalent pluralist ideology. Much pluralist ideology derives its sustenance from Alexis de Tocqueville's classic *Democracy in America,* written in the 1830s on a government mission from France. Tocqueville lauded social and political pluralism in the United States, emphasizing its role in channelling grievances to the government, in protecting individual liberties, and particularly in providing opportunities for personal development through group association. Current mainstream political theory provides continuing reinforcement for this idealistic vision of American society and government.

Olson implicitly questions the unqualified virtues of the pluralist model by pointing to the inherent bias in democracy against collective goals—in particular, economic growth. Tocqueville, however, feared another bias that is inherent in pluralism under private enterprise: the extraordinary power of one interest group—big business. It is Olson's neglect of the critical role of business in interest-group politics that partially prompts this essay.

---

3. This is not to say that state governments have successfully retained all their constitutional rights. Recent trends show federal power growing in certain areas that constitutionally belong to the states: natural resources, education, and welfare are prime examples.

4. Sometimes hypocritically: for example, the gun lobby, or (not the same thing!) organized crime.

Contemporary Pluralist Theory

The dominant school of thought in contemporary American political theory is pluralist, representing politics as essentially interaction among interest groups. Government acts as an arena for resolution of group conflicts. This view implies that conflicts between, for example, organized labor and corporate business are resolved by such government proxies for labor and business as the Department of Labor and the Federal Trade Commission; but it also suggests, according to its primary expositor, Robert Dahl, that few groups (in the U.S.) that are determined to influence government and that are organized, active, and persistent can fail entirely to influence government officials.[5]

Certain sociologists and institutional economists also see the world through pluralist eyes, though they may not share the political theorists' language. In contrast with the latter, they focus on pluralism in the private sector and view government less as an arena for conflict resolution than as an umpire. Economists of this ilk include Adolf Berle and Gardiner Means[6] and John Kenneth Galbraith.[7] Writing in the thirties, Berle and Means were the first to perceive that corporate managers, as separate from owners, could initiate unilateral action outside the government process. They suggested that corporate interests are constrained not only by government but also by organized labor, the market, and a "corporate conscience." Two decades later, Galbraith deemphasized the latter two when he invented the concept of "countervailing power" to rationalize labor's need to organize to constrain corporate interests.[8]

Since our concern is with the connections between pluralism and government policy as it affects growth, I will concentrate on pluralist and antipluralist *political* analysis, relegating the literature from sociology and institutional economics to the background.

Dahl uses the term "polyarchy" to reflect the pluralist notion that popular participation in governance occurs in practice through interest groups, rather than via representation on the simple basis of enfranchised

5. Robert A. Dahl, *A Preface to Democratic Theory* (Chicago: University of Chicago Press, 1956), esp. ch. 5.
6. Adolph A. Berle and Gardiner C. Means, *The Modern Corporation and Private Property* (New York: Macmillan, 1933).
7. John Kenneth Galbraith, *American Capitalism: The Concept of Countervailing Power* (Boston: Houghton Mifflin, 1956).
8. For a good explanation of the arena/umpire distinction, see William E. Connally, ed., *The Bias of Pluralism* (New York: Atherton Press, 1969), ch. 1.

body counts as implied by the traditional term "democracy." Charles Lindblom estimated in 1977 that polyarchy exists in only twenty-eight of the world's 144 nations:

Australia	Italy
Austria	Jamaica
Belgium	Japan
Canada	Luxembourg
Costa Rica	Netherlands
Denmark	New Zealand
Federal Republic of Germany	Norway
Finland	Philippines
France	Sweden
Greece	Switzerland
Iceland	Trinidad and Tobago
India	United Kingdom
Ireland	United States
Israel	Venezuela

And, Lindblom suggests, "Some on the list are questionable, or were or will be. . . ."[9]

Is Olson's growth thesis applicable only to polyarchies, only to these twenty-eight countries at most? Certainly all countries he mentions are on this list. And if interest groups impose their growth-inhibiting externalities only via formal political power, as we surmise is the case in politically developed countries, his thesis can apply only in polyarchies by definition. In any case, I will confine my attention to the *political* influence of interest groups, and therefore to polyarchies.

I turn now to a taxonomy Dahl formulated that characterizes what he called *democratization* along two dimensions: popular participation and public contestation. I will show in the next section that each of these characteristics is necessary if collective goals are to be articulated and realized democratically; there, I will also show that polyarchy is nevertheless in practice seriously flawed. It is these flaws, I will argue, that underlie the conflict in polyarchies between such collective goals as growth on the one hand and participatory democracy on the other.

---

9. Charles E. Lindblom, *Politics and Markets: The World's Political Economic Systems* (New York: Basic Books, 1977), p. 131.

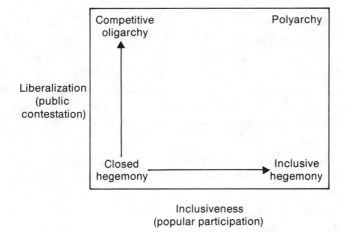

Figure 12.1.   Dimensions of Democratization

Polyarchy in Theory: Its Democratic Virtues

Dahl's taxonomy identifies two characteristics in democratization: popular participation, or ''inclusiveness,'' and public contestation, or ''liberalization.'' Nonparticipatory regimes without opportunity for contestation he terms *closed hegemonies*. Participation without contestation defines *inclusive hegemony;* contestation without participation defines *competitive oligarchy;* and contestation with participation defines *polyarchy*. Polyarchies are ''relatively (but incompletely) democratized regimes.''[10] All this is illustrated in figure 12.1.

I will define the democratic ideal not, as is usual, in terms of liberalization and inclusiveness, but as ''the articulation and realization of collective goals in accordance with popular will.'' How well can each of these regimes meet this criterion? I begin with closed hegemony.

Closed Hegemony

Deny for the moment human greed and lust for power, and assume, heroically, that a regime is perfectly altruistic or benevolent. This removes the most obvious need for contestation (though as I shall argue below,

10.   Robert A. Dahl, *Polyarchy: Participation and Opposition* (New Haven: Yale University Press, 1971), ch. 1.

contestation serves another purpose besides limiting the abuse of power).
Can the regime then approach the democratic ideal, lacking as it does
popular political participation?

The answer hinges on its information system: whether it can articulate
collective goals without perfect omniscience. Economists of liberal per-
suasion would argue that most so-called collective goals are best provided by private arrangement through the market, which articulates par
excellence preferences for private goods and should do so for public goods
as well. Those with less faith in laissez-faire argue that for the market to
begin as and remain an unbiased indicator of popular preferences even for
private goods would require virtual government omnipotence: the power to
distribute initial endowments of wealth equitably, to ensure equal economic and educational opportunities, and to limit unequal outcomes to the
extent that they cumulate as inequality in market power. Such extraordinary power would surely place an unrealistic burden on benevolence.

But the liberal economist's minimization of a need for political participation is also vulnerable on grounds particular to public goods and
public policy. His case rests on the naive assumptions about preferences
implicit in standard economic theory.[11] The latter takes all preferences as
given, including those that may have involved complex judgments and,
perhaps, ethical considerations. Economists generally avoid analysis of
preference formation, limiting themselves to the axiom of "revealed preference": what you chose, by definition, you wanted. This assumption has
proved workable for the analysis of price- and income-determined choice
among marketable goods and services, though at the cost of fostering
among economists the opinion that tastes for most goods are almost
primordial.

The revealed preference assumption is, however, absolutely inadmissi-
ble for political analysis because in that realm choice begins not with given
preferences but with a set of complex issues about which considerable
deliberation is required. As Lindblom puts it, "Choices are volitions. For
understanding political choices we need a concept that will identify not a
datum but an emergent act of will. Only after political choices are made can
they be referred to as data."[12]

Thus even granting the closed hegemonic government both perfect be-

11. Anthony Downs's seminal work, *An Economic Theory of Democracy* (New York: Harper &
Brothers, 1957) can hardly be termed naive. Nevertheless, he applies market choice theory directly to
politics.
12. Lindblom, *Politics and Markets*, p. 135.

nevolence and absolute omnipotence to ensure equal opportunity, and even assuming that "dollar votes" accurately translate private preferences into final output, such a government cannot possibly possess the omniscience necessary to formulate the demand for public goods and public policies. That is, the glaring deficiency in closed hegemony, even by the rather restricted democratic criterion, is that there are no political avenues by which preferences or volitions concerning collective goals can be popularly formulated. This process of formulation is crucial, since preferences are not static but emerge over time, with the outcome critically dependent on political dynamics.[13] Particularly in a pluralistic society, in which political dynamics are potentially complex, closed hegemony cannot even approach the omniscience necessary to govern. It is questionable enough whether data can be knowable; it is impossible conceptually that "emergent acts of will" can be knowable.

Of course no political system can act with the assurance of omniscience, but will public-policy formation under inclusive hegemony be easier?

Inclusive Hegemony

Assume the existence of consensual ethics: moral and ethical values are shared throughout the population. Everyone thinks alike in the sense that after deliberation, perhaps quite considerable deliberation, each citizen comes to the same conclusion when confronted with any particular issue.

Even under this assumption, inclusive hegemony is problematic. It places extraordinary strain on altruism. Public policy by definition imposes one good, service, or regulation on many individuals. Though all may think alike, not all are in the same boat; of the diversely situated, only the most Christ-like will come to the same conclusion. For example, ethical opposition to killing may be shared to the degree that everyone after discussion and deliberation opposes abortion; nevertheless, women and the young are affected differently and their self-interest may preclude a consensus. Thus consensual ethics is insufficient to guarantee consensual politics unless altruism dominates all other dimensions of the moral code; but consensual ethics help: witness the exceptional ability of the Japanese to achieve public consensus without overt interest-group conflict.

Inclusive hegemony *is* superior to closed hegemony in one important respect. Political choices, involving as they do complex volitionary delib-

---

13. The notion of a political dynamic is what distinguishes my thesis about growth under polyarchy from Olson's; this will become clear in the final section.

eration, cannot possibly be made without considerable and frequent input from the population at large. Partly, the advantage derives simply from dividing the labor of volitionary deliberation; but more than that, it derives from the ability to gather information from individuals in widely different circumstances.

The limitations of inclusive hegemony become apparent upon dropping the benevolence assumption, the consensual ethics assumption, or both. Dropping benevolence means that greed and lust for power will cause those governing to put their personal interests above those of the body politic. This could be countered by contestation. That is, the opportunity for contestation, Dahl's liberalization dimension, acquires a positive function—that of a counter to the self-interested exercise of power.

Dropping consensual ethics also assigns a positive function to liberalization, for if persons in different boats can no longer agree about the principle that decides who sinks if one boat develops a leak, an arena for arbitration helps articulate that collective goal. Again, contestation acquires value.

Polyarchy

Participation therefore moves government closer to the democratic ideal. Given participation, liberalization moves it closer still; thus the superiority of polyarchy over the three alternative regimes. But is the democratic criterion served by liberalization per se, beginning from a closed state, with zero public participation? That is, does competitive oligarchy provide more democratic government than closed hegemony? Not necessarily.

Competitive Oligarchy

Recall that, given public participation, contestation acquired value once the assumptions of benevolence or consensual ethics were dropped. But contestation per se provides no guarantee against the arbitrary exercise of power. There is no reason to assume that the self-interested winner of a power struggle will be any more attuned to the public interest than the uncontested oligarch (though potential entry of competitors may constrain outrageous pecuniary profiteering in politics just as it constrains the monopoly business firm). Nor does contestation per se guarantee that the issues over which oligarchs compete are at all related to the issues that divide the population at large.

In short, contestation (liberalization) does not necessarily move government one iota closer to the democratic criterion unless it is accompanied by public participation. Even then, the gains from liberalization diminish as government is benevolent, and as popular ethical consensus is greater, particularly concerning altruism.

To assume these latter is heroic in the extreme: economic theory since Adam Smith has assumed precisely the opposite. Yet illiberal regimes that, sincerely or otherwise, rationalize their existence ideologically assume all three: governmental benevolence, popular ethical consensus, and healthy doses of altruism. The theory of polyarchy, in contrast, assumes, as does liberal economic theory, that both governments and individuals are strictly self-interested and that tastes differ. On two grounds polyarchy is flawed precisely as the liberal economy: vulnerability to power inequalities and vulnerability to externalities. It is to these defects of polyarchy that I now turn.

Polyarchy in Practice: Its Defects in Collective Enterprise

Recall that the democratic criterion was the articulation and realization of collective goals in accordance with popular will. There are three aspects of polyarchy that limit its ability to meet this criterion:

  a. Cost externalization.   Benefits from many if not most political decisions are concentrated, accruing disproportionately to one or more particular interest groups. Costs, on the other hand, are often dispersed: they do not fall sufficiently on particular interest groups to provoke a response. Alternatively, benefits may be dispersed but particular groups may not incur their share of the costs. To generalize, for many political decisions *net* benefits accrue to one or more interest groups, but not to society as a whole. Society then bears net costs that have been externalized by such groups.
  b. Unequal representation.   Some interests can more easily internalize political benefits and externalize costs. Moreover, some politically achievable goals coincide neatly with the interests of groups already organized for other purposes. Other interests remain loosely organized or not organized at all. Unequal representation therefore results from differing incentives to organize, on the one hand, and differing costs of organizing, on the other.[14]

14. The marginal utility of both time and money differs among interest groups. "Volunteer" groups unequally represent the interests of persons whose time in alternative activity is less valuable (at least to them); other groups unequally represent the interests of those to whom the marginal utility of money is

   c. Unequal access to power.   Once organized, interest groups' access to power is uneven owing to constitutional arrangements. In fact many constitutional arrangements permit a minority to veto a consensual majority. Also, if majority opinion is polarized, opposing interest groups may negate one another, leaving control to a minority opinion. Under polyarchy, such constitutional arrangements reflect the priority accorded to liberalism, defined here as limitations on government to ensure interest-group power.

Olson's growth-retardation hypothesis derives from *a*. Nevertheless, in a passing comment he seems to suggest that *a* would be inoperative without *b* and *c*: "If all groups in society were symmetrically organized . . . inefficient policies would rarely pass." I disagree.

Olson's suggestion ignores the transaction costs of collusion. Defect *a* results in situations like the following: In one interest group the per-capita incentive to lobby for growth-retardant policy exceeds the per-capita incentive in all other interest groups to lobby against it. However, the aggregate incentive to lobby against the policy exceeds the aggregate incentive to lobby for it. Assume all interests to be symmetrically organized in senses *b* and *c* above: that is, each is represented by a group, and each group in turn has equally effective access, in proportion to its membership, to the relevant policy makers. Then it is nevertheless the case that the growth-retardant policy could pass because of costs of collusion between groups. *Even with symmetric organization of interest groups, cost externalization retains its potential to inhibit growth unless the transaction costs of collusion between interest groups are lower than the costs externalized.*

But more important, I wish to emphasize the converse: that interest group politics cannot be understood by relegating *b* and *c* to the background, as Olson has done. Whether or not asymmetry of organization is *necessary* to block collective efficiency, it is nevertheless *sufficient*. Unequal representation and constitutional arrangements cut across the interest-group fragmentation that Olson (quite correctly) identifies with cost externalization. Asymmetry may retard or reinforce the effects of fragmentation, but it is unlikely to prove irrelevant.

---

below average (for instance, the rich, if one subscribes to the axiom of declining marginal utility from income as income increases). A testable hypothesis is that the interests of groups with leisure time (consumers? conservationists? animal lovers?) will be represented by such labor-intensive lobbying as door-to-door campaigning or nonprofit research, whereas those of groups with money (oil companies, perhaps) will be represented by such pecuniary lobbying as campaign contributions and paid advertising.

I have identified two types of asymmetry: defects *b* and *c*. In the next section I will argue that, under free enterprise, defect *b* operates to exaggerate political representation by business interests, since the costs of organizing business interest groups are so low and the potential benefits are so high.

Defect *c* operates archetypically under the constitutional arrangements of the United States. There, checks and balances were explicitly designed to allow a (sizable) minority to block majority action. Moreover, the U.S. committee system grants great de facto leverage to certain individuals. As I argued in the first part, these constitutional and de facto arrangements have served to exaggerate the power of minority interest groups. Again, constitutional features of the U.S. and most other federal governments exaggerate the veto power of regional interests. Finally, there is the problem familiar in all polyarchal governments: a minority candidate or party may gain power because majority popular opinion is polarized and votes are cast for the minority position to block one of the majority positions.

Therefore, I submit, the ability of polyarchy to realize collective goals is flawed on three grounds. Olson rests his argument, that (fragmented) interest groups deter growth, on one of these—a version of our defect *a*. How, one might ask, does modern polyarchy realize *any* collective goals given the additional two defects I have noted?

One answer is that (except in wartime) polyarchies are incapable of major collective enterprise.[15] Economic growth might not be thought to count as politically collective enterprise because the "invisible hand" can guide economic affairs efficiently. Yet Olson's persuasive argument is sufficient to undermine this view: special-interest groups arise to inhibit economic efficiency. A major raison d'être for interest groups is an attempt to resist the invisible hand's pressure to level factor prices under efficient, competitive conditions. Moreover, other groups—conservationists and environmentalists being the best current examples—go beyond simply externalizing the growth-inhibiting aspects of their self-interests: they lobby explicitly against growth.

Thus, it is tempting to conclude that in modern polyarchies, the political cards are stacked against collective ends and against growth in particular. Why this is not necessarily so is my next subject.

15. I reject this answer, as will become clear in the next section. The building of the railways in the United States and Canada was arguably a collective enterprise: success was virtually ensured by the cooperation of business and government.

Polyarchy and the Market: A Paradox of Modern Democracy

To understand how modern polyarchies resist their inherent antigrowth bias, I return to Lindblom's list of the extant twenty-eight. A peculiar fact emerges: though not all free-market economies are polyarchies, without exception all polyarchies are free-market economies.[16] This is true both in the sense that consumer goods and services are distributed via markets (as is indeed true in socialist countries), but also in the sense that markets in the factors of production are relatively free. It is the latter feature that makes them *private enterprise* economies. Thus private enterprise appears, in practice at least, to be a precondition for polyarchy.

Why is this so? Probably because most polyarchal interest groups are based on livelihood: industrial associations, trade unions, farmers' organizations, professional associations. Part and parcel of private enterprise is the freedom to organize to enhance one's market position. Such organization supplies the interest groups that constitute a precondition for polyarchal government, but this is *not* the mechanism for representative popular participation that the pluralist model describes. Rather, interest groups are disproportionately livelihood-based. Under free enterprise, groups based on livelihood find the costs of organizing low and the potential benefits high. Defect *b* operates in practice to enhance representation by livelihood-based groups.

Over time, moreover, the power of these interest groups is likely to accumulate.[17] Interest groups based on livelihood can use market position to enhance political power and vice versa. These are not ordinary interest groups; they possess economic as well as political power. As their economic and political positions reinforce each other, they will inhibit free markets in the means of livelihood. Why, then, at this point in polyarchal history, have not factor markets been so undermined by special interests seeking to supersede them as to have disappeared? How has free enterprise survived polyarchal government?

---

16. This contention is not without its disputants. As Robert Solo, reviewing Lindblom's *Politics and Markets*, retorts, "Are we then to consider the slave-based city states of ancient Greece, or the feudalities that produced the Magna Carta and the parliaments, to be market-oriented private enterprise systems? What he [Lindblom] means is that fifty years ago a single state, and during the past three decades a handful of others, in total two significant instances (two unique cultures without democratic antecedents) became planned socialisms, and neither is a polyarchy. This is hardly a discovery and certainly no sufficient basis from which to deduce a law of history." *Journal of Economic Issues*, vol. 13 (March 1979):208–09.

17. Limits to the accumulation of power are set by entry of competing groups, competing issues, countervailing groups, organizational constraints, and suffrage according to head count rather than property.

The answer, I submit, is the extraordinary power among livelihood-based groups of *business* interests. Granted that labor unions possess considerable political leverage and sizeable revenues, they do not compose a genuine power elite. Business does, because of its both unique and potentially cumulative command over resources: capital both commands and accumulates. Business corporations even count as "persons" before the law, a clear victory for liberalism over popular participation.

There is considerable recent literature on business as a power elite, much of it evolving from attempts to counter the pluralism of Dahl and of Lindblom's early work. Though American antipluralism goes back at least to Thorstein Veblen, modern work takes off from C. Wright Mills's *The Power Elite* and ranges through Henry Kariel, Gabriel Kolko, Herbert Marcuse, Ferdinand Lundberg, Robert Paul Wolff, the later work of John Kenneth Galbraith, Michael Parenti, and G. William Domhoff.[18] Much of this literature is sociological, associating power elites with class, occupation, or networks of personnel. The literature is typically weak methodologically, since it usually infers power from "positioned" elites but fails to document the processes by which these elites actually exercise power. (Domhoff is an exception; see footnote 27.) Nevertheless, this evidence, coupled with increasing recognition of the major role played by government itself as a collection of interest groups, has in recent years unquestionably diminished the persuasiveness of pluralist thought.

The most extensive argument to date that corporate interests dominate modern polyarchy is Lindblom's. At some length he propounds the thesis that in the inter-interest-group struggle to dominate polyarchal politics, business wins greatly disproportionate influence. Further, he suggests that "businessmen achieve an indoctrination of citizens so that citizens' volitions serve not their own interests but the interests of businessmen."[19] In terms of the democratic ideal I defined above, not only is the realization of popular will dominated by business, but also its articulation. A thesis such as this is particularly startling from Lindblom, who as an erstwhile

---

18. C. Wright Mills, *The Power Elite* (New York: Oxford University Press, 1956); Henry S. Kariel, *The Decline of American Pluralism* (Stanford: Stanford University Press, 1961); Gabriel Kolko, *Wealth and Power in America: An Analysis of Social Class and Income Distribution* (New York: Praeger, 1962); Herbert Marcuse, *One Dimensional Man: Studies in the Ideology of Advanced Industrial Society* (Boston: Beacon Press, 1964); Ferdinand Lundberg, *The Rich and the Super-Rich: A Study in the Power of Money Today* (New York: Lyle Stuart, 1968); Robert Paul Wolff, *The Poverty of Liberalism* (Boston: Beacon Press, 1968); John Kenneth Galbraith, *The New Industrial State* (Boston: Houghton Mifflin, 1971); Michael Parenti, *Power and the Powerless* (New York: St. Martin's Press, 1978); G. William Domhoff, *The Powers That Be: Processes of Ruling-Class Domination in America* (New York: Vintage, 1979).

19. Lindblom, *Politics and Markets,* p. 202.

coauthor of Dahl has long been identified with the pluralist mainstream of American political theory.

If, then, one accepts Lindblom's argument that all polyarchies have private enterprise economies, and further that all polyarchies accord business extraordinary power, the apparent polyarchal biases against growth are undermined. The polyarchal biases against free factor markets and growth that derive from Olson's defect *a* are to a major extent counteracted by the extraordinary power enjoyed by a set of interest groups that tend to identify their net benefits with free factor markets and growth: business interest groups. *Defects* b *and* c *are pitted in opposition to defect* a.

Thus the paradox of modern democracy:

> Free factor markets are necessary to foster polyarchy, modern pluralistic society's imperfect approach to democracy via popular participation and liberalization.

> Polyarchy undermines free factor markets and therefore its own preconditions unless its participatory features are undermined by granting business disproportionate power. That is, liberalization prevails over popular participation.

All this is not to deny the powerful antigrowth role played by certain interest groups, in particular those that are based on livelihood and that seek narrow economic privilege to the collective detriment. It is this role to which Olson has incisively drawn attention. To his thesis I add, however, two observations: first, of all interest groups, those of business are the most powerful; and second, business exerts a predominantly (though by no means exclusively) pro-growth role. It is the *dynamic* between anti- and pro-growth forces that I wish to emphasize. That dynamic is essentially political in nature and its outcome depends both on the relative ease with which various interests can organize and on their relative access to power.

An Alternative to the Olson Thesis

To recapitulate the argument thus far:

1. Polyarchy, or government by interest groups, is an approach to democracy that evolves readily out of a pluralist society.
2. Polyarchy can be characterized along two dimensions: liberalization and popular participation.
3. If democracy is defined as "the articulation and realization of

popular will,'' liberalization does not necessarily contribute to democracy unless it is accompanied by popular participation.

4. In the oldest polyarchy, Britain, liberalization has a longer and stronger tradition than does popular participation. To a lesser extent this is true also of such younger polyarchies as the United States and France. Liberalization has manifested itself as constitutional liberalism, resulting from the efforts of interest groups to limit government in order to ensure their own power.[20]

5. Three defects in polyarchy inhibit the democratic articulation and realization of collective goals:

    a. Externalization of the costs of policies that benefit particular interest groups.

    b. Unequal representation by pluralistic interests, reflecting different relative costs and benefits of organizing.

    c. Unequal access to power owing to constitutional arrangements in the liberal tradition.

6. Collective goals can in fact be realized under polyarchy, but only by sacrificing symmetric participation of interests. Defects *b* and *c*, that is, can be used to counter defect *a*. Specifically, the collective goal of economic growth is advanced under polyarchy to the extent that a growth-oriented interest group enjoys disproportionate power, but is inhibited to the extent that groups with other goals exercise power.

7. Olson's thesis states, in effect, that narrowly based interest groups proliferate only as democracies mature and that such interest groups inhibit economic growth. The second point follows from what I have termed defect *a* in polyarchies' ability to achieve collective goals. To this cost-externalizing defect I have added two others which have the potential to work in opposition. Defect *b* flows from the fact that polyarchies necessarily have free-enterprise economies, which in turn encourage organization by some interests but not others. In particular, business representation and therefore growth is enhanced. Defect *c* provides a

---

20. This is not to imply that British nineteenth-century liberalism enhanced the power of business more than did eighteenth-century mercantilism. In fact, quite the reverse occurred, as the political clout of guilds, trading companies, and the like was eroded along with the power of government. However, accumulation of capital and economic power by business under freer nineteenth-century markets led to neomercantilistic business political power in the twentieth century: this illustrates the ''democratic paradox'' above.

governmental context which permits such uneven interest-group representation: constitutional arrangements emphasizing liberalism over popular participation. Defect *c* is my alternative to Olson's first point; defect *b* is my alternative to his second.

This alternative thesis demands further elaboration. The liberal dimension of polyarchy has a longer tradition than does popular participation. Liberalism has been codified constitutionally, archetypically in the United States, as limitations on the power of government. Individuals and non-government groups are guaranteed rights, and government power is restricted internally by checks and balances of the various levels against each other.

I noted, with Lindblom, that free enterprise is in practice a precondition for polyarchy. I ventured that this is because interest groups are usually livelihood-based, and free enterprise, as the term suggests, provides relatively unrestricted opportunity for such interest groups to organize. Just as constitutional arrangements encourage liberalization by granting power to nongovernment groups, free enterprise should enhance broad participation, at least among livelihood-based groups, by providing a wide range of economic bases for participation.

Paradoxically, however, over time free enterprise seems to have worked *against* the participatory dimension of polyarchy by encouraging extraordinary business power. Although there is not unanimity as to how the evidence should be interpreted, most informed students would agree that business concentration in free-enterprise economies has increased substantially since the early nineteenth century.[21] The foremost manifestation is the modern corporation, now multinational in its reach. Although there has been less consensus among (non-Marxist) sociologists and political scientists about the extent of a ruling class and business hegemony of power, particularly in a society as apparently pluralistic as that of the United States, evidence and agreement seem to be mounting on this score as well. Modern corporate enterprise organizationally facilitates communication

---

21. This point, however, ought not be pushed too far. Increased concentration in older industries has to some extent been offset by the rise of new industries in which competition is keen either because of the nascent industry's growth or because of less marked economies of scale (for instance, the service industry). There is also a strong antitrust bias in United States government, though it has hardly been highly effective. Finally, the 1970s in particular saw the rise of "public" interest groups—representing consumer, environmentalist, and civil rights interests—that have enhanced the participatory dimension.

among business elites. Lindblom's recent "conversion" to this view is particularly notable since he was once identified with the pluralist view.

To the extent that business interest groups are more powerful than others, defects *b* and *c* operate to counteract defect *a* where it inhibits the collective goal of economic growth. Of course, the individual interests of business may not coincide with growth at the aggregate level, but if, as would seem plausible, growth-oriented business constitutes over 50 percent of the private sector, since *big* business especially seems to be dominantly growth-oriented, it is reasonable to conclude that business is interested in aggregate economic growth. There is the offsetting possibility of cost-externalizing, nongrowth self-interest on the part of individual firms or industries. But recent evidence, particularly from Domhoff,[22] argues strongly that business interests are on balance hegemonic.

Business Interest Groups

It is curious that Olson fails to treat business interest groups as politically important. Perhaps this is in part because he implicitly associates size of membership with potential for growth inhibition. He lists as the three "largest interest groups in at least the United States" labor unions, farm organizations, and professional associations. Granted, this list is provided in a context: namely, his elaboration of the "selective incentives" necessary for organization toward common purpose. Nevertheless, these three seem to be the interest groups he has in mind when it comes to growth inhibition.

Size of membership of interest groups may, it is true, be loosely related to growth inhibition, particularly that which occurs through nonpolitical channels. Indeed the three growth-retarding classes of activities that Olson mentions (reducing economic efficiency, blocking innovations, and limiting entry into industries and occupations) do not depend exclusively on political legitimation. Nevertheless, serious extralegal interference with the market can usually be challenged in the courts. Most interest group growth retardation and growth promotion does depend heavily on formal political power. Size of membership is far from a good proxy for such power, especially in the case of interest groups that represent business.

Business, particularly the modern corporation, possesses political power quite unrelated to its size or to the sizes of the interest groups it

22. Domhoff, *The Powers That Be.*

sponsors as measured by individual membership. Indeed, "individual membership" is hard to define for modern business: does one mean directors, managers, employees, major stockholders, all stockholders? It is therefore political strength, not "membership" strength, of business and its interest groups that is of concern. The political role of business under polyarchy is far more critical to the economy than that of any other interest group. As Lindblom argues,

> In the eyes of government officials . . . businessmen do not appear simply as the representatives of a special interest. . . . They appear as functionaries performing functions that government officials regard as indispensable. . . . When a government official asks himself whether business needs a tax reduction, he knows he is asking a question about the welfare of the whole society and not simply about a favor to a segment of the population, which is what is typically at stake when he asks himself whether he should respond to an interest group. Any government official who understands the requirements of his position and the responsibilities that market-oriented systems throw on businessmen will therefore grant them a privileged position. . . . Businessmen cannot be left knocking at the doors of the political systems, they must be invited in.

Lindblom then lists some of the privileges that corporation executives seek and obtain:

> autonomy for the enterprise, tax favors and subsidies, restrictions on unions, a great variety of monopolistic privileges (tariffs, patents, retail price maintenance, weak anti-trust enforcement, encouragement of mergers, fair trade restrictions on competition, occupational licensing, permissive regulation of public utilities).

I might add that partial capture of regulatory agencies by the industries they are designed to supervise is recognized by such a variety of economists as to be orthodox wisdom.

It is of course arguable whether all of these, particularly monopolistic privileges, encourage economic efficiency and growth. Lindblom's implicit answer to this seems to be that entrepreneurial effort is critical to growth and that entrepreneurship must perforce be induced by government: "[Often] the businessmen . . . will . . . risk capital, reputation, or the solvency of an enterprise in order to undertake an entrepreneurial venture . . . only when sufficiently indulged." Or, more sinister: "If spokesmen for businessmen predict that new investment will lag without tax relief, it is only one short step to corporate decisions that put off investment until tax relief is granted.''[23]

In other words, Lindblom is arguing, contrary to neoclassical economic theory, that under free enterprise economic growth is not assured by the spontaneous emergence of market demand but by governmentally pro-vided inducements to entrepreneurship. To the Keynesian who fears the fragility of the ''animal-spirits'' that inspire investment optimism, this thesis may seem plausible; so too to the Galbraithian who believes that consumer demand has a limited life of its own. For others, a ''second-best'' thesis may improve Lindblom's plausibility: business is increasingly heavily taxed and regulated; this second-best world demands offsetting privileges. The latter have indeed emerged in the form of tax credits for investment,[24] government underwritten research and development, gov-ernment-provided defense plants, and government loans to failing enterprises.

The Business/Labor Political Power Balance

What of labor unions? Olson treats them as the predominant special-interest group. This may seem plausible as a result both of their large membership and of their control over huge pools of dues and pension funds. Moreover, in Britain, Canada, and some European countries, they are explicitly connected to political parties. In Britain, they can exercise considerable veto power over business decisions; in Yugoslavia and even West Germany and Sweden it is arguable that they also exercise on en-trepreneurial role.

Lindblom disputes the political dominance of labor unions, both the-oretically and empirically. At the level of theory, he argues that whereas business can choose between entrepreneurship and the status quo, workers cannot choose between work and idleness, an argument reminiscent of the classical economists. Workers must work to survive. Therefore labor will work with or without government inducement, but business will not neces-sarily invest.[25]

At the empirical level, Lindblom presents statistics that estimate the political expenditures of various interest groups. Unfortunately, his statis-

---

23. Lindblom, *Politics and Markets,* pp. 175, 188, 176, 185.

24. ''Forty percent of net investments in manufacturing equipment in the United States in 1963 was estimated to be attributable to the investment tax credit of 1962.'' Ibid., p. 177.

25. Ibid., p. 176.

tics are out of date, and he uses them somewhat casually. Nevertheless, comparable data have not been assembled elsewhere and Lindblom's are worth summarizing here.

For the United States in the 1950s, the following groups were estimated by a Congressional committee to have spent these amounts to influence legislation:

173 corporations	$32.1 million
Farm organizations	0.9 million
Labor unions	0.55 million[26]

For Britain's 1964 election campaign, press and poster expenditure came from the following major sources:

Conservative Party (itself financed largely through corporate contributions)	£ 950,000
Aims of Industry (an industrial association)	270,000
Steel Federation (an industrial association)	621,000
Stewards and Lloyds (a single corporation)	306,000
Labour Party	267,000

In the United States, though most kinds of corporate election contributions are illegal, circumvention is extensive—as was partially demonstrated by Watergate. Of nearly $400 million in campaign expenditures during 1972, the union contribution was only $13.5 million. The 1974 election reform laws attempted to broaden the contribution base by legalizing political action committees; nevertheless, these are predominantly sponsored by corporations (see Appendix).

In terms of numbers of organizations, business again is predominant among interest groups. There are roughly 40,000 U.S. corporations with at least 100 employees, each of which is concerned with public policy. Among about 4,000 national associations in the U.S., the 1949 distribution was as follows:

Business	1,800
Professional	500
Labor unions	200
Women's	100
Veterans and military	60

26. These and following data are from ibid., pp. 195–97.

Commodity exchanges	60
Farmers	55
Blacks	50
Public officials	50
Fraternal	25
Sports and recreations	100
Other	1,000

Again, Domhoff's most recent evidence of a dominant and hegemonic ruling class is consistent with dominant and hegemonic business power but not with labor.[27] His ruling class is defined as that 0.5 percent of the population that holds about 22 percent of personal wealth and a much higher percentage of corporate stock. This is not a labor elite. Domhoff's study traces its power through the "special-interest, policy-formation, candidate-selection, and ideology process." Most important, he argues that this is a *hegemonic* elite on important issues. To the extent that hegemony holds, business interests are not only dominant under polyarchy, they are undissipated through jousts over narrowly defined issues. My polyarchal defects *b* and *c* would then prevail over Olson's defect *a* to facilitate the articulation and realization of collective business goals, among which economic growth is perhaps the most basic.

The Olson Thesis and Further Research

The Lindblom evidence that business interests dominate, as well as the Domhoff evidence that they are hegemonic, is by no means conclusive. Lindblom's, for example, is seriously out of date. It has been my purpose in this essay simply to argue that Olson's thesis is incomplete to the extent that business interest groups enjoy significant power and pursue hegemonic, growth-oriented goals.

Olson's thesis would become *invalid* if, as polyarchies age, business interest groups gain power relative to labor or become increasingly hegemonic relative to labor. The evidence is not strong enough to support these propositions, but neither is it strong enough to reject them. I consider them plausible.

27. Domhoff, *The Powers That Be*. Most previous evidence was of the "positional" variety and drew conclusions about the exercise of power from observations of elites positioned in government posts. Domhoff's evidence, in contrast, is process-oriented, documenting the processes through which power is exercised. According to the process view, elites being positioned in formal power is neither necessary nor sufficient evidence that they act in their class interest.

Olson's thesis, then, is not inconsistent with mine, but is incomplete. His exclusive concern with growth-retardant interest groups leads him to underplay the political role of business in growth. Thus, he omits one-half of a critical political dynamic, between growth-retarding groups on the one hand and business on the other. His polarity, between fragmentation and "encompassingness," is undoubtedly important, but it is only part of the issue. Degree of explicit concern with growth is the other. This cuts across the fragmentation dimension. As just argued, business groups, though more fragmented in form than labor, are more powerful politically and may also be more hegemonic in goals.[28]

Olson also misses the constitutional element. Polyarchies have tended to codify constitutional liberalism ahead of popular participation, and under free enterprise this has encouraged extraordinary business power. Nevertheless, polyarchal constitutions differ in the degree to which the power of the state is limited, as well as in the degree to which nonbusiness interests, especially labor, are granted formal power. One need look no further than the United States and Britain to illustrate both points. In the United States, the veto powers between various levels of government enable interest groups, including small interest groups, to exercise far greater influence than in Britain. On the other hand, Britain, unlike the United States, has a labor party in parliament.

Further research into the political determinants of growth in democracies should explore at least four issues. First, there is the issue of interest-group fragmentation that Olson has so astutely raised. Can measures of fragmentation be developed that allow comparisons internationally and through time? Second, independently of fragmentation, interest groups should be classified according to the nature of their goals and activities (growth-promoting or growth-retarding) and their relative political strengths. The balance of power in this political dynamic varies crucially between countries and over time; in fact it is, I would venture, the critical element in the growth process. That is why Olson's thesis, which has introduced us to one-half of the dynamic, is so important. In free enterprise economies, the position of business vis-à-vis other groups deserves particular attention, but the analysis could in principle be applied to socialist economies as well, to the extent that political power is decentralized. Third, is it the case that the strength of pro-growth interest groups is

---

28. Britain, according to Olson, is the archetypical case of growth sacrificed to fragmented special interest groups, primarily labor unions. Yet Britain's economic woes are as readily attributable to managerial ineptitude as to labor unions: that is, to the other half of our "political dynamic."

associated with the extent of free enterprise, rather than, as Olson suggests, with political youth? Thus, the pro-growth and antigrowth interest groups should be compared internationally and over time with the degree of private enterprise in their respective economies. Fourth, constitutional arrangements should be compared internationally and over time according to their relative emphases on liberalism versus popular participation. These factors could then be correlated with the relative political strengths of pro-growth and antigrowth interest groups. Finally, constitutional arrangements should be analyzed over time, with an eye to the motives for and implications of increased popular participation. I will close by briefly addressing this last issue.

Participatory Democracy and Growth

It is Olson's hypothesis that, as democracies mature uninterrupted by war or similar crises, fragmentary interest groups proliferate. I venture the similar suggestion that popular participation is gradually nourished as polyarchies age. Olson's rationale is basically that organization takes time. I would agree but add that the powerful role played by polyarchal business in articulating goals has retarded the evolution of a popular role.

Recall the argument above that most choices are not between givens but rather are volitional, requiring complex deliberation as well as a continuous process of formulation. Business has been better organized to deliberate. It has also been well organized to sell ideas, both as private goods through advertising and as public goods and policies through political pressure. Therefore business has dominated popular participation in the goal-articulation process. Nevertheless, one might expect the Olson half of the political dynamic to come into play in the articulation as well as the realization process, as indeed it has.

In articulating goals, business has given high priority to economic growth; but, as the late Fred Hirsch has argued, growth yields disappointing fruits owing to the inherent scarcity of "positional" goods.[29] As growth is sustained, Hirsch suggests, society's preoccupation with growth gives way to such other concerns as distribution, collective provision, and state regulation.

For whatever reasons, racial minorities, environmentalists, and consumers have in recent years asserted themselves in the United States,

29. Fred Hirsch, *Social Limits to Growth* (Cambridge, Mass.: Harvard University Press, 1976).

regionalists and a cultural minority in Canada, labor in Britain, and women worldwide. Is growth, like the caterpillar, extinguished when the butterfly of popular participation takes flight? Certainly in some cases economic goals suffer, both as interest fragmentation increases à la Olson and as business influence is circumscribed according to the dynamic I have been emphasizing. Hesitating to grant economics priority over democracy, one finds oneself in a dilemma.

It may well be that the popular will is for less growth than business interests articulate. More precisely, some of the policies that the public wants may, as a side effect, lower the growth rate: environmental purity or conservation, equality of opportunity or outcome, security of employment or income, or simple leisure. A second possibility is that the public through its interest groups pushes merely for a different mix of goods than business provides. This may not prove growth-reducing. A third possibility is that some of the popular demands that government, under conservative pressure from business, resists would turn out to be growth-enhancing rather than the reverse. In any case, despite the evident distortions of popular interest-group politics, I believe that it should be encouraged even at economic cost.

APPENDIX

Political Action Committees[30]

The United States is currently experiencing the evolution of an important new brand of interest group—the political action committee (PAC). PACs grew out of the sweeping 1974 (post-Watergate) election reform laws. The 1974 legislation limited the amount a candidate for federal office can receive from a single contributor. Concurrently, the new legislation allowed companies to establish PACs to solicit funds for donation to individual candidates. The intent of the legislation was to broaden the base of contributors. In practice, however, PACs receive the bulk of their funds as donations from upper and middle management, and firms themselves are permitted to pay for the PACs' administrative expenses and costs of soliciting funds.

The Federal Election Commission (as of February 1980) records

30. Thanks are due to Alex Rorke for research assistance.

844 active PACs. Of the 844, 266 are sponsored by labor unions. It is generally acknowledged by labor, consumer, and business groups that corporate PACs are greatly outspending their rivals.

Corporate PACs are becoming institutionalized parts of the political process. There are even coordinating groups such as BIPAC (Business Industry Political Action Committee). Atlantic Richfield's PAC has held 205 meetings with legislators over the past year. Almost $10 million was spent by PACs in the 1977–78 Congressional campaigns, and observers predict spending of double that amount on the current campaign.

Unions have recently tried to reduce the power of corporate PACs. For example, the International Association of Machinists filed a suit against the PACs of General Motors and other large corporations, charging that by soliciting money from career employees who do not have union protection, the PACs were obtaining contributions under implicit threat. Another recent suit attempted to enact legislation which would lower from $5,000 to $3,000 the amount a PAC can contribute to an individual candidate in a general election or a primary.

Part IV: Conclusion

13: The Political Economy of Growth and Redistribution

DENNIS C. MUELLER

The preceding essays attempt to evaluate the importance of political factors in explaining differences in countries' growth rates. Although Olson, Choi, and Murrell each present empirical support for the Olson thesis, there is obvious disagreement over how much of the difference in country growth rates can be explained by political factors in general and by Olson's thesis in particular. In this final essay I shall not attempt to weigh the various arguments and conflicting pieces of evidence that have been presented and somehow strike a balance for or against the Olson thesis. Instead, I shall try to relate the thesis to some of the rest of the public choice or political economy literature, and from the latter draw some additional inferences that might be used to test the validity of the Olson hypothesis and some of its complements and substitutes.

To Grow or Not To Grow?

Figure 13.1*a* presents two standard production possibility frontiers for commodities X and Y. PP represents today's opportunities given today's labor force, capital stock, and technology. $P'P'$ represents the set of opportunities the country could achieve tomorrow if it pursued a pro-growth set of policies, whatever they may be. While it is obviously simplistic to assume that the choice is limited to growth or no growth, the assumption suffices for illustrative purposes.

Figure 13.1*b* presents transformations of the two production possibility frontiers into utility space. A and B can be viewed as individuals in a two-person economy or as representative individuals in a two-class economy. The $U'U'$ frontier contains points that are Pareto-preferred to any status quo point S. Thus, a movement from UU to $U'U'$ could make all individuals in the economy better off. If such a movement does not occur

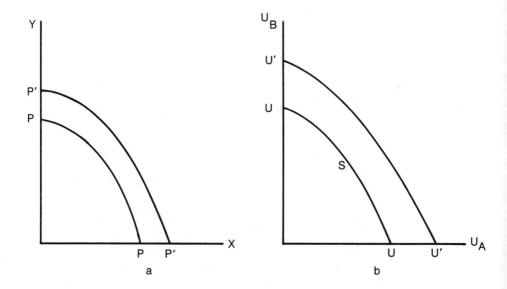

Figure 13.1   Production and Utility Possibility Frontiers

automatically, but only as a consequence of a conscious, collective decision to adopt some growth-generating policies, or not to adopt some
growth-retarding policies, then growth is a public good. From a public
choice perspective the question then is, under what circumstances will a
society make a collective decision in favor of growth-oriented policies, and
under what circumstances will it not?

Should a society not decide to move to $U'U'$ it still must make a collective decision whether to remain at S or to move to some other point on UU,
a pure redistribution choice. One of the primary objectives of interest
groups is to bring about redistribution for their members. If A and B are
viewed as representative individuals from two interest groups, then the
clash of interest groups in a democracy can be viewed as a battle for
positions along utility possibility frontiers like UU. One of the assumptions
underlying the Olson thesis is that the efforts by interest groups to jockey
for position along UU stand in the way of adopting policies that would lead
society to $U'U'$. This possibility can arise in at least two ways. First, to the
extent interest groups do battle within the democratic arena, redistribution
and growth may be direct substitutes for one another during the time

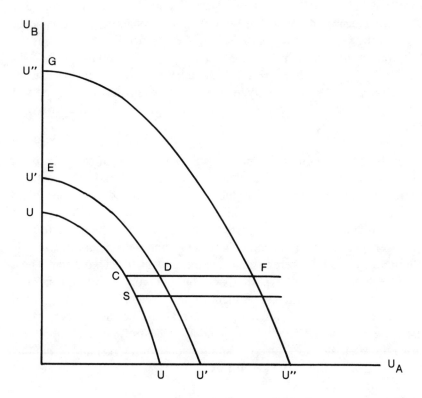

Figure 13.2. Shifting Utility Possibility Frontiers under Rapid and Slow Growth

available to the democratic bodies to make decisions. Growth-inducing or growth-fostering politics may be shoved off the democratic agenda by debate over redistribution. Second, the policies used to achieve redistribution may be in direct conflict with those required to achieve growth. A tariff increase to protect an industry conflicts with a liberalization of trade that might improve overall efficiency and stimulate growth. A rise in the minimum wage conflicts with full employment and with the stimulus to growth the latter brings.

Suppose that interest group B expects with probability P_r to be able to move to point C (in Figure 13.2) along UU by pursuing a given redistribution policy that conflicts with a movement to $U'U'$. The group will clearly abandon the redistribution objective if it expects to reach the range of outcomes that are Pareto-preferred to C, with a higher probability than P_r.

If we treat all points along $U'U'$ as equally likely outcomes from any collective decision in favor of growth, then the probability that B is better off under the growth policy is $ED/U'U'$. This probability increases as the utility possibility frontier is shifted outward by the growth policy ($GF/U''U'' > ED/U'U'$). Thus, we reach the unsurprising conclusion that interest groups will be more likely to abandon their growth-retarding pursuit of redistribution as the potential gains from a growth policy become greater.

The end of World War II found Western society in a state that was extremely, perhaps uniquely, conducive to a general pursuit of growth policies. World War II and the Depression before it had left great disparities between the levels of production economies and those they could achieve by investment in and adoption of the technologies available at that time. "Catching-up" was a particularly attractive strategy to follow. Moreover, groups most concerned with zero-sum redistribution, which is debilitating to growth, were in many countries weakened by the war. Thus, one expects the catch-up hypothesis not only to work well in this period, but one predicts from the Olson theory that the catch-up hypothesis will work better during this period than in most others. The Olson theory offers a possible explanation for both the general success of the catch-up model during the post–World War II era and for some of the residuals from that model—the British experience, for example.

Allocation, Redistribution, and Political Economy

Consider a country with a weak interest-group structure. Vote-seeking politicians find it difficult to form winning majorities by offering to serve well-defined and organized private interests. An appeal to the voters on the basis of broad common goals and public-good-type issues is relatively attractive. Since these issues can by definition win broad support, consensual politics emerges in an era of weak interest-group structure. Winning majorities are expected to be large, and the governing parties should be able to hold office for long periods of time, barring scandals unrelated to policy choices.

In contrast, an era dominated by the pursuit of narrow private goals as represented by interest groups should be one of narrow and unstable majorities. Anthony Downs, in his classic treatise on political economy,[1] depicts

1. Anthony Downs, *An Economic Theory of Democracy* (New York: Harper & Brothers, 1957).

candidates as running on platforms made up of the most favored issues of several interest groups. Such platforms can inevitably be defeated, however, by yet other platforms that include most of the members of the previous winning coalition but substitute one or two new minority interests for one or two of those in the original coalition. Downs's model of platform formation by logrolling interest groups leads to a revolving-door political system with each incumbent candidate or party headed for defeat.

Pure redistribution is a zero-sum game: no core to this game exists, no stable winning coalition can be formed. Downs's description of candidate competition is consistent with a view of politics as a zero-sum game with each interest group seeking redistribution in favor of itself.

Riker has also depicted politics as a zero-sum game.[2] He develops this assumption to predict that only minimum-winning coalitions form. If the object of politics is to redistribute from the losing side, then one wants the losing side to be as large as possible while remaining the losing side. Grand coalitions will seldom appear, and when they do they are short lived.

These considerations allow us to formulate some predictions about the electoral outcomes one expects to observe under Olson's theory. In countries where interest groups were destroyed or where the opportunities for catch-up existed, stable winning coalitions—perhaps representing large majorities—should have been observed. In contrast, the countries with entrenched interest groups and slow growth should have been characterized by oscillating governments, and narrow (or narrower) winning majorities.

Perhaps the most unusual characteristic of the two decades following World War II, in contrast with other times, is the relatively rapid growth of *all* developed countries. While some countries did considerably better than others, virtually all countries enjoyed fairly rapid economic growth in comparison with other twenty-year stretches over the past century. Table 13.1 presents some representative growth rates.

The post–World War II period was also characterized by relative political tranquility at least until the late sixties. The parliaments of almost all developed countries were ruled by single parties either alone or as dominant members of coalitions. Table 13.2 summarizes the periods of single-party or stable-coalition rule in various developed countries. During the first two decades after World War II several parties won by substantial majorities, and a few grand coalitions even appeared. The Liberal Demo-

2. William H. Riker, *The Theory of Political Coalitions* (New Haven: Yale University Press, 1962).

Table 13.1. Annual Average Rates of Growth of Gross Domestic Product Per Worker, Selected Periods, 1950–70

	First Boom	Second Boom	Third Boom	Fourth Boom
Japan	5.38%	9.20%	8.50%	8.64%
W. Germany	5.60	4.80	4.32	4.66
Italy	3.58	4.56	4.47	5.41
France	n.a.	4.40	5.27	4.88
Netherlands	3.75	3.78	3.60	4.73
Denmark	n.a.	3.51	3.88	3.03
United Kingdom	1.95	2.09	2.18	2.81
Austria	n.a.	4.20	4.27	6.79
Norway	3.81	3.44	4.17	3.34

	First Boom	Second Boom	Third Boom
Canada	3.67%	1.78%	1.11%
Belgium	2.72	3.35	3.56
United States	1.88	2.57	1.08

SOURCE: F. Cripps and R. Tarling, *Growth in Advanced Industrial Countries* (Cambridge: Cambridge University Press, 1973).

NOTE: Boom periods are peak-to-peak and correspond roughly to 1950–56, 1956–60, 1960–65, and 1965–70. For Canada and the U.S., the third and fourth cycles are combined. The cycles in Belgium are of roughly six-year duration.

crats in Japan often controlled over 60 percent of the seats in Parliament and never less than 55 percent up through 1972. A grand coalition between the People's and the Socialist Parties, with 90 percent or more of the vote, ruled from 1945 to 1966 in Austria. In West Germany the Christian Democrats (CDU) were dominant alone or in coalition with the Free Democrats through 1965 and then formed a grand coalition with the Social Democrats that lasted until 1969, when the CDU finally lost control of the government. In France, the period of postwar consensual politics began only in 1958 with de Gaulle's first major victory. This political event coincided with the important collective decision to enter the EEC. Entry into the EEC is an obvious public-good-type issue and appears to have both stimulated France's growth and reinforced the consensual support enjoyed by the Gaullists at least until the general's death. Majorities substantially in excess of 50 percent also were given to the incumbent majority party or coalition government in Australia, Norway, Sweden, and the U.K. The first two decades following World War II were clearly not ones of revolving-door politics in most developed countries. Voters continually ex-

Table 13.2.   Periods of Political Stability and Instability
in Selected Developed Countries

Country	Period of Stable Rule by One Party or One-Party-Dominated Coalition	Party or Parties	Percentage Growth in Real GDP 1970–77
Australia	1949–72	Liberal/Country	14%
Austria	1945–66	People's/Socialist	30
Belgium	None		17
Canada	1963–79	Liberal	36
Denmark	1953–68	Social Democratic	5
France	1958–81	Gaullist	26
W. Germany	1949–69	CDU alone or in coalition	16
Greece	1949–64, 1967–74	Conservatives, Dictatorship	70
Ireland	1957–73	Fianna Fail	35
Italy	1948–62, 1962–68	CD, Center/Left	21
Japan	1948–present (weaker recently)	Liberal Democratic	27
Luxembourg	1959–74	Christian Socialist	−1
Netherlands	1945–72	Catholic People's	27
Norway	1945–65	Labor Party	38
Spain	−76	Dictatorship	67
Sweden	−76	Social Democratic	11
Switzerland	*		3
U.K.	1951–64	Conservatives	6
U.S.	*		27

*See text.
SOURCES: Political data obtained from Thomas J. Mackie and Richard Rose, *The International Almanac of Electoral History* (New York: Free Press, 1974); Arthur S. Banks, *Political Handbook of the World: 1978* (New York: McGraw-Hill, 1978). Gross domestic product growth figures are taken from OECD, *Main Economic Indicators,* September 1975 and July 1978.

pressed confidence in the ruling parties by returning them to office, and they often did so by very large majorities.

Switzerland's parliament was not dominated by a single party or coalition in the post–World War II period, but it was also not subject to revolving-door instability. As Lehner's essay above makes clear, the dominant federalist nature of the Swiss political system, combined with the powerful threat of calling a national referendum, forced the national legislature to engage in consensual politics. Thus, consensual stability and a relatively high rate of growth characterized Switzerland during the fifties and sixties despite the absence of a single, dominant party at the national level.

Given that all countries grew rapidly, at least relative to their previous experiences, one should not be surprised to find that dramatic differences do not appear across countries in levels of political stability. Belgium appears to be the only country on the Continent, with the exception of Switzerland, whose parliament was not dominated for at least a part of the postwar period by a single party or coalition, although the Christian Social Party came close to playing that role within a stable three-party system until 1965. Belgium also grew somewhat more slowly than did the other European countries, with the exception of the U.K. (see table 13.1). Interestingly enough, Belgium's economy also did not follow the same business cycle pattern that the other Common Market countries did over this period, despite its small size. More interesting, perhaps, is that Belgium is one of the four countries standing highest on Choi's (unadjusted) ranking of countries that suffer institutional sclerosis.

The laggards in growth over the post–World War II period have, of course, been the Anglo-Saxon countries: Canada, the U.K., and the U.S. These three countries, along with their Anglo-Saxon cousin New Zealand, are also on the top of Choi's institutional sclerosis lists (adjusted or unadjusted). Whether or not these countries have been characterized by revolving-door politics is a matter of interpretation. All three are essentially two-party democracies. In Canada, however, neither party secured more than 50 percent of the seats in the House of Commons in two successive elections from 1953 to 1977. In that year the Liberals returned to office with 53.4 percent of the seats in the House, only to be turned out of office two years later. Although the Liberals have been in office more often than not since World War II, and continually from 1963 to 1979, their majorities have regularly swayed back and forth over the 50 percent mark.

The Conservatives were in firm control of the House of Commons in the U.K. from 1951 to 1964. Thus, the U.K. does not differ from other European countries in having experienced a period of sustained single-party rule following World War II. It is worth noting, however, that the period of single party rule came to an end earlier in the U.K. than in any other European country save Italy and excepting Belgium, where it never existed. If one treats the period of stable three-party rule in Belgium as comparable to an era of consensual politics then Belgium's political history would resemble Britain's quite closely. Belgium's three-party system began to crack in 1965—one year after the Conservatives were turned out of office in the U.K.—with the increased showing of the Flemish Nationalists. This parallel is significant because Belgium had the slowest growth of the continental EEC countries during this period and was second only to the

U.K. in slowness of growth among the present EEC members. Important parallels between the U.K. and Italy also appear in Lady Hicks's essay. We shall return to these in the following section.

The Democrats have controlled both houses of Congress in the United States for all but one term since World War II. The extreme importance of the presidency in this country, however, suggests that the control of this office be considered when judging the stability of party control. Since 1952 (since 1945, if one treats Franklin D. Roosevelt as a special case), control of the executive branch has passed between parties every eight years. After the first four years, the incumbent party's candidate has been returned to office by a substantial majority. After the second four-year term, the incumbent party's new candidate has lost by a narrow margin. This cycle shows no sign of changing, except that its periodicity may have dropped to four years.

Although it is hard to argue that the Anglo-Saxon countries were characterized by political instability over the post–World War II period, their governing parties did not receive support that was as substantial, consistent, or sustained as it was in most other developed countries.

Since the mid-1960s, every developed country except Japan and Switzerland has witnessed at least one change in government. In dramatic contrast with the preceding era, the recent period has seen numerous minority governments, unstable majority coalitions, and generally narrower majorities for the party or coalition in office. Even in Japan, where the Liberal Democrats have successfully remained in office, they were able to capture in 1976 only 249 of 511 seats. Only Switzerland continues to return after every election the same set of parties with almost identical percentages of seats as they held before.

Allocation, Redistribution, and the Growth of Government

Since the mid-1960s, redistribution has emerged in virtually every developed democratic country as *the* political issue; this is apparent in some of the essays in this volume. Over the same period of time, growth of the size of government has become conspicuous and an object of much concern in both Europe and the United States. These two developments may be related. In one of the pioneering essays of the public-choice field some twenty years ago, Gordon Tullock demonstrated how majority rule can lead a community to add items to an agenda that essentially result in redistributions from the losing coalition members to the members of the winning coalition.[3] In the context of this volume, logrolling to achieve redistribution can be regarded as the formation of coalitions of interest groups to elect candidates or pass legislation. The legislation that passes, however, does not typically take the form of direct transfers from one group to another, even though it is distributionally motivated, but rather appears under the guise of special regulations, price supports, tariffs and quotas, tax relief, and directed expenditure programs. Thus, the use of majority rule to achieve redistribution in a democracy dominated by interest groups results in the growth of the government's size.

The link between the pursuit of distributional objectives and the growth of government and government intervention is clearly brought out by Lady Hicks. In both the U.K. and Italy the government has sought to achieve redistributional objectives by offering various tax and subsidy advantages to different industries or regions and, more dramatically, by establishing programs of regional development and by direct nationalization of certain firms and industries. The growth of the welfare state, which is largely fostered to achieve distributional objectives, accounts for a large fraction of government growth not only in the U.K. and Italy, but in all developed Western countries. As Lady Hicks points out, these government policies, which are primarily oriented toward redistribution, have an impact on the incentives and efficiency of the remainder of the economy. Thus, the redistribution-economic efficiency (growth) political debate, upon which this volume focuses, can be recast as a debate over the proper size and scope of the government.

An examination of the recent political histories of the developed democratic countries reveals that growth of government/redistribution issues have dominated political events and help to explain the erosion of consensual politics. In the Scandinavian countries, the left-of-center parties were in control during the period of broad political consensus and rapid economic growth following World War II. The disappearance of political consensus in these countries has, therefore, taken the form of an increase in the strength of right-wing parties. In Norway and Sweden this movement has appeared simply as increased political support for the established conservative parties that remained in opposition in the years after the war. In Denmark, the reaction has taken the more dramatic form of the creation of the Progress Party, which together with other antitax parties captured nearly a quarter of the vote in 1973.

---

3. "Some Problems of Majority Voting," *Journal of Political Economy* 67 (December 1959):571–79.

In the majority of continental countries (France, Germany, Italy, Luxembourg, and the Netherlands), right-of-center parties were in office during the period of broad government support of the fifties and sixties. Here the era of narrow government majorities, minority coalitions, and unstable governments was marked by the rise in ascendency of the left-of-center parties. On the Continent, a political stalemate has evolved between those who press for further expansion of the welfare state, further socialist reform, and government intervention and those who think that these policies have gone too far.

Here again, Switzerland appears to be the exception that goes to prove the rule. The decentralized nature of its political system and the importance of direct democracy and the referendum make it more difficult in Switzerland to introduce, *and pass,* redistributional issues. The agenda is limited perforce to allocation-efficiency-type issues—issues capable of winning consensual support. Thus, Switzerland has not experienced the same growth in government since World War II as the other continental countries have and has enjoyed the same political stability in the seventies that it did in the fifties and sixties (see chapter 10, above).

In the Anglo-Saxon countries, in contrast, redistribution issues have come increasingly into the forefront. In Canada, the issue appears largely in the form of regional distribution among the various subregions of this vast country. The Liberal Party's ability to stay in power from 1963 to 1979 can be attributed largely to its ability to contain the hottest distributional issue, the status of Quebec, within the bounds of Canada's federalist structure.

In the U.K., as on the Continent, the Conservatives were in power during the period of sustained political consensus following World War II. Labour's victory in 1964 made possible the introduction of such traditional socialist demands as nationalization of various industries. Since then virtually every possible kind of redistributional issue (regional, class, and interest-group) has taken its turn in the center of the U.K.'s political arena. Lady Hicks discusses several of the government's proposals that feature largely distributional objectives and hold possibly important consequences for economic growth and efficiency. The recent, resounding victory of the Conservative Party, led by a forceful and outspoken critic of the growth of government and government intervention, can be interpreted as a backlash to these trends, albeit one that might further polarize British politics.

Redistribution was not a political issue of major significance in the U.S. during the fifties and early sixties. Ideology was thought to be at an end, and growth was the major economic objective of the Democratic administrations that governed during this period. In the mid-sixties and seventies the issue has taken hold. The size of government programs that deal with direct redistribution has grown tremendously over the last decade. Beyond this the government is involved in promulgating and enforcing myriad antidiscrimination regulations with direct distributional consequences. Debate over redistribution here, as elsewhere, appears in large part as debate over the optimal level of government activity.

Thus, the general slowdown in growth rates during the seventies has been associated with both a shift in emphasis to distributional issues and an intensification of political strife and instability. Here, the major conclusion Asselain and Morrisson draw from the French experience should be stressed and generalized. The causal links between growth and interest-group strength—between growth and an emphasis on government redistribution policies—may run in both directions. The slowdown in Western growth rates in the seventies, partially attributable to the achievement of catch-up by several European countries, partially to the world recession caused by the oil crisis, would in itself lead to intensified pressure from interest groups for redistribution and could have further strengthened their political support. This increased political strength should in turn foster further emphasis on redistribution, further retardation of economic growth, and further political instability as governments become caught in the centrifugal forces of revolving-door, redistributional politics.

If this line of argument holds, we should find that countries that did not experience political instability and narrow majority governments grew faster over the seventies than did the others. The last column of table 13.2 presents real domestic product growth rates for several developed countries between 1970 and 1977. The two outliers on the list are Greece and Spain, with growth rates more than double the average of the other countries. Both of these countries have experienced the political stability of dictatorship for a majority of this period and have perhaps further benefited from the leap forward both politically and economically that accompanies the lifting of dictatorial rule. Canada and Japan are the only two democracies that have been ruled by one party throughout the seventies, and their growth rates have been high relative to those of other developed democratic countries. Virtually all of the countries that have done quite badly over the seventies in terms of growth have also experienced rule by narrower majorities or minority governments (notably, Australia, Belgium, Denmark, West Germany, Luxembourg, Sweden, and the U.K.). The chief exception to this generalization is Switzerland, which has grown almost not at all, but whose national politics seem the same now as in the fifties and sixties.[4] Norway is an exception on the other side. Although distributional issues and the size of government have been hotly debated there, its growth rate is the highest of any developed country that has been democratically governed over the entire 1970–77 period.

While these figures do not prove anything, they do seem broadly consistent with the thesis that a link exists between the level of economic growth in a country, the intensity of debate and action to achieve redistribution, and the amount of consensus enjoyed by the governing party or party coalition.

Efficiency and Equity as Political Goals

Debate over distributional issues and the political instabilities such debate fosters show little sign of abatement. Inflation in most countries is high. Inflation places additional pressures on interest groups to use the political process to recoup recent "losses" in real income due to inflation relative to some other benchmark group. In Switzerland, where the inflation rate has been near zero and real incomes are among the highest in the world, such pressures have not been present and this may help to explain this country's political stability in spite of a poor growth performance. In addition, most wages and salaries in Switzerland are changed according to the same national formula. Thus, in Switzerland, neither the incentive to push for changes in one's relative income position nor the opportunity to achieve them may be as great as in other countries. Outside of Switzerland, however, inflation rates have been high and are probably rising. Pressures to redress recent inflation-related setbacks exist and will be directed in part toward the government. Demands for income policies, subsidies, rent controls, tariff protection, and a variety of similar policies with significant distributional consequences and harmful efficiency effects can be expected to occupy political platforms for some time to come. Perhaps they should. Many political scientists view the political process as mainly a means for resolving distributional issues and arbitrating property rights.[5] The political game is inherently zero-sum. There should be no difference between the *types* of political issues that arose in the seventies and those of the

4. Switzerland has continually had coalition governments at the national level.
5. Riker, *The Theory of Political Coalitions,* p. 174; Brian Barry, *Political Argument* (London: Routledge and Kegan Paul, 1965), p. 313.

sixties and fifties or, for that matter, of the forties. While I think distributional questions are and should be a part of the political agenda, I think that
they should be only a *part* of that agenda and that their significance does
vary over time.

Since most of the contributions to this volume have avoided the norma-
tive issues that growth and redistribution raise, it is perhaps appropriate to
close the volume by briefly addressing them. First, note that growth need
not imply simply growth in the private sector of the economy. If redistribution raises trade-off issues, they are of the efficiency-versus-equity kind.
Greater efficiency can be used to yield private or public goods, and the
latter can be defined to include clean air, conservation of the environment,
and the elimination of any other externalities caused by activity in the
private sector. Growth as a political objective differs from redistribution in
that *all* citizens can potentially be made better off from the growth in output
of public or private goods, while only some are made better off from
redistribution. Thus, growth has the advantage as a political issue of
achieving consensual support. Although consensual politics may not be an
interesting subject for political theorists to study, it presumably is a game
that politicians like, at least occasionally, to play. Consensual issues also
have the advantage for society of strengthening support for the political
process itself. When a given policy proposal is favored by a large majority
of voters, both the governing party and the process of government are
strengthened, for it is the latter that makes it possible for the proposal to
come forth. If the process of government never casts up proposals that win
consensual support, then more than the governing parties are at fault.
Eventually, the system of government itself is called into question.

People who participated in World War II either as soldiers or on the
homefront, particularly in the U.K., often remark that in many ways these
were the best years of their lives. A sense of purpose and solidarity with
their friends and fellow citizens existed then that did not exist before and
has not existed since. Winning the war is obviously a public good of the
purest kind, and in a war like World War II, for which there is substantial
consensual support, loyalty to one's nation and political system are given a
great boost, even at a time when some democratic freedoms are, by consensus, set aside.

Similarly, reconstruction following a war, catching up with the economic leaders of the world in standard of living, are also consensual issues.
All members of society, regardless of class, religious, or ethnic background, were significantly better off in terms of real income and consump-

tion at the end of the sixties than they were in 1948, and all would have been even better off than they are today had growth rates continued through the seventies at the same levels that existed in the fifties and sixties. A government that successfully pursues growth wins support not only for the party in control of the government at that time, but for the democratic order that brought that party into power. Conversely, when each successive government fails to achieve growth or any other objective that commands consensual support, a shadow falls over the entire democratic process.

Today, much of the democratic world seems to be under this shadow. Discontent with government, as represented by the present ruling party or coalition, or by the leader of the present government, or, more fundamentally, discontent with the system of government itself, is widespread. Expression of this discontent takes a variety of forms: opposition to big government and public bureaucracies; complaints about the quality of candidates available today in contrast with, say, the fifties and sixties; simple absence from the polls. Giovanni Sartori, in his careful analysis of party systems, notes a loss in strength by parties in the center of the political spectrum to parties at either extreme.[6] What has been described as a shift from consensual government to revolving-door governments Sartori characterizes as a shift from center-based governing coalitions to polarized, extremist governments. This trend, coupled with the increase in the number of viable parties occurring in several countries, threatens the existence of multi-party rule in the European democracies. These developments have gone furthest in Italy, which Sartori already classifies as being "polarized pluralism," a classification he also applies to the Weimar Republic, the Fourth Republic of France, and Chile from 1961 to 1973. But "polarized politics" is in evidence elsewhere. The Conservatives' victory in Britain has polarized the political environment there, and the increase in the number of viable political parties in Belgium and in some of the Scandinavian countries has brought them to the brink of "polarized pluralism."[7] This polarization of the political process and consequent political instability is precisely what one expects when distributional issues are the focal point of political competition. Some writers, like Samuel Brittan,[8] foresee this situation continuing or even worsening, and thus fear even the end of liberal democracy in the West.

6. *Parties and Party Systems,* vol. 1 (Cambridge: Cambridge University Press, 1976).
7. Ibid., pp. 131–85.
8. "The Economic Contradictions of Democracy," *British Journal of Political Science* 5 (April 1975):129–59.

276 Dennis C. Mueller

What can be done to avoid this? Perhaps nothing can be done, short of abolishing either the capitalist-based economic system or the pluralist-based political system, or both. As I interpret Bowles and Eatwell and Dean, capitalism must inevitably raise redistributional issues, which the system's major interest groups—business and labor—will take to the political arena. If the pluralist political process is incapable of resolving these redistributional issues without sapping the efficiency of the market-oriented, capitalist system, as Olson's theory contends, then one or the other has to go.

To avoid this apocalypse, clearly what is needed are issues or candidates capable of achieving consensual support. A war would do, but in a nuclear age this form of medicine is worse than the disease. Lacking a war, perhaps a war hero of charismatic stature can be found. But the stock of World War II heroes is by now all but depleted, and outside of Israel no more recent war has produced any heroes. Growth will not do, for it, in the post-catch-up period, is no longer easy for most countries to achieve, and since growth is typically thought of as antienvironment, it is less of a public good now than it was in the fifties and sixties. The welfare state is a dream partly realized, partly shattered. Further expansion of the welfare state seems unlikely to generate a new consensus. Perhaps the preservation of democracy itself can become an issue to rally behind. Suggestions for constitutional reform in the U.S. and Europe seem motivated by the recognition that changes of this magnitude are necessary to restore the democratic process to a healthy state. Such reforms would seem to require political procedures, which somehow sever the Gordian knot between allocative efficiency improvements and redistributional issues. These procedures would furthermore have to provide political mechanisms for achieving efficiency improvements that can be collectively achieved, while at the same time resolving the real distributional issues every community faces. All of this must be accomplished without destroying the consensual fiber that holds a polity together. But what crisis can precipitate a constitutional convention of this magnitude? And where are the Madisons and Hamiltons to guide us when we get there?

Answers to these questions must await the events of the eighties. Whatever these answers turn out to be, they will require knowledge of the interrelationships between the polity and the economy. The essays of this volume are a contribution in this direction.

Contributors

MOSES ABRAMOVITZ
  Coe Professor of American Economic History (Emeritus)
  Stanford University

JEAN-CHARLES ASSELAIN
  Professeur des sciences économiques
  Université de Bordeaux I

SAMUEL BOWLES
  Professor of Economics
  University of Massachusetts, Amherst

KWANG CHOI
  Visiting Professor of Economics
  University of Wyoming

JAMES W. DEAN
  Professor of Economics
  Simon Fraser University

JOHN EATWELL
  Fellow of Trinity College
  Cambridge University

JEAN-FRANÇOIS HENNART
  Associate Professor of International Business
  School of Business
  Florida International University

JOHN HICKS
  Professor Emeritus
  All Souls College
  Oxford University

URSULA K. HICKS
  Linacre College
  Oxford University

FRANZ LEHNER
  Professor of Political Science
  Ruhr-Universität Bochum

CHRISTIAN MORRISSON
  Professor
  Université de Paris I (Pantheon-Sorbonne)
  Laboratoire d'Economie Politique
  Ecole Normale Supérieure, Paris

DENNIS C. MUELLER
  Professor of Economics
  University of Maryland

PETER MURRELL
  Associate Professor of Economics
  University of Maryland

MANCUR OLSON
  Distinguished Professor of Economics
  University of Maryland

FREDERIC L. PRYOR
  Professor of Economics
  Swarthmore College

Index